94390

D0269690

European
Management
Systems

European Management Systems

Towards unity out of cultural diversity

Ronnie Lessem and Fred Neubauer

McGRAW-HILL BOOK COMPANY

London · New York · St Louis · San Francisco · Auckland · Bogotá · Caracas
Lisbon · Madrid · Mexico · Milan · Montreal · New Delhi · Panama · Paris
San Juan · São Paulo · Singapore · Sydney · Tokyo · Toronto

Published by
McGRAW-HILL Book Company Europe
Shoppenhangers Road, Maidenhead, Berkshire, SL6 2QL, England
Telephone 0628 23432
Fax 0628 770224

British Library Cataloguing in Publication Data
Lessem, Ronnie
  European Management Systems: Towards
  Unity Out of Cultural Diversity
  I. Title II. Neubauer, F. -Friedrich
  658.0094

  ISBN 0–07–707908–6

Library of Congress Cataloging-in-Publication Data
Lessem, Ronnie.
  European management systems: towards unity out of cultural
  diversity / Ronnie Lessem and Fred Neubauer.
     p. cm.
  Includes bibliographical references and index.
  ISBN 0–07–707908–6
  1. Management—Europe. I. Neubauer, Franz–Friedrich. II. Title.
HD70.E8L46 1993
658'.0094—dc20   93–29857
                                                          CIP

12345 CUP 97654

Typeset by Pentacor PLC, High Wycombe, Bucks
and printed and bound in Great Britain at the University Press, Cambridge.

To our parents, who passed on to us our European heritage

Contents

Part I

Introduction

1

Introduction to European management systems

The post-capitalist society will be divided by a new dichotomy of values, between intellectuals and managers, the former concerned with words and ideas, the latter with people and work. To transcend this dichotomy in a new synthesis will be a central philosophical challenge for the post-capitalist society.

Peter Drucker, *Post-Capitalist Society*, 1993

How European diversity can be put to work productively
Of the world's seven most industrialized countries, two are North American—the United States and Canada—one is Asian—Japan—and the other four are European—Germany, France, Italy and the UK. In other words, the majority of the G7 economies are European. That having been said, the conventional wisdom on 'Western' management is American, and the unconventional wisdom has come from Japan. Europe, at least from a conceptual point of view, has been left out in the cold. In fact, the advance of political and economic unification within Europe has not yet been accompanied by a purposefully differentiated and subsequently integrated approach to European management. While strategic alliances, pan-European production and marketing, and cross-cultural teamwork gather apace, managers have yet to recognize, and indeed harness, the full potential of our cultural, economic and personal variety. As a result, the quality of our business and organizational synergy, of our product and market individuality, and of our personal and social harmony in Europe is heavily constrained.

In this book we shall therefore be identifying how European diversity can be put more productively to work, so that we can take our rightful place alongside our American and Japanese counterparts, as a force to be recognized both in our organization behaviour and in our business strategy. Drawing upon our recent research into Europe's cultural, economic and institutional foundations, we shall be illustrating possible ways in which four distinct and complementary strands of capitalism— *personal, communal, managerial* and *cooperative*—can be differentiated and integrated.

Having recognized these culturally and philosophically laden strands of management we will explore how best to harness them. Before doing so, however, it is necessary to position European management within a global perspective.

Positioning Europe within a global perspective
The motivation for our producing this book, as we have indicated, arises from the dominance of primarily American and secondarily Japanese concepts and techniques in the teaching of management as a discipline. That both should occupy a prominent role is for good reasons. The dominance of the former is historically based. After the Second World War the US economy was the strongest in the world; it produced a standard of living for its people that the rest of the world might have envied. The progress of the American economy, moreover, was accompanied by a rapid growth in the field of management as a discipline. One development influenced the other's progress. Practitioners found pragmatic solutions of their problems for which the academics had provided the theoretical underpinnings. Academic researchers developed concepts and tools many of which were welcomed and put to work by practitioners. Due to the pressure to publish in American universities, this body of knowledge also became well documented in the literature. In addition, such documentation appeared in a language that was understood internationally by academics and practitioners alike. This greatly facilitated the spread of American management thinking. Such a development, moreover, was reinforced by the prolific movement of American firms abroad; they naturally took their management methods with them, and passed them on to local managers. Furthermore, the non-American community was ready to absorb the American approaches, and incorporate them into their teaching. In many cases they even imitated the educational technology, that is, the case method.

More recently, however, Japanese management methods have also made inroads. On the one hand, the threat that many people felt to be emanating from the Far East has prompted them to study Japanese management practices. This fear, at least in some quarters, was mixed with admiration for Japanese successes. As a result, a widespread desire arose to understand the Japanese better, and, if possible, to copy them. On the other hand, the presence of Japanese management approaches in the academic curricula and in the offices and factories of non-Japanese firms is far more limited than the influence of American thinking. The inaccessibility of the Japanese language and culture to those of us in the West, North and South has often proved overwhelming.

There is, of course, nothing wholly wrong with these developments. They have actually helped to raise the standards of management education and practice around the world. The question needs to be asked, though, as to whether the relative predominance of the Anglo-American approach, as business spreads across the world, is fully desirable. In fact, in 1984 exactly 50 per cent of the first 50 firms of *Fortune's* largest multinationals were non-American. Only seven years later, in 1991, almost 70 per cent of the same sample came from outside the USA. This development alone should lead us to conclude that a more pluralistic treatment of management thinking is in order. Moreover, in his latest book *Head to Head* MIT's Lester Thurow (1992) advances the thesis that it will be Europe rather than America or Japan who will win the economic race in the years to come. Yet our appreciation of the European approach to management, or, alternatively, the constituent approaches of the French, the Germans, the Dutch, the British, the Italians, the Spanish, the Swedes or the Swiss remains negligible.

The quartet at a glance
Our starting hypothesis was that there were at least four major schools of European management thought and practice that needed to be taken seriously. Taking the national cultures of Britain, France, Germany and Italy as our composite European base, we uncovered four internally consistent approaches to management.

In Fig. 1.1 we make a graphically based attempt to position these *vis-à-vis* the American approach, on the one hand, and the Japanese, on the other, drawing on a technique first used by Knut Bleicher (1989) at Switzerland's University of St Gallen. The least controversial, in this preliminary classification, is the position of the UK relative to the USA. Moreover, our opinion that the German approach is probably closer to the Japanese is supported by other observers, including Michel Albert (1992). The most controversial positions are those of Italy and France. Although their approaches to management are clearly different to those of Japan and Germany, they seem to be closer to these countries than to the Anglo-Americans. However, it is the purpose of this book to explore these maters in greater depth, starting with Europe's underlying philosophical foundations.

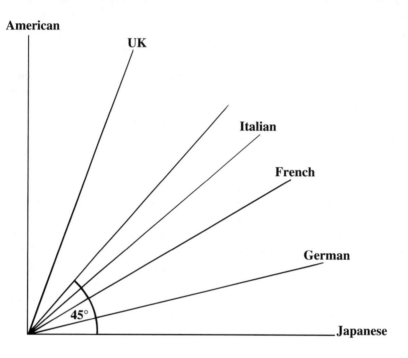

Fig. 1.1   A spectrum of management approaches

Our philosophical foundations
Business enterprise in the European Community has not emerged from a vacuum. It has evolved out of the Continent's particular cultural heritage. That distinctive and composite heritage is reflected in both arts and artifacts and also in the core philosophies that have developed over the past millennium. At the same time, of course, diverse European people and communities have evolved as well as multifaceted sciences and institutions. Yet none of these elements 'speaks for itself' as clearly and comprehensively as its seminal philosophies.

Philosophy, in effect, brings clarity and meaning to careers of individuals, nations and civilizations:

Such is the strength of tradition that men have always tended to accept the particular philosophy or religion prevailing in the group into which they were born. Human beings, primitive or civilized, educated or uneducated, cannot escape from philosophy. Philosophy is everybody's business.

(Lamont, 1965)

Philosophers, then, are supposedly our experts in integration; they form a general staff for coping with the increasing fragmentation of our culture:

They are the liaison officers among the many different and often isolated branches of knowledge; between the civilizations of the past and present; between the great living systems of belief that move the various nations of our day. Philosophers are always reminding people of the interrelatedness of things, always bringing together what has artificially been torn apart from disunited.

(Lamont, 1965)

They should, therefore, serve us well in our attempt to create managerial unity out of our inherent European variety. Philosophy, moreover, underpins knowledge.

Spanning the European quartet

In fact, as Europe develops its knowledge-based economy so the need to replace the materially based factors of production—land, labour and capital—with knowledge-based ones becomes paramount. The four most pervasive sources of knowledge, or philosophies, as we see it, are *pragmatism*, *rationalism*, *wholism* and *humanism*. These in turn, and as we shall see, give rise to experiential and professional, developmental and convivial approaches to business.

Those generic philosophies, in their turn, have produced diverse economic concepts and applications that precondition European business activity. Yet only one of these concepts, that of the market economy and its derivative business practice of free enterprise, has seen the full light of our European economic day. As for the other three philosophies, their time is only now beginning to come, both in theory and in practice. Now that Marxism has suffered its demise in Europe and we are left with the limiting prospect of only one economic ideology—capitalism—dominating the scene, notwithstanding Europe's richly diverse cultural heritage, the time has come both to deepen and extend our business and economic foundations.

In other words, should we wish both to differentiate and integrate European management we will need to link back to our diverse philosophical roots, and for the first time purposefully connect them all to our respective managerial attitudes and behaviour. In the course of this book, therefore, we shall be probing, in turn, the predominating cultures, philosophies and institutions of Europe, and their influence—both actual and potential—on business and organizational concepts as well as on managerial attitudes and behaviour.

Reconstituting the factors of production

In his most recent book *The Competitive Advantage of Nations* Michael Porter (1990) assesses the comparative economic performance of particular developed and rapidly developing countries. In so doing he argues that four interacting elements have to be systemically taken into account in assessing competitive advantage. These are the *factor costs*; the *demand conditions* in each industry; the *structure, strategy and rivalry* of firms within it; and the status of the *industry cluster*, that is, supporting and related industries.

These elements of Porter's, we would argue, are empirically (pragmatically) oriented, and thereby culturally and philosophically biased. In fact, by focusing on the individual firm as his structural unit, and on competitive advantage as his dynamic force, Porter is displaying an empirical–pragmatic–utilitarian–individualist bias. Such an orientation is increasingly being labelled 'Anglo-Saxon' (Albert, 1991), although its influence on management education around the world is all-pervasive. Britain does make up a significant part of the European Community, America is still an important economic influence in Europe, and the pragmatic approach is culturally amenable to the Dutch and the Scandinavians as well as to the English. Nevertheless, we shall be arguing here that Porter's partial and derivative preconditions be replaced by a set of generic constituents of our Europeanness, that is, by extensions of *pragmatism, rationalism, wholism* and *humanism*. For as we move around the European Community we shall find that the generic business orientation, both in process and structure, shifts its 'factorial' ground, progressively evolving from 'firm' part to 'socio-economic' whole.

First, competitive enterprise within a free market thrives upon pragmatism; second, coordinated organization in a *dirigiste* economy draws upon rationalism; third, collaboratively based industry within the context of a social market is nourished by wholism; finally, what might be termed a socio-economic network, as illustrated by the economic historians Piore and Sabel (1984) in their book *The Second Industrial Divide* draws upon humanism.

Covering both 'intercultural' and 'intracultural' ground
In developing 'models' of the European 'businessphere' we run the risk of covering either all the ground extremely superficially or of only a part of it in depth. Here we have decided to go for depth rather than for breadth, concentrating our focus, as it were, horizontally—'intercultural' —but more particularly, vertically—'intracultural'.

The whole of the European 'businessphere' can be divided in two ways. First, and horizontally, there is the geographical terrain. This covers intitially the 'European Community', subsequently the whole of 'Western' Europe, and ultimately our entire continent—what Mikhail Gorbachev called our 'European home'. We shall be focusing upon the former rather than the latter, at least for the time being. Second, and vertically, the Euopean 'businessphere is composed of different levels. The extent of potential coverage—from the surface to the profound depths—extends over four distinct levels, each divided into, respectively, explicit and implicit layers (Table 1.1).

Table 1.1 European management levels

Level of terrain	Externalized quality	Internalized quality
Attributes (1)	Personal behaviour	Managerial attitudes
Models (2)	Institutional frameworks	Organizational concepts
Ideas (3)	Economic policies	Societal philosophies
Images (4)	Natural and cultural heritage	Art and religion

Each level and layer is of equal importance to managers, although the influence of surface features will be much more visible than that of deeper features. It is, in fact, because of this 'invisibility' factor that it has taken us so long in Europe to realize that our management approach is so strongly influenced by America.

The four descending levels, in fact, can also be envisaged as a systemic progression towards ever greater complexity, that is, from the managerial subsystems on the level 1 surface towards, ultimately at level 4, the cultural 'suprasystem'. We have decided to focus our attention on the underlying philosophical, economic and social grounds rather than the more accessible, surface managerial features for two reasons. First, because these deeper levels are least visible they have been most neglected by academics and practitioners alike. Second, these levels form the bedrock, that deep foundation upon which shallower soils rest. Management is affected by such underlying grounds often indirectly and unconsciously, rather than directly and consciously. As a result, more reflective consideration is required of them than of more commonplace applications.

For a number of reasons Fig. 1.2 is of crucial importance for this book. First, it serves to summarize and to metaphorically synthesize our generic concept of 'intercultural' management. Second, it indicates that the discussion of a given management system can take place at any one of four layers, something that is often ignored by those managing across cultures. Yet by neglecting this layered cultural reality we bypass the fullness of our European management systems. Because the notion of cultural layers is such an important one we have shown it in the form of a 'tree' in Fig. 1.2, thereby hoping that we can make this concept more easily understood. It was the great Spanish writer and philosopher, José Ortega y Gasset, who once said that 'The metaphor is probably the most fertile power possessed by man.'

In Fig. 1.2 we have therefore used the metaphor of the tree to present the ideas expressed in Table 1.1. Within it the leaves of the tree symbolize the first layer of managerial attributes; the second layer, the branches, depicts the organizational frameworks; the third, the trunk, represents the seminal idea out of which philosophies and policies have emerged,. Finally the roots of the tree, at level 4, represent the formative images which circumscribe a particular culture, predominantly made up of its natural, social and cultural heritage. We shall be referring continually to this metaphorical tree during the course of this book.

As a result, we need to continually bear in mind that the relationships between the different parts of the tree are organically connected rather than separated from each other. It is for this reason that we refer to 'European Management systems' made up of interconnected attributes, frameworks and philosophies. Individual elements of these systems, because the latter are internally coherent, cannot be separated from each other and transferred discretely into another system.

European management as systems
It may be possible to transfer analytical tools or techniques from one system to another, particularly if they are not culture-bound. However, when copying more complex elements such as the German apprenticeship system or co-determination, there are likely to be problems. Unless their philosophical foundations are understood and specific preparation in the host environment is made, the transplantation of such 'foreign bodies' can be easily rejected.

A sobering example in this context was the attempt to introduce co-determination into the British Post Office in the late 1970s. In those years

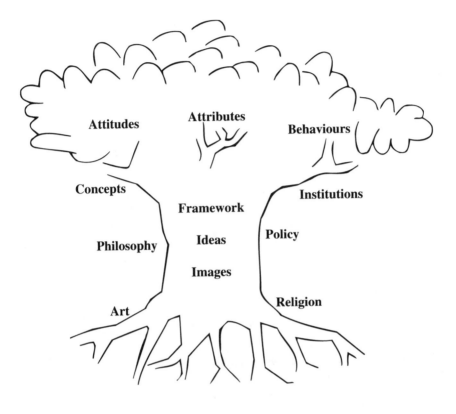

Fig. 1.2   European management levels

Britain embarked on an experiment in industrial democracy by giving union representatives parity with management on the board of the Post Office (Backhaus, 1987). The Post Office, in fact, is traditionally strongly unionized. The attempt failed for a number of reasons. First, there was no parity presentation between labour and capital, as in the German system. Second, the union representatives were unable to embrace a role different from their traditional one of collective bargaining; they could not bring themselves to become entrepreneurial partners but retained their traditional adversarial role. Third, no incentives were given to both sides to make the experiment work. Instead, both unions and management were interested in completing the experiment and reverting to the previous situation.

The problem of transplanting isolated elements is that the managerial approaches prevailing in the four countries of the 'European quartet' are systemic. Barsoux and Lawrence (1991) make this point explicitly with respect to the French approach 'The French model is a coherent whole'. Wever and Allen (1992) say the same for the German model: 'It is precisely in the system that the real lessons of the German model lie.' Through Fig. 1.3 we have attempted to illustrate a systemic approach, in this case the German one, as a dynamic, open one. For building blocks we use the different aspects of the German management system, which will be elaborated upon in this book. All the elements are important for the system. It would be inconceivable to modify one and leave the others untouched. Think of a drastic change in the role of the banks in Germany; massive reverberations would be felt within the whole European system as a consequence.

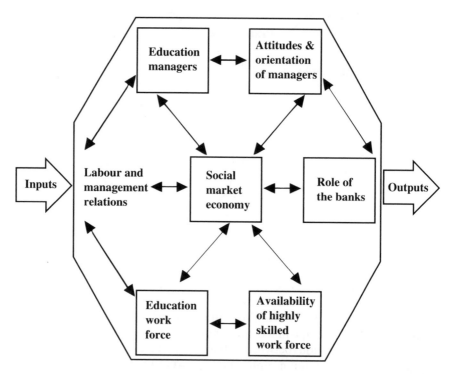

Fig. 1.3   The German management system

We close this section with a quote from Wever and Allen (1992):

So what can managers learn from Germany? An important lesson: in the global economy, is that competition is not just between companies; it is between entire socioeconomic systems. These systems set the all important context that shapes the actions and the fortunes of individual companies. For this reason, what managers do outside the company—in their relationships with other companies, unions, providers of capital, and government—is as important as what they do inside.

What holds true for the German model, as we shall see, also applies to the French, British or Italian management systems.

The plan of this book
We begin by providing a bird's-eye view of the European quartet of France, Germany, Italy and the UK, together with the rationale for selecting these countries. This enables us to get an early 'feel' for management in the European Community. In Part I we introduce our overall conceptual model for both 'intercultural' and 'intracultural' management. This constitutes our 'managerial toolkit'. In Parts II, III, IV and V we then describe the four management systems that make up our European quartet. By way of conclusion, in Part VI we integrate our findings with a view to creating a European 'school' of management, also relating our intercultural approach to professional, corporate and industrial cultures. Let us begin, though, with our bird's-eye view of management systems in France, Germany, Italy and the UK.

2

Towards the European businessphere

Significant differences of variety within a relatively narrow field of unity account for the typically European gift of quality.

Salvador de Madariaga, *Portrait of Europe*, 1968

Capitalism–Communism: the politics of division

The collapse of the Berlin Wall in 1989 within the Germanic heartlands of Europe symbolized (if not yet materialized) the rebirth of a continent. As such, we have the chance of creating a new global unity out of Europe's renewed variety. The sudden demise of Communism in Europe is calling for a new unified world view, albeit this time born out of variety. This variety-in-unity, as we shall see, is contained within what we shall term the inner, as well as the outer, businessphere.

Both capitalism and Communism were born out of partial, monolithic views of the world. Nominally European in origin, neither doctrine attempted to capture the cultural richness of the continent, an endeavour taken up by artists rather than political economists. Whereas Adam Smith, by implication, called upon the merchants of the world to unite, Karl Marx invited the workers to do the same. Each appealed to one class of society rather than to another, and neither appealed directly to Scottishness, to Englishness, or to Germanness, not to mention African-ness or Asianness. In the same way as European cultural variety was ignored by both the great ideologies, so was the variety of cultures in the world at large. Capitalism or Communism was assumed to be of unilateral appeal, north of the equator or south, Eastern hemisphere or Western.

For the past 150 years, and particularly during the course of this century, global politics and economics have been marked by two sets of divisive rather than dialectical forces. While the so-called East/West division has been caused by warring capitalist and Communist factions, the chasm between North and South has divided the rich nations from the poor. Whereas the collapse of the Berlin Wall symbolizes a break-up of the former divide, the crises in Africa represent a continuity of the latter. For poverty and ignorance inevitably breeds social and political strife. Interestingly enough, the great divides within Europe—the capitalist West versus the Communist East, and the rich North versus the poor South—are reflected worldwide. The two-way, polarized state of Europe has spread, symbolically if not in fact, across the world (Fig. 2.1).

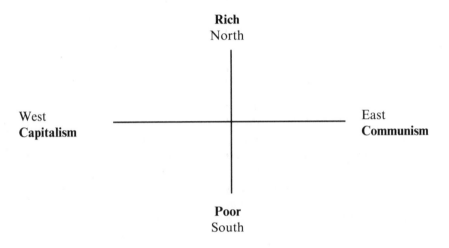

Fig. 2.1   The great divides

These old symbolic maps, however, increasingly misrepresent economic and political reality. Not only has Communism been eroded in Eastern Europe but it has also been losing its grip of the whole Eastern hemisphere, notably in 'Red' China. Paradoxically, meanwhile, that rising star Japan, while having espoused capitalism economically and politically, has retained its communalism (as opposed to Communism) culturally and psychologically. The time has come to transform our vision of global reality, and outward-looking Europe, having implanted the original set of polarities, will need to take the lead in creating new ones. *It is the aim of this book, at least within a managerial context, to do just that.*

Events in Europe have already overtaken the old economic and political divisions. Over the course of the past three decades the colonels in Greece, Franco in Spain and Salazar in Portugal have been replaced. Dictatorship accompanied by poverty and ignorance have given way to democracy, accompanied by rising living and educational standards. So the old North–South divide has begun to erode within Europe although not in the world at large. The European country that has the greatest responsibility for bridging the cultural and economic gap is Italy, straddling North and South. Similarly, it is now Germany, having become unified economically and politically though not yet psychologically, which has the greatest responsibility for transcending the divisions of East and West. Yet, and worryingly at the same time, the spectres of the Mafia, on the one hand, and the Nazis, on the other, hover in the wings. The forces of evil are never quite able to leave the forces of good, at least as long as psychological and socio-economic imbalances remain in place.

Management of integration: thinking/feeling; sensing/intuiting

UNITY THROUGH VARIETY

While the imagery of East and West, if not also North and South, in political and ideological terms has now become outmoded, its symbolical importance in cultural and psychological terms has grown. Essentially, as we move from the politics of division to the psychology of integration, contradition between opposing forces is replaced by complementarity between opposites, and rivalry between factions is transformed into unity through variety. How might this be coming about, both within ourselves and without? To help us along the way, we introduce the concept of the 'businessphere'. Within this global sphere of business a variety of philosophies and practices co-exist, each rooted in a different part of the world, both geographically 'out there' and psychologically 'in here'.

The outer businessphere

THE ADVENT OF POLITICAL ECONOMY

Business has always been a characteristically outgoing activity. Unlike philosophical, religious, artistic or even scientific activity, it has involved extraverted rather than introverted attitudes and behaviours. The aggressive, individualistic and competitive 'Western' (Anglo-Saxon) nature of business enterprise has in fact dominated human consciousness to the exclusion of the collective, cooperative and communal aspects which are also intrinsic to business as a whole.

These latter aspects, however, are more characteristic of the 'non-Western' quarters of the globe—northern, southern and eastern—in which business and management theory and practice had been much less clearly differentiated. In fact the two dominating images of business activity, the one capitalistic and the other communistic, are subject to this imbalance. Whereas the former is strongly based in Adam Smith's *laissez faire* economics and Charles Darwin's 'survival of the fittest' biology, the latter has a much less well-developed heritage. Meanwhile, Marx's view of business was essentially an antithetical one, so that communality is thereby left out of the business reckoning, on both capitalistic and socialistic counts. No wonder that competitive strategies in the context of an economic battleground continue to dominate the global business mind, notwithstanding the advent of ever more varied business cultures—particularly Eastern as well as Western—and strategic alliances.

THE TEMPORAL DOMAIN

In this book we have hopefully made a fresh start, viewing economic activity as part of a so-called businessphere, in the same sense as biological activity forms part of an ecosphere and geological activity forms part of the geosphere. Within such a global sphere, be it physically or economically based, unity and variety not only co-exist but continually enrich one another through their relentless interplay. Like the geosphere 'out there', which is made up of temporally differentiated geological layers and of spatially differentiated land masses, the outer businessphere is composed of organizations at differing stages of development and of management philosophies rooted in differentiated cultures.

These all-important temporal variations totally bypass the great capitalism/Communism and First World/Third World divides. Businesses, if they are to grow and develop, evolve from parochial enterprises and nationally based institutions, into transnationals and ultimately global corporations. Hitherto, management theorists and practitioners have only been able to differentiate clearly between small enterprises and large-scale organizations. However, qualitative differences between mono-cultural and multi-cultural, intra-organizational and inter-organizational requirements are now becoming apparent.

THE SPATIAL DOMAIN

Similarly, businesses, if they are to prosper over the long term, need to draw on their indigenous cultural soils. While the business ethos in America is demonstrably different from that in Japan—and these two countries combined have recently dominated the businessphere—further variants, including those within Europe, have remained substantially hidden. It is as if a geologist is unable to differentiate, at least in any fundamental way, granite rock formations in the Pyrenees from limestone cliffs in Wales. The implication is that volcanic rock in Japan and coal shale in America are the only clearly visible rock formations in the geosphere.

The old ideological divide, whereby either the marketplace (capitalism) or the State (Communism) reigned supreme, served to hide such businesspheric variations. Such perceived differences were restricted to easily visible surface phenomena, 'topsoil', or what might be termed 'surface' attributes, such as culinary habits, susceptibility to corruption, and time keeping. Substantive 'bedrock' or 'root' differences were lumped together under the respective guises of capitalism or socialism, with a so-called mixed economy being seen to lie somewhere between.

For all the evident cultural differences between, for example, the French and the English, the American and the European, none of these have entered into the forefront of the outer businessphere. It as if political and economic duality have concealed cultural and psychological variety. Why should this be?

The inner businessphere

THE ADVENT OF ORGANIZATIONAL PSYCHOLOGY

Until comparatively recently, that is, within the last thirty years or so, culture and psychology were considered to be entirely peripheral to business activity. Economics and politics, coupled with technology, ruled the commercial roost. One of us can well remember, as a young aspiring businessman in the late 1950s, being told by the then Minister of Finance, in colonial Rhodesia, that psychology was for 'backroom boys'. Still to this day, business in its raw and primal context is much more concerned with buying and selling than personal development and cultural evolution. Similarly, economics, as a rationally based science underpinning business activity, is concerned with culture-free concepts of 'monetarism' or 'scientific socialism'.

In fact, whereas at least since the 1960s, industrial and organizational psychology, if not also anthropology, has entered into mainstream MBA curricula, economic policy at large has remained dominated by the capitalism–socialism polarity. To that extent, such evolved European philosophies as French rationalism, Italian humanism and Germanic wholism have remained on the periphery of the businessphere, eclipsed by the empirical Adam Smith and the dogmatic Karl Marx. This oppressive duopoly was apparently first broken by the Japanese, and their overtly successful brand of collectivism (Lazonof, 1991), which seemed to bypass the conventionally polarized economic wisdom.

However, the most viable alternative to the ideological duopoly was probably developed by that globally minded European, the psychoanalyst Carl Jung (1875–1961), as early as in the 1930s, and was adopted by management psychologists in the 1970s. At the same time, while Jung in the 1930s was seen to be totally disconnected from the world of business, the Myers Briggs (1980) inventory developed in the 1970s has become largely disconnected from Jung! We need to remind ourselves of what Jung had to say about individual, psychological types.

PSYCHOLOGICAL TYPES

Carl Gustav Jung

People, according to Jung, both perceive (become aware of) and judge (come to conclusions about) their worlds in different ways. Specifically, he says, there are two ways of perceiving, that is, alternately sensing and intuiting. Through conscious sensation we become aware of people and objects directly through our senses. Through unconscious intuition, conversely, we perceive people and objects indirectly via ideas or associations which the unconscious attaches to the perceptions coming from outside. At the same time, for Jung, there are two contrasting approaches to forming conclusions or making judgements. One is by objective thought, an impersonal and logical approach; the other is by feeling, that is, a process of subjective appreciation, bestowing a subjective value on people and objects.

According to Jung, moreover, each individual is characterized by a dominant and subordinate personality attribute. Whereas the one is perceptual the other is judgemental, and vice versa. For example, while one person may combine thinking with intuiting, another may combine feeling with sensation. A particular individual, therefore, can neither be characterized by both thought and feeling nor by both sensation and intuition.

In fact each of us carries what Jung calls a 'shadow'. For the person whose dominant trait is thinking, his or her shadowland will be occupied by feeling; for the individual who is predominantly a sensation type, his or her shadow will be cast in the form of intuition.

Finally, and perhaps most notably, Jung distinguishes between the introverted (or inner-directed) and the extraverted (or outer-directed) person. Whereas the former is preoccupied by his or her inner world the latter is predisposed towards the outer world. The introvert is a typical researcher; the extravert is a typical salesperson.

Isabel Myers Briggs

In the 1950s a remarkable American woman, Isabel Myers Briggs, managed to develop an inventory, based on Jung's typology, which has since become the most popular tool for 'psychological typing'. Managers, in particular, have responded to this so-called 'MBTI' indicator, which divides personality into 16 discrete types. As can be seen in Figure 2.2, each is made up of four types of either introverted (I) or extraverted (E); sensing (S) or intuitive (N); thinking (T) or feeling (F); as well as judgemental (J) or perceiving (P).

The intravert–extravert preference is relatively easy to spot. It describes the source and focus of your energy (Kroeger and Thuesen, 1988). Extraverts are sociable, outer directed, speak and then think. Introverts are reserved, inner directed, think and then speak. Equally easy to identify is a person's lifestyle orientation, judgemental or perceiving. Judgers are structured, controlled, decisive and scheduled; perceivers flow, are adaptive, wait and see and act spontaneously.

Information gathering can be specific, practical, down-to-earth and realistic—sensing; or general, ingenuous, head in the clouds and conceptual—intuitive. Intuitives look for the meaning of an event while sensors tend to examine its various components. Most difficult of all to identify is the individual's decision-making function—thinking or feeling. The thinking and feeling processes, whereby we critique, evaluate and decide about the information we have gathered, is a highly personal one. It can be difficult to tell at any moment whether someone's opinion is an objective (thinking) or subjective (feeling) one. Whereas thinkers seek objective clarity, feelers seek harmony with people; whereas thinkers tend to be consistent and uniform in the way they apply their decisions, feelers are situational and variable.

CULTURAL/PSYCHOLOGICAL TYPES

Anglo/Saxon—ST

As can be seen in Fig. 2.2, the sixteen psychological types that emerge (we have adapted the descriptions from Kroeger and Thuesen's *Type Talk*) can be applied not only to individuals but, more or less, to societies. As we can see, the Anglo-Saxons are pragmatically sense based, supported by thinking. Moreover, they alternate between extraverted—typically American and Australian—and introverted—typically English and Canadian. Finally, while entrepreneurs tend to accentuate perception, managers are more judgemental.

The free market, in effect, is a macro-economic reflection of an eStp micro-outlook on business. More specifically, it is extraverted, or customer focused; primarily sense oriented, whereby it reacts immediately to short-term market signals; secondarily thoughtful in that it logically adapts its supply function to market demand; and finally

The fun of *problem solving*
inTp

Complexity is there
to be managed
inTj

One exciting <u>*intellectual*</u>
challenge after another
enTp

We plan to lead
enTj

FRANCO-NORDIC
RATIONALISM

GERMANIC-JAPANESE
WHOLISM

Life's *dependable*
administrators
eStj

A high sense of
duty
isFj

<u>*The ultimate*</u>
<u>*entrepreneur*</u>
eStp

Ready to *try*
anything once
iSTp

Force of order
and harmony
esFj

Performing
noble deeds
iNFp

Doing what should
be done
iStj

An *inspiration*
to others
inFj

ANGLO-AMERICAN
PRAGMATISM

LATIN-ITALIAN
HUMANISM

Doing things for the
joy of it
isFp

Living for the *moment*
esFp

Natural *motivator*
of people
enFj

Enthusiasm for *social*
and community life
eNfp

Fig. 2.2   Psychological and national types

perceptive in that the free marketeer goes with the flow, as a proverbial risk taker.

The pre-eminence of the gifted amateur, the proliferation of venture capital, and the characteristic short-termism of the Anglo-Saxons is a reflection of their prevailing psychological type. Interestingly enough, Revans's (1980) focus on action learning is a further reflection of the ST pre-emphasis. When it comes to individual managers, moreover, the experiential orientation is entirely consistent with the 'can do' approach, albeit that the differences between introversion and extraversion, as well as between judgers and perceivers, create variations on the ST theme. Whereas the STP emphasis is appropriate for the small business, the STJ orientation befits the larger one. Finally, and as we have already stressed, this 'ST' orientation is characteristic of the business entrepreneur throughout western and northern Europe, and spreads most particularly into parts of Holland and Scandinavia. In other words, it is characteristically, but not exclusively, Anglo-Saxon.

Franco/Nordic—NT

Rationalism, quintessentially associated with France, emerges from an NT orientation, most typically inTj. The predominance of thinking leads to the French preoccupation with planning, both at a macro *dirigiste* and at a micro level, and to the overall emphasis on intellect in French schools and polytechnics. In this general NT respect, the Nordic countries, notably Sweden, has much that is rationally in common with its Gallic European counterpart. Both European regions are unwilling to wholly subjugate themselves to the ST forces of the market. Thinking, moreover, in these Franco-Nordic instances, is supported by intuition insofar as an orientation towards the future is predominant. The judgemental perspective in France accords with the elitist structure of its meritocracy and the hierarchical nature of its institutions. Conversely, the perceiving orientation of the Nordic countries leads to an altogether more egalitarian approach embodied in their social welfare-based societies and flat management structures.

Not surprisingly, bureaucracy plays a strong part in an INTJ type culture, and scientific management—*à la* Henri Fayol (1949)—has taken its pride of place. In no country in Europe has the professional administrator attained as much prominence and status as in France. Moreover, in France, as in Sweden, public service plays a prominent and respected part in the nation's destiny, albeit that in Sweden of late there has been considerable reaction to the overpraised strengths of social welfarism. In fact, with individual personalities as with whole nations, over done strengths dissolve into weaknesses.

Finally, it needs to be emphasized that the NT orientation, with its emphasis on structure and function, is essential to any company, as it develops in scale and scope, whether in the Anglo-Saxon or Franco-Nordic worlds. In effect, it has been easier for America, with its melting-pot society, to assimilate these rationally based elements than for the 'culturally purer' Britain. That having been said, Scotland is more rationally oriented than the rest of the United Kingdom, and the south of France is much less NT than the rest of that country. Similarly, the French-speaking parts of Belgium and Switzerland have much in common with France itself.

Nippo/Germanic—N/SF

France and England exhibit, in effect, the 'purest' forms of personality and cultural type among our European quartet. When we come to Germany the situation is much less clear. In this book we have associated Germany, from a philosophical perspective, with wholism or Idealism, which accords with an NF orientation, that is, specifically infj. The search for the whole that transcends the parts is a reflection of an intuitive outlook, and the yearning for an ideal accords with the feeling for unity. Moreover, the inevitably judgemental orientation of the Germanic people leads directly to the systematic approach that is so much part of that country's cultural personality.

However, and thereafter, the picture begins to blur. Whereas the combined FJ perspective remains fairly constant at all levels of Germany's cultural and managerial being, the N/S factor is more variable. To begin with, the country's ability to marry marketplace and society within the social market represents an inclination to combine the S and N worlds, that is, the specifics of the market with the integrity of society. Similarly, the country's noted apprenticeship schemes are an amalgam of FS—an affiliation with the place of work and its product, with FN—an orientation towards integration of the individual with the organization, and individuation, of the person over time. Similarly, the so-called developmental manager in Germany is, on the one hand, concerned with product specifics rather than managerial generalities (FS), but, on the other, is oriented towards the long term within the context of the developing industry as a whole (FN).

Interestingly enough, the Japanese represent a purer NF type than their close economic relatives, the Germans. Both business cultures, in their orientation towards participation and consensus within the firm and without, favour the 'inclusive F' mode over the 'exclusive T' one. The Japanese, however, with their pre-emphasis on quality circles, just-in-time production and *kaizen* approach to product development, combine intuiting with perceiving to flow into management rather than to compulsively pre-structure it. At the same time, the interaction between 'N' and 'F' creates a degree of inspiration and idealism that is more marked, in business circles, in Japan than in Germany.

What Germans and Japanese do share, however, is a pervasive orientation towards the practicality of work, product and production, and away from abstracted management *per se*, which is much more ST or NT in nature. Similarly, in both the Idealist and Taoist philosophies of Germany and Japan, in turn, there is an inherent capacity to assimilate opposites, polarities or dialectics. In such intuitive world views *both and* prevails over *either or*, so that manager and worker, product and market, small company and large, business and environment, are juxtaposed rather than opposed. In fact it is this particular world view that serves to integrate a Japan Inc. or a Germany Inc. through which manufacturer and banker, employer and employee, government and industry combine forces rather than engage in adversarial relations. To some degree, such an approach applies in the Netherlands, as it does within all those large companies that have become involved in joint ventures across Europe, if not also across the world, thereby entering what Bernard Lievegoed calls the integrated phase of business development (see Chapter 12).

Italian/Latin—FS/N
Whereas wholism is the philosophical extension of personal intuition, and is economically embodied in the social market, humanism is an extension of individual feeling, and is economically and organizationally embodied in what has been termed 'flexible specialization'. Italy, like Germany, is more of a personal and cultural amalgam than France or Britain. Northern Italy, to begin with, often combines an N orientation with T rather than F, so that an Italian brand of rationalism supplants humanism. Southern Italy, meanwhile, is so steeped in F and S that an immediacy of impulse and outlook often prevents any economic activity of an enduring nature. It is central Italy, in effect, which is most distinctly FN in character, combined with an extraversion and a perceiving orientation that makes for a characteristically southern enfp.

The extraversion, which is typically and flamboyantly Latin, fosters an outgoing, customer-focused approach to business that, combined with a perceiving orientation, lends itself to risk-taking entrepreneurship. In fact this Latin, feeling-centred approach to family-based enterprise is the counterpart to the Anglo-Saxon, more thought-centred variety. The socio-economic network that serves to combine small, family businesses together, communally, is typified by the Prato region in central Italy. Moreover, the extraverted nature of such communal integration, combined with its 'go with the flow' character, gives it a more convivial flavour than its Germanic counterparts. The Germanic force of order and harmony is supplanted by a Latin love of spontaneity and community. To some extent, Spain and Portugal, as well as Southern Ireland, share this personal and cultural orientation. Moreover, the inefficient bureaucracies, in most of these countries, lack the rationality of the Franco-Nordic countries.

The reinventing of small-scale craft-based production, in effect, is ideally suited to such NFP (as opposed to NTJ) enterprises, where the N supplies the new technology, the F the communal bonding and the P the market responsiveness. These three together, combined with the extraverted desire to make an impact on the business world, create a unique form of economy. The bonding of social and economic networks is more family centred, localized and flexible than is the case in Germany, though Bavaria, for example, would be closer to this Italian model than, say, north Germany. So much, then, for the psychological and cultural types as they have been represented in our book. For this developmental perspective we have to part company from Myers Briggs and return to the master himself: to Jung.

INDIVIDUATION

From the vantage point of this book, and for reasons which will soon become apparent, Carl Jung is likely to play the role within the global businesssphere of the twenty-first century that Smith and Marx played in the previous three (Van der Post, 1978). Jung's role, on the one hand, was to break down the duopoly in political and economic thought and to replace it with a quaternity, in psychological and cultural as well as managerial and ultimately commercial terms. On the other hand, and of equal importance to us, is his concept of *individuation*.

Jung argues that the function of people in the second half of their lives—usually senior management—is to sustain the culture that supported their youth. By following the imperative to individuate, we become as complete human beings as we can within the context of our culture, and in so doing we perform the highest functions for the wellbeing of society, as well as for the personal fulfilment of our lives (Stevens, 1980).

For Jung, unlike for Myers Briggs, a psychological or managerial typology could only be useful if it were an essentially dynamic set of concepts. He insisted, in fact, that all typological possibilities are inherently available in the Self. Viewed in this light, getting to know one's psychological type is not to put oneself in a straitjacket but to become aware of where there is room left for personal development. The same applies, in our context, within each part of the European whole. Redemption, individually and societally, is achieved by recognizing and integrating these unknown elements of the soul. This, for us, is the essential mission of European integration.

The whole problem of individuation consists in resolving the thesis of one's or society's 'pure nature' and the antithesis of the opposing nature into the synthesis of conscious nature. The relation of people in nature, or the French or Italian, British or German managers in Europe, is that of the subject and object. The 'object' is literally what is in opposition, or facing you; the 'subject' is at the mercy of the object. But the object can only attain life through the subject. So Europe can only realize its integrated self-as-object through the separate selves of its constituent nations-as-subjects.

The task of the first half of European life consists in establishing these subjects so firmly that they are capable—whether as French or English, German or Italian—of acting as equal and opposite poles to one another. The psychic state reached as a result of the interaction between these equal but opposite poles is both richer and better informed than one based on one or other set of cultural and managerial intentions.

The ultimate position is neither one nor the other but a third, previously unimagined, possibility: the achievement Jung attributed to the transcendent function of the self. To live ethically is to choose to develop the best possible personality that one's individuation will allow. In the Anglo/Saxon case the evolution of free enterprise towards a learning company is subject to the emergence of an F force—with a Latin infusion—to balance the T, under the guidance of an evolving S. For such a development, as subject, Britain is dependent on its European counterparts as objects. Similarly, in the Franco-Nordic case, the development of an organization that is 'requisite' to human nature is dependent on the emergence of an S force—with an Anglo/Saxon infusion—to balance the N, under the guidance of an evolving T. Furthermore, in the Germanic or Japanese case, the full development of a hitherto closed system into an open one is contingent on the emergence of T—with a Franco/Nordic infusion—under the guidance of an evolving N. Finally, in the Latin case, the full emergence of an exclusive family-based enterprise into a more inclusive socio-economic network is dependent on the emergence of N—with a Germanic infusion—under the guidance of an evolving F.

The transcendent function is the psyche's means of evolution, through which it moves towards a more complete realization of its destiny to become whole. Moreover, intimate collaboration between ego and self is not only crucial to individuation but also indispensable to the achievement of genius. Shakespeare and Mozart possessed the supreme gift of transforming unconscious intuition into the conscious lineaments of great art. Individuation, like art, depends on fruitful propinquity between ego and self, producing a series of psychic metamorphoses.

The great paradox of the whole process is that in realizing one's full humanity one is, at the same time, actualizing one's unique individuality. To individuate, in Jung's terms, is to defy the tyranny of received opinion and to confront the primordial symbols in the collective unconscious—in one's own unique way. Only thus does one become individual, a separate, indivisible unity or 'whole' (Stevens, 1980). Individuation means precisely the better and more complete fulfilment of collective qualities which are invested in the self. Individuation does not shut out the world but gathers the world to oneself.

Our quaternity of psychological types, of management domains, and of evolutionary stages are thereby mutually interdependent rather than mutually exclusive, in both space and time. In other words, as a manager or organization develops over a life span or spreads across the world, each will need to migrate across the quaternity. For unlike capitalism and Communism, which shut each other out, the inner worlds of sensing, intuiting, thinking and feeling will welcome each other if growth takes place.

The dynamics of development

CUMULATIVE DEVELOPMENT

As individuals, organizations or societies grow and develop, each needs to advance both internally and externally. Starting in life with a strong parochial bias, each must grow geographically and psychologically if it is to evolve. This is exactly what happened to the Japanese and the Germans after the Second World War as they—admittedly by force—were opened up to the West. As far as European business today is concerned, it needs geographically to reach out to America and Japan, both of which it has already done, and psychologically to reach into those intuitive and feeling sides of its nature which have been hitherto repressed by the sensing and thinking functions. In the latter respect the cultural influence of Southern and Eastern Europe, if given half a chance, will have an important part to play. Similarly, in Clinton's new America, indigenous and exogenous populations must meet, thereby creating unity-in-variety.

While a particular individual or enterprise, nation or continent retains its personal and cultural stamp over time, it needs to follow a particular pattern of development if it is to successfully evolve. The youthful, pioneering organism requires a combination of primal enterprise and community, predominant in the sense-bound West. Britain within Europe and the United States in the world have both ruled the primal domain, with free and independent enterprise as the overriding business form.

The adultlike, established entity needs, over and above the primal qualities, a combination of rationally based freedom and order, prevalent in the thinking-oriented North. Scandinavia, France and Switzerland, within Europe, rule the rationally based business domain, with dependable and accountable but also flexible management and organization as the be-all and end-all.

The individual or institutional entity in midlife, at a time of personal or collective re-integration, requires—over and above the primal and rational qualities—an intuitively Eastern combination of developmentally oriented individuation and harmonization. A united Germany within Europe, looking across from west to east, and Japan in the wider world, may rule the developmental domain, with mutual and interdependent association becoming the guiding force.

The human organism in maturity, at a time of total transformation, over and above the three sets of former qualities, requires a metaphysically based combination of vision and energy. This we find, albeit thinly spread, in the South, stretching from Father Arizmendi, who created the Mondragon cooperatives in Spain, to Albert Koopman, who established the Cashbuild 'rights organization' in South Africa (Koopman, 1991).

ANIMUS AND ANIMA

At any one stage of individual or organizational, economic or cultural development the captain needs a mate. In other words, tough-talking enterprise (sensing) needs to be allied with tender-hearted community (feeling) at the outset of business. Jung alludes to a dominant and auxiliary function of personality, which we have extended to parallel functions of business, nationhood or even 'Europeanness' or globality.

Thinking and sensing, mind and will have been the dominant functions of male-run businesses, albeit that there are many national, regional and local variations on this prevailing theme. Jung also referred to our 'animus' and 'anima'. In effect, therefore, every male carries within him a female aspect (anima) and every female carries within her a male aspect (animus). A balanced personality, organization or society will have primary and auxiliary functions that cut across the animus–anima divide. In overall terms the western and northern parts of the businesssphere are animus-prone, and the eastern and southern are anima in spirit. Whereas mind and will predominate in Europe, expecially in its western and northern climes, heart and soul predominate in the east and south. However, this is not the end of the story.

LIGHT AND SHADE

Just to make matters a little more complicated Jung argues that each of us carries a shadow. This means there is a side (one of the four psychological functions) to our individual, corporate or national personality that is hidden from us. In effect, it is that 'shadow' side which yearns for recognition, having been cast out for so many years of youth and adulthood, before we enter a midlife crisis. Interestingly enough, the European continent, as a whole, and its major constituent organizations have now reached such a crisis.

While the sense-bound 'West' has abandoned the function of intuition to its shadowlands, thought-bound Northern Europe has cast out feeling. While businesses in America and Europe, not to mention the former imperial colonies, functioned adequately as either parochially based enterprises or nationally based organizations, the well-lit sensing and thinking functions appropriately ruled the economic domain. However, as organisms approach their third developmental stage of evolu- tion—becoming transnational, transorganizational and transfunctional in orientation—then intuition needs to overtake thought as the predominant and integrative function. Japan, in global terms, and Germany, in European terms, therefore take over from America and Britain as dominant economic powers. They emerge, as it were, from out of the shadows. In the same way, as we shall see, the newly evolved production function (eastern) overtakes marketing (western) and finance (northern) as the predominant influence within the businessphere.

Interestingly enough, the same psychological need for the individual, at midlife, to emerge from the shadows is what the impending crisis is all about. The proverbial crisis is only ultimately resolved, thereby paving Jung's way to individuation, if a person comes to terms with his or her shadow.

Conclusion

BUSINESS AND MANAGERIAL INDIVIDUATION

As global business advances from image to reality it needs to provide scope for individual managers, institutions and nations to grow and evolve. As such, they will be encourged to develop as sensing, thinking, intuiting and feeling personalities over the course of their youth, adulthood, midlife and maturity. This is only likely to materialize if the western and northern parts of the businessphere not only assert their own selves but also open themselves to the eastern and southern parts of their global being. This global awakening, of course, will need to be enhanced by a similar unfolding within each individual, organization, nation and continent.

The greatest difficulty we shall have, according to Jung, is to come to terms with our shadow. As dominantly mindful and wilful northerners and westerners we struggle to cope with Eastern intuition and Southern feeling. Interestingly enough, the latter is the dominant function of our Japanese competition. No wonder they have left many of us in the shade. Breadth of intuition and depth of feeling, interestingly enough, develop progressively—if we choose to let them in—with age. These latter psychological functions are much more commonplace in Europe in the arts, where Southern and Eastern countries have made their major contributions, than in the sciences or in the commercial world.

The global manager's inner space has its mirror image in the global business's so-called outer space. The West is endowed with lots of common sense; the North with a level head; the East with feminine intuition; and the South with intensity of feeling.

The truly global corporation, having reached maturity, spans the whole of the businessphere not only geographically but also psychologically. While it retains its indigenous bias, it becomes whole through its interactions with other psychological and geographical domains. It thereby creates an action-centred enterprise, a rationally structured organization, a quality product and an inspired culture. To the extent that it succeeds in such a global endeavour such a corporation embraces a cast of eight charcters, representing the hard and soft sides of each of Jung's four psychological types.

STRATIFICATION

A business leader like John Harvey-Jones is located in the Anglo-Saxon West, poised between enterprise and community. A manager of change like Jan Carlson as SAS stands in the North between freedom and order. A corporate architect like Reinhard Mohn is located towards the East, between evolution and harmony. Finally, a visionary like Mondragon's Father Arizmendi, with his Southern European heritage, was based in Catalonia, poised between energy and spirit (Fig. 2.3).

PLUMBING THE DEPTHS

None of us, as individuals or as continents, can afford to stand still. If we are to grow, to change, to develop, and ultimately to transform ourselves we have to transcend our innate cultural bias. In the past we have relied on wars to achieve this, notably and most recently in the cases of Germany and Japan. In the future, we would hope, such cultural assimilation can be achieved by a conscious act of will, directed at our evolution as a business and as a species, rather than through an act of creation that follows great destruction. Such assimilation, moreover, can only be achieved if we are willing, with Jung, to plumb the individual and

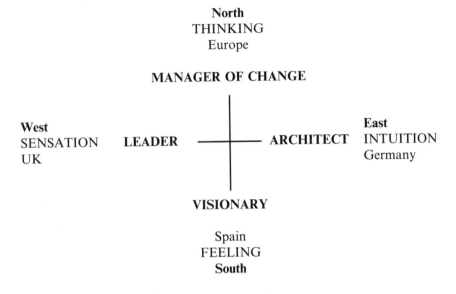

Fig. 2.3 Global cast of characters

Table 2.1. Geological layers

(1) *Topsoil*—the primal ego, harbouring personal instincts and local customs, commonly connected with sensing

(2) *Subsoil*—rational consciousness, containing structured intelligence and national institutions, commonly associated with thinking

(3) *Bedrock*—an unconscious layer of personal insights and underlying national traits, hidden from the visible surface, often associated with intuition

(4) *Core*—a collective unconscious, inhabiting the individual imagination, and containing the myths and legends of an entire continent, drawn from the world of feeling

societal depths. In fact, using a geological metaphor, we would need to probe through topsoil towards bedrock (Table 2.1).

In the course of evolving from the surface to depth structure of ourselves, Jung tells us, we shall have to come to terms with our shadow. As individuals, businesses and nations we are all incomplete. Unless the Anglo-Saxons, post-Reagan and post-Thatcher, can turn part of their competitiveness into a more cooperative and interdependent whole; unless the French can turn part of their secular efficiency into a more transcendent unity; unless the Germans can turn part of their collective individuals, businesses and nations we are all incomplete. Unless the Anglo-Saxons, post-Reagan and post-Thatcher, can turn part of their competitiveness into a more cooperative and interdependent whole; unless the French can turn part of their secular efficiency into a more transcendent unity; unless the Germans can turn part of their collective nature into a more evolved form of individualism; unless the Italians can turn part of their tribal energy into a more all-embracing spirit of community—we shall all, as Keynes said, in the long run be dead.

Conversely, if we do manage to draw appropriately from one another's inner and outer domains of being, our business and human prospects, in the world at large, should be universally bright. In fact, a key factor in such cultural interfusion will be the part played by the spatially intermediate nations. The Dutch are already playing a dominant part in conceptualizing approaches to cross-cultural management, the Norwegians have taken an ecological lead, and it was the Czechs, through Havel (1988), who posed the question as to what we Europeans are doing here on Earth! We have no doubt that the exclusively competitive business ethic, alongside Britain's former prime minister, is now hopelessly obsolete. It needs to be replaced by a cosmopolitain ethic which the business world as a whole needs to bring about: made up of sensible Western competition; thoughtful Northern coordination; heartfelt Eastern cooperation; and inspired Southern co-creation. Such global integrity would accommodate not only the four stages of managerial, organizational and societal development but also the totality of the inner businessphere, on the one hand, and the outer businessphere, on the other. It is a long and arduous path for European business and management to follow, but the alternative, surely, is physical, economic, political and social disintegation. We now turn to Chapter 3, where our own particular journey towards European management will begin in earnest.

3

The European businessphere

The European force field

In Chapters 1 and 2 we introduced you to our European quartet in general, without attempting to tease out significant conceptual differences. This is what we now wish to do. In fact, from now on we shall be setting out to uncover a field of European management, in both theory and practice, that is a unified sum of varied parts. Those four parts are derived from contemporary European philosophies that have emerged over the past five hundred years, drawing, in turn, upon a classical Greek and Roman heritage. At the same time, moreover, it is important to recognize that business is now passing from an industrial into a post-industrial era, from what Harvard sociologist David Riesman has called a more 'outer-directed' to a relatively 'inner-directed' approach.

For the first time in its history the whole of Western Europe, at least, is developing interdependently from within, rather than its constituent parts battling independently, without. At the same time, knowledge work rather than physical labour, human as opposed to financial capital, information rather than energy, philosophy rather than economy have become the primary resources. Empirically oriented market economies, therefore, may, for example, need to evolve from an industrial era of free enterprise, marked by a spirit of self-help and drawing on the classical economist's factors of production into a post-industrial era of the learning organization, characterized by self-development and drawing upon our 'factorial' European philosophies.

THE SPATIAL DIMENSION

Philosophical and managerial types
Of the four post-industrial factors of 'European production', *pragmatism* is strongly rooted in English culture but has a clear affinity with the Dutch

and the Scandinavians. Such empiricism has given rise to the experiential manager. While its positive manifestation is in free-spirited individualism its negative form of expression is in rampant materialism. *Rationalism* is strongly grounded in Gallic soil, and also in parts of Germany, Scandinavia, Northern Italy and also the French-speaking part of Switzerland. It has given rise, in its turn, to the professional manager. While its positive manifestation is that of a meritocracy its negative expression is in its stereotypical bureaucracy. *Wholism* has emerged from a longstanding Germanic philosophical tradition, inclusive of Austro-Hungary and part of Switzerland. It has given rise to what may be termed a developmental manager. While its positive manifestation is wholistic, its negative expression is totalitarianism. Finally, *humanism* is strongly rooted in Italian art and culture, whence came the first European Renaissance, while having distinct branches in Greece, Spain and Ireland. It has given rise to what may be called the convivial manager. While its positive manifestation is in its communal nature, its negative expression is in the form of nepotism and corruption.

Psychological types

Each philosophy is part of a pan-European whole. In fact, Europe has been noted for the intense interplay between its diverse philosophical systems. Alas, until now the same could not be said for our business and organizational systems.

Whereas Jung's sensing type is empirically oriented, and his thinking type rationally disposed, his intuitive type is typically idealistic, and his feeling type characteristically humanistic. Moreover, we are all combinations of at least two personality types, albeit that one remains dominant.

Interestingly enough, the European force field, as we can see in Fig. 3.1, constitutes more or less the learning cycle popularized by the American organizational psychologist, David Kolb (1974). The 'experiential' orientation applies a pragmatic philosophy to management in active mode; the professional orientation applies a rational philosophy in thoughtful mode; the 'developmental' orientation applies a wholistic philosophy in intuitive mode, the 'convivial' orientation applies a humanistic philosophy in feeling mode. Following the basic methodology of scientific method, European learners, depending upon their philosophical outlooks, will start in one or other of the four positions, but will need to complete the cycle in order to wholly learn. In that respect they will become fully European!

Because in explicit management theory (if not in implicit business practice) it is the empirically oriented, competitively focused, personality and enterprise-based outlook which has predominated, our collective learning has been inhibited. The other three perspectives—rationalist,

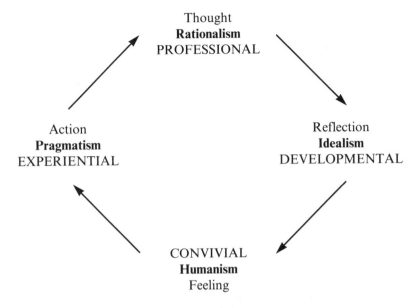

Fig. 3.1   The force field of European management

idealist, humanist—have been much less clearly differentiated, let alone integrated into an overall European or even global economic world view. The result has been the over-generalized (and hence ultimately destructive as opposed to creative) tension between capitalism and Communism. Clearcut differentiation is a necessary prelude to coherent integration. We start, then, with pragmatism.

Pragmatism

> Originating in or relying on factual information; relying on experience or observation rather than system or theory; the practice of emphasizing experience, especially of the senses, or relying on sensation rather than intuition, induction rather than other rationalistic means in the pursuit of knowledge.
>
> (*Webster's Third New International Dictionary*)

FROM FREE ENTERPRISE TO LEARNING COMMUNITY

'Pragmatism', the doctrine that all knowledge is acquired through experience, is firmly imbedded in the 'empiricist' philosophical soils of Britain, most particularly within England. To some extent, the Dutch and the Scandinavians within Europe, and to a greater extent the Americans and Australasians without, share this individually centred, experientially based philosophical outlook. It has dominated the global economic scene, prior to the emergence of the Japanese as an industrial power with a rival philosophy to the Anglo-Saxon. It also preconditioned Britain's independent outlook at Maastricht (see Table 3.1).

Table 3.1 Features of pragmatism

Aspect	Attribute
Kindred philosophies	Empiricism, utilitarianism
Unit focus	Entrepreneur, enterprise
Business outlook	Competition, transactional
Managerial orientation	Experiential
Psychological type	Sensing, action oriented
Path of evolution	Self-help—self-development; free enterprise—learning company

Pragmatism shares its analytical bent with rationalism, and its practical orientation with Italian humanism, but it stands, as Michel Albert has recently revealed in his book *Capitalism against Capitalism*, in polar opposition to 'Rhenish' idealism. Hence the great divide between Adam Smith's 'realistic' capitalism and Karl Marx's 'idealistic' Communism.

THE IDEA OF PRAGMATISM

The seminal 'empiricist' philosophers Thomas Hobbes and John Locke as well as the classical economists Adam Smith and Jeremy Bentham were all of a pragmatic bent. Common law based on precedent, behavioural psychology based on directly observable phenomena, and classical science based on visible blocks of matter, all stem from this Anglo-Saxon 'feet on the ground' approach. Empiricism is also eminently suited to the early, entrepreneurial phase of business, when it is essential to be 'close to the customer' and to have a 'bias for action'. In fact Will Durant (1962), the popular American historian of philosophy, claims that

> English thought took its spirit from a life of industry and trade, and looked up to matters of fact with a certain reverence. This tradition had turned thought in the direction of things, mind in the direction of matter, the materialism of Hobbes, the sensationalism of Locke, the scepticism of Hume, the utilitarianism of Bentham were so many variations on the theme of a practical and busy life.

The Industrial Revolution in Britain, though born of a little science, stimulated more as, for example, Robert Boyle and Humphry Davy opened up the treasures of chemistry and Michael Faraday made the discoveries that would electrify the world. These were all scientists who 'managed by wandering about', keeping their ears close to the ground. The worlds of the technician–craftsman and that of the scientist–technologist were never far apart.

THE EXPERIENTIAL MANAGER

The seminal influence on empiricism, from a managerial perspective, was, interestingly enough, Francis Bacon in seventeenth-century England. His work on the inductively based advancement of learning did for the scientific revolution what Adam Smith's treatise on the wealth of nations did for the industrial one. Following in the footsteps of Adam Smith, the Victorian biographer Samuel Smiles distilled from emerging nineteenth-century free enterprise the concept of individual self-help that underpinned it. Subsequently drawing on Bacon's inductively based approach to learning, the contemporary and experientially based English management philosopher, Reg Revans, has distilled from emerging twentieth-century 'action learning' the concept of manager self-development that underpins it. In empirical, experiential summary:

- The *subject* of European pragmatism has been the individual manager, duly evolving in orientation from self-help to self-management.
- Its *object* has been the independent enterprise, duly evolving in its structure from a *free enterprise into a learning company*.

Rationalism

The notion that reason is in itself a source of knowledge superior to and independent of sense perceptions, as contrasted against sensationalism or empiricism; knowledge can thereby be deduced from *a priori* concepts; such rationality is opposed to nonrational emotion or intuition.

(*Webster's Third New International Dictionary*)

FROM FORMAL ORGANIZATION TO REQUISITE BUREAUCRACY

Where empiricism is inductive, rationalism is deductive. The seventeenth-century French philosopher, René Descartes, was as seminal an influence on the latter as Francis Bacon was on the former. According to Durant (1962): 'Beginning in philosophy with clearly perceived institutions which he regarded as comparable to the axioms of geometry, Descartes, a mathematician of the first rank, constructed by deductive reasoning his complete cosmic theory'. Thought-centred rationalism shares with empiricism its functional orientation and with idealism its structural perspective, but it stands in polar opposition to Italy's feeling-centred humanism. While most strongly rooted in France, there are manifestations of such rationalism in such diverse European regions as Scotland and Northern Germany, Northern Italy and Scandinavia. In many ways it is the most quintessentially European, or northern, as opposed to western (American), eastern or southern, of all four philosophies. Moreover, it is of particular applicability when a commericially based enterprise evolves into a managerially directed organization (Table 3.2).

Table 3.2   Features of rationalism

Aspect	Attribute
Kindred philosophies	Positivism, scientism
Unit focus	Management, organization
Business outlook	Coordination, hierarchical
Managerial orientation	Professional
Psychological type	Thinking, analysis oriented
Path of evolution	Functional—structural; bureaucracy—requisite organization

THE RATIONAL IDEA

In the economic arena the Physiocrats, the immediate predecessors of Adam Smith, were 'rationalists who set out to find self-evident truths in the light of reason rather than with the help of experience' (Roll, 1954). However, the direct counterparts to the British classical economists were the French socialists. The best known is the nineteenth-century pamphleteer Henri Saint-Simon (1675–1755), who considered the forces of the market as conducive to anarchy rather than as instruments of discipline. However, he upheld private property in strong terms but grounded it in social utility rather than as an absolute right. From each according to his capacity to each according to his works, Saint-Simon saw all producers, employers and employees united in a huge class of 'industrialists'. For the rationalists, whether in Paris or Stockholm, *dirigiste*-style planning supplants free market economics, constitutional law transcends common law. Moreover, the social sciences become dominated by such structural/functionalists rather than empirically based behaviourists. What of the rational management perspective, which is objectively depersonalized rather than experientially personalized?

THE PROFESSIONAL MANAGER

The management thinker who followed in the functional line, with mechanical Descartian precision, was the redoubtable turn-of-the-century engineer and European industrialist, Henri Fayol. In America, moreover, whereas the economy at large has always remained true to the empirically based free market, management thought has been heavily impregnated with rationalism by such people as Frederick Taylor and Henry Ford. More recently in Europe, a structural advocate who has drafted a general theory of bureaucracy is the Canadian, resident in Britain, Elliot Jaques. Henri Fayol deduced his clearcut business and managerial functions, and subsequently Jaques (1989) has articulated his requisite organizational and management structures. In rational, management summary:

- The *subject* of European rationalism has been depersonalized management, duly evolving in its orientation from a functional to a structural one.
- Its *object* has been the enterprise as an institution, dependent on the *dirigiste* state, duly evolving in its structure *from formal organization to 'requisite' bureaucracy* (i.e. complex).

Wholism

FROM CLOSED TO OPEN SYSTEMS

> A conception of something in its highest perfection; a theory that affirms that mind, or the spiritual or ideal is of central importance in reality, asserting either that the ideal element in reality is predominant, or that the intrinsic nature of reality is consciousness.
>
> (*Webster's Third New International Dictionary*)

Commercial realism, whether pragmatically or rationally founded, has all too often been contrasted with social Idealism. In fact it has hitherto epitomized the capitalist–socialist divide. However, this oversimplified division has been challenged in recent years by the Japanese. For, as Pascale and Athos (1982) have written, it has been Honda's or Matsushita's ability to unite matter and spirit, real and ideal, that has underpinned their success. More recently Michel Albert (1991) has indicated that the Germanic and Japanese models of business and management are very similar (Table 3.3).

Table 3.3   Features of wholism

Aspect	Attribute
Kindred philosophies	Idealism, historicism
Unit focus	*Primus inter pares*, industrial association
Business outlook	Cooperation, systemic
Managerial orientation	Developmental
Psychological type	Intuiting, reflectively oriented
Path of evolution	Differentiation—integration; closed cartel—open system

THE PHILOSOPHY OF WHOLISM

Bacon in England, Descartes in France, Hegel in Germany—there lies a formidable European trinity. For Friedrich Hegel, the idealist:

> Every condition of thought or of things—every idea and every situation in the world leads irresistibly to its opposite, and then unites with it to form a higher or more complex whole. History is made only in those periods in which the contradictions of reality are being resolved by growth, as the hesitations and awkwardness of youth pass into the ease and order of maturity

Marx, in his turn, also emerged from this dialectical, developmental mould. Ironically, it was his very failure to follow through with this 'historicist' logic which led him and his followers towards their static state socialism.

In contrast, the German advocates of the social market, the so-called 'Ordo-Liberals', have tried to avoid the excesses of both Communist and Fascist totalitarianism, while retaining, like the *gestalt* school of psychology, the Germanic sense for the social totality. Such a sense also underlies, at least in part, the Dutch notion of the civic economy and the Scandinavian brand of social democracy. Idealism therefore shares with rationalism a notion of partnership between public and private interests, and with humanism a sensitivity for the interdependence between an organization and its environment. However, it stands directly opposed to the brand of economic freedom embodied in Adam Smith's *laissez faire* or in Darwin's survival of the individually fittest.

THE DEVELOPMENTAL MANAGER

Germanic management thinking, as we shall see, has not been made accessible to the world at large. In effect, the Dutch management thinker Bernard Lievegoed, following in Goethe's footsteps, has come up with an approach to the developing organization that is better known than any German version. It also systemically and organically represents a higher rationalism than the systematic and mechanistic bureaucracy which Weber himself articulated and yet so despised because it cut across the developmental, idealist grain. In developmental, industrial summary:

- The *subject* of European idealism has been developing groups of industrialists, duly evolving from differentiated bureaucrats to integrated organizers.
- Its *object* has been the industry, duly evolving in its structure from a closed *cartel* into an open industrial *system*.

Humanism

> Pertaining to the social life or collective relations of mankind; devoted to realising the fullness of human being; a philosophy that asserts the essential dignity and worth of man, relating to the arts and humanities, to the 'good' things of life.
> (*Webster's Third New International Dictionary*).

FROM FAMILY BUSINESS TO SOCIO-ECONOMIC NETWORK

Europe's cultural heritage is richly bestowed not only with the fruits of science and technology, strongly connected with its empirical and rational philosophies, but also with arts and artifacts, represented in 'the humanities'. Such humanistic elements are most strongly rooted in those southern European climes—in ancient Greece and Rome as well as in modern Italy and Spain—where 'taste' is so important. It is also in those parts of Europe where passion, as opposed to mere thought or action, predominates, and where sociability is so prized. (Table 3.4).

Table 3.4 Features of humanism

Aspect	Attribute
Kindred philosophies	Aestheticism, classicism
Unit focus	Family group; social community
Business outlook	Communal, networked
Managerial orientation	Convivial
Psychological type	Feeling, concretely oriented
Path of evolution	Patriarch/social architect; family business/ socio-economic network

THE PHILOSOPHICAL PERSPECTIVE

Renaissance humanism was first and foremost a revolt against the other-worldliness of medieval Christianity, a turning away from preoccupation with personal immortality to making the best of life in this world. For the Renaissance the ideal human being was no longer the ascetic monk but a new type—the universal man, the many-sided personality, delighting in every kind of earthly achievement. The great Italian artists, Leonardo da Vinci and Michelangelo, typified this ideal. The Humanist intellectual awakening consisted largely of a rediscovery and a return to the Greek and Latin classics.

Ferdinando Galiani (1728–87), an eighteenth-century Italian abbot in diplomatic employment in Paris, condemned the dogmatic rationalism of the French Physiocrats, and he called for flexible policies in line with historical and geographical conditions rather than for adherence to immutable principles of allegedly universal applicability. Galiani's doubts about the power of reason to deduce eternal truths reflect the influence of Italy's seminal philosopher, Giambattista Vico (1668–1744), who opposed the antihistorical rationalism characteristic of French Cartesianism. In his approach to history Vico stressed the evolution of social institutions.

Galiani's historical sense made him see value not as an inherent quality of goods but as one that will vary with our changing appreciation of them. He recognized the effect of social forces and stressed the role of fashion as a determinant of our desires and thus values. A historical perspective, for Galiani, gave feeling-centred humanism a *relativist* connection with idealism and a *pragmatic* link with empiricism, maintaining, however, its polar opposition against thought-centred rationalism.

THE CONVIVIAL MANAGER

The flexible specialization cited by economists Piore and Sabel (1984) is the direct antithesis to formal bureaucracy and to large-scale mass production. As such, it directly reflects Galiani's doubts over undiluted rationality. It also draws upon the aesthetic sensitivities, highlighted by Alberti in the fifteenth century.

Leon Battista Alberti (1404–72) was a humanist who had not yet lost his faith in our capacity to act effectively in human affairs. Alberti's confidence in our capacity to organize the world led him to assert that humanity achieves its highest expression in two arts: plastic and political. In the former art we discover order and harmony in nature; in the latter we translate that order and harmony into social terms. A perfect example of the latter has been the industrialist and humanist Aurelio Peccei who, as founder of the 'Club of Rome', attempted to bring a 'human quality' into the global business environment. In humanistic, societal summary:

- The *subject* of European humanism has been the politically and artistically based *impresario*, duly evolving in orientation from patriarch or matriarch to *impannatore*.
- Its *object* has been the community, duly evolving in its structure from a *family business into socio-economic network*.

So much for the separately differentiated European parts. We now need to turn to the dynamically integrated European management whole.

THE EUROPEAN BUSINESSPHERE

Complementary forces

The combined Western–Eastern (empiricist–idealist) and Northern–Southern (rationalist–humanist) dimensions provide a basic template, a force field of creative tension for European and for global management.

Within this 'European businessphere' will be the adjacent countries; without lies the rest of the business world. Inevitably and globally they interpenetrate.

As we traverse such 'outer space' we shall in Jungian terms cross an equivalent 'inner space'. In so consciously doing we move, in accordance with Jung's psychological types (popularized by Myers Briggs) from sensation-oriented *pragmatism* towards thought-centred *rationalism*; and from intuition-based *wholism* towards feeling-centred *humanism*. The totality, albeit made up of differing degrees of emphasis, of light and shade, of colour and contrast constitutes the whole personality.

For Jung the fully functioning individual, on the one hand, is able to move back and forth between his or her primary and secondary psychological types. In other words, an empirical (sensing type) orientation is often combined with (thinking type) rationality. This was, interestingly enough, the case for Adam Smith and also for Isaac Newton who effectively linked induction with deduction.

Contradictory forces

On the other hand, the fully functioning individual—or business or economy—needs to come to terms with what Jung has called the shadow. The shadow side of our personalities stands in opposition to our primary selves, as empiricism does to idealism. In Jung's view, if we fail to acknowledge this opposing force it will unconsciously subvert our conscious purposes. For example, in the UK—in the absence of a healthy idealism—an ideologically based class war subverts its pragmatically based market economy. Conversely, the individualizing thrust of Anglo-Saxon influence on collectivist Germany after the Second World War helped that nation to regain a dynamic balance. Similarly, the relative success of central Italy, *vis-à-vis* the north but more particularly the south, is because it has succeeded in balancing, at least to some degree, the opposing forces of thought-centred rationality and feeling-centred humanism.

Interestingly enough, moreover, if the shadow side of management, as with personality, is shunned it assumes its most primitive form. For example, while experientially based education is limited in Germany and Japan, trade associations in Britain and America are of limited economic influence when compared to their multifaceted German and Japanese counterparts.

European management as a dynamic whole represents an interplay between the four psychological or philosophical types, albeit with different shades of emphasis in the various European regions. Whereas Michel Albert has identified a major east–west polarity separating the free market/empiricist Anglo-Saxons from the social market-idealist Nippo–Germans, we would argue that there is an equally important north–south tension between rationalism and humanism.

In the final analysis, though, all four philosophical factors are required for integrated managerial learning and organization development. Moreover, as and when space is transformed into time, experientially based enterprise develops into professionally based organization. Thereafter, and in turn, the developmentally oriented industrial association ultimately develops into the convivially networked economy and society.

Conclusion

THE EUROPEAN MANAGEMENT WHOLE

While it is obvious for all to see that, for example, the Japanese and the British come from very different cultures, which in turn affect their management and business behaviours, it may not be so clearly apparent that different European regions and nations have fundamentally different philosophical traditions. These, in their turn, radically precondition the art of the possible, in management as in life as a whole (Table 3.5). They are the generic factors of European production. Within a particular European company, we ignore these at our peril.

Table 3.5 The European management whole

Generic philosophy	Management type	Process	Orientation
Pragmatism	Experiential	Competition	Transactional
Rationalism	Professional	Coordination	Normative
Wholism	Developmental	Cooperation	Integrative
Humanism	Convivial	Co-creation	Transforming

FROM EUROPEAN CULTURE TO MANAGERIAL BEHAVIOUR

Having described the proposed European 'businessphere' it is now necessary for us to reveal the significance of the different levels of analysis, before revisiting each of the philosophical and managerial domains in turn.

4

Mapping the European terrain

We shall now outline all the four 'intracultural' levels with which you were initially acquainted in Chapter 1. In each case we shall specify the managerial question which most appropriately arises out of a particular layer—respectively explicit and externalized, and implicit and internalized —within each level and then address it in outline (see Table 4.1).

Level 1—Managerial 'attributes'

1/1 EXPLICIT MANAGERIAL BEHAVIOUR
How can I get the best out of a particular British, French, German or Italian employee/colleague/boss/customer/supplier/official?

Comparative behaviour
At this surface level we notice—tangibly and overtly through specific behaviours—the action-centred leadership of the experientially based manager concerned with making things happen, in contrast to the reflective orientation of the developmental manager, who is more concerned with making things work. Similarly, whereas the professional manager is characterized by his or her formality and intellectual virtuosity, the convivial manager is noted rather for his or her flexibility and political acumen.

Strongly localized
Externally visible managerial behaviour is not only the most immediately accessible of all the layers, it is also the most strongly localized. For that reason, the visible behaviour in France of the Lyonnais is bound to be somewhat different from that of the Parisian, as will that of the Yorkshireman compared with the Cornishman in England. Such local variations, though common, are complicated to detect and knowledge

Table 4.1 The European management terrain

	Personal	*Managerial*	*Cooperative*	*Communal*
A T T R I B U T E S	Making things happen	Intellectual virtuosity	Making things work	Political cultivation
M O D E L S	Free enterprise	Formal bureaucracy	Production system	Family business
	Learning company	Requisite organization	Systemic industrial association	Flexible specialization
I D E A S	Free market	*Dirigiste* economy	Social market	Socio-economic network
	Empiricism	Rationalism	Idealism	Humanism
I M A G E S	Drama/literature	Art/architecture	Classical music	Dance/opera

about them is best acquired through extensive first-hand exposure. This behavioural layer, in effect, most lends itself to exposure of the senses, that is, to sight and hearing, touch, taste and smell. Powers of direct observation are therefore at a premium, spread over a wide range of specific contexts and within informal as well as formal settings.

Experientially based

In a training context, video playbacks on comparative behaviour in the classroom as well as role plays on cross-cultural communications and negotiations will be particularly appropriate. Such training methods, moreover, should be intertwined with good food and drink, combined with storytelling and folk music that is representative of the local cultures involved. Such practical books as those of John Mole (1991) and Barzini (1974) provide suitable reading in this context, covering the tangible specifics of the culture, such as styles of greeting and parting, patterns of time keeping, social customs, body language and, of course, the indigenous language.

1/2 IMPLICIT MANAGERIAL ATTITUDES

How can I respond better to the members of my team across British, French, German or Italian cultural boundaries?

Comparative attitudes

Whereas, implicitly and internally, experientially based managers are conscious of themselves as individuals, their developmental counterparts are managerially comparatively unaware, being more oriented towards product rather than personal quality. Similarly, while rationally based managers maintain their professional and logical integrity, their convivial counterparts are more inclined to bring their artistic outlook to bear upon everyday commercial, technical and social transactions.

Thought about behaviour

Attitude, like behaviour, is specific to an individual but, unlike behaviour, it cannot be directly observed. For attitudes are implicit rather than explicit, internalized rather than externalized. They are therefore less readily accessible to the senses than observed behaviour, and have to be inferred with the help of ready-made questionnaires or suitable inventories. The respondent, in effect, has to think about his or her behaviour rather than merely produce it. In a training context, therefore, management inventories are required to help to measure attitudes and subsequently predict behaviour in a cross-cultural setting. Such questionnaires need to be supplemented by exercises whereby attitudes are compared and contrasted, and appropriate feedback is given on perceptions and misperceptions. Particular aspects of managing across cultures include those relating to motivation, communication and, of course, leadership.

Culture's consequences
The best known of the questionnaire-based approaches in the cross-cultural field is that of Geert Hofstede (1991), the Dutchman who based his research on the responses of IBM managers worldwide. It is interesting to note that the other major research in this area has been that conducted by another Dutchman, Fons Trompenaars (1993). There seems to be something in the cultural air in Holland that gives the Dutch a particular kind of analytically based sensitivity towards cultural differences. Hofstede categorized his sample population, after thousands of IBM employees had completed carefully designed questionnares, according to their *individuality* (IDV), *masculinity* (MAS), *uncertainty avoidance* (UAI), and what he termed *'power distance'* (PDI), that is, their desire to exercise power over others.

We now turn from personal behaviour and managerial attitudes (attribute level 1) to institutional frameworks and organizational concepts (model level 2).

Level 2—'Models' of management and organization

2/1 EXPLICIT INSTITUTIONAL FRAMEWORKS
What rules and procedures, systems and procedures, facts and figures do we need to be on top of, in the different European countries, as an employer, as a producer, as a distributor, and as a citizen of the country?

Comparative frameworks
Whereas experientially based managers relish the individualistic and somewhat chaotic nature of free enterprise, their professional counterparts are more at home within the orderly and somewhat depersonalized, formal bureaucracy. Similarly, while developmental managers are attuned to workflow within the production system their convivial European counterparts are more inclined towards social relations within the family network.

Know what
In the 1990s there has been a proliferation of practical books and articles on European institutions affecting management and organization. A major point of focus has been upon pan-European institutions of a technological, economic, political and legal nature. The information on these has been characteristically depersonalized, structural and functional, factual and statistical. More widespread, though, has been the literature on comparative institutions across the European communities.

Particular emphasis has been placed at a macro level on education and training, banking and finance, trade unions and trade associations and governmental relations with industry and commerce. Conversely, at a micro level a comparative approach to the structures and functions of management—technology, people, finance and market based—has been undertaken.

Hard data

At both macro and micro levels, moreover, account needs to be taken of key and comparative statistics that affect the institutional infrastucture. At a macro level, demographic trends, climatic features, legal statutes, political developments, economic facts and figures need to be accounted for. At a micro level, customer profiles, lifestyle trends, promotional patterns, prevailing technologies, as well as comparative access to factors of production require analytical and practical consideration. Training programmes therefore need to be filled with relevant data, practical cases, authoritative presentations from institutional representatives and visits to the pertinent institutions themselves. In effect, a case study orientation, at this institutionally and functionally based level, is wholly appropriate.

2/2 IMPLICIT ORGANIZATIONAL CONCEPTS

How can we design inherently British, French, German or Italian organizations, and subsequently conceptualize a generically European model, with a view to adapting our organizational structures and functions to indigenous conditions, thereby enhancing composite performance?

Beyond the threshold

It is at this particular point that conventional European wisdom reaches its *cul de sac*. Our implicit models of organization and management are largely American, even though the Americans in their turn may have originally—say, half a century ago—drawn on European models. Yet it is these implicit models, invisible though they may be, that predetermine our management and organizational stuctures, as well as functions, in Europe. If managerial attributes make up the subsystems, then organizational models comprise the underlying system below.

Comparative models

Experientially based managers, with their characteristically inductive approaches, are inherently disposed towards a bottom-up approach to what is now being termed the *learning company* (Lessem, 1991). Conversely, their rationally based counterparts, with their deductive orientations, incline towards a top-down *requisitely* structured organization (Jaques, 1991), with hierarchical strata to accommodate progressively decreasing levels of cognitive complexity. Similarly, whereas developmental managers evolve their large-scale organizations towards a point of systemic industrial association (Lievegoed, 1990), their convivial counterparts retain smallness of scale, within the context of regionalized socio-economic networks (Piore and Sabel, 1984).

Alternating contexts

Geert Hofstede (1991) has uncovered four 'implicit models of organization' around the world, somewhat similar to our own. Three of these, he perceived, had particular application in Europe.

For Hofstede, in the German 'workflow bureaucracy', work processes are rigidly prescribed but not relationships. In a 'full bureaucracy', as in France and Italy, everything is rigidly prescribed whereas in Britain's 'market model' relationships among people or among work processes are not rigidly preset. A comparative portrayal of European, American and Japanese organizational concepts in an educational context would establish the contextual richness required to evoke such reflective thinking. Seminal management books need to replace business cases, and didactic teaching methods of a Socratic nature are required instead of experientially oriented approaches to management education. However, models of management and organization, both explicit and implicit, are embedded within a deeper infra-structure.

Level 3—Economic and philosophical 'ideas'

3/1 EXPLICIT ECONOMIC POLICIES
How can our own activities influence the economic or industrial policies in the respective countries in which we are operating, so that our industrial or commercial productivity and productive relations can be enhanced in line with the countries' own economic and social development?

Comparative economic policies

At this third level, explicitly characterized by its economic policies, management is subsumed by a 'suprasystem' that transcends its particular organization. In other words, both the institutional frameworks and the organizational models are embedded within the industry and the economy of a region, if not of the country at large.

The four European domains we are covering are respectively characterized by the free market so dear to the competitor, the social market more attuned to the cooperator, the *dirigiste* economy favoured by the coordinator and the socio-economic networks preferred by the co-creator, albeit with variations on these themes. Moreover, although the development of a globally based economy in some respects overtakes such regional and national contextual variations, it is the exploitation of such differences which creates added value at this third, policy-making level.

Enhancing productive relations

In order to participate as management in a truly effective way at a wider policy-making level, you need to have more than 'good connections'. Such connections are important at the ground level 1, in the same way as it is essential, at level 2, to know your facts and figures, rules and procedures. At level 3, though, it is of the greatest importance to be aware of the historical and philosophical context from which the economic policies have emerged. An understanding of Adam Smith and the empirically based classical economic tradition needs to be supplemented, for example, by an appreciation of the 'romantic' economists and of the developmentally inclined 'Ordo-Liberals', who emerged in Germany after the Second World War.

Education in context

Management education therefore needs to incorporate economic history within its curriculum, set in its appropriate cultural and philosophical context. Our manager operating in Germany would not only make a point of being on the *Aufsichtsrat* or Board of several associated companies, but would be in a position to shape the development of his or her industry, because of an appreciation of the wider, level 3 context. In that respect, moreover, he or she needs to develop synthetically based intuitive faculties that transcend but remain inclusive of analytically based thoughts.

3/3 IMPLICIT PHILOSOPHY

How can we become so finely attuned to the philosophical base of countries in which we operate that their economic and social development, together with our organizational growth and evolution, will become one and the same?

Comparative philosophies

Pragmatically based empiricism, as we have already indicated, has given rise to experientially based managers whereas dialectically based idealism has created developmentally oriented managers. At the same time, while deductively based rationalism has led to analytically and numerically adept professionally based managers, humanism has resulted in socially and politically adept convivial managers. While these four sets of philosophies have their most strongly established respective bases in

England, Germany, France and Italy, there are many regional variations on these broad themes.

Philosophical dissonance and resonance

If there is dissonance between a country's longstanding philosophical heritage and its current economic policy, as is the case in Britain today, the national economy will duly falter. Such dissonance can arise for two distinct reasons. First, which is not the case in Britain, there may be a gap between, say, its empirically based philosophy and market-based economy. Second, which is the British case, the generic philosophy may not have been reviewed, updated and adaptively incorporated into its renewed organization and management.

To the extent that one is able to turn nationally based economic dissonance into resonance, one will thereby enhance industrial or commercial performance on a large scale. Interestingly enough, this has been at least partially the case for the Japanese in Britain. They have brought their brand of 'peoplism' into the communal Welsh valleys and the parochial 'Geordie' heartlands while also providing for a touch of Anglo-Saxon individualism along the way. In fact, Sony and Nissan, for example, have managed to blend in the 'action learning' orientation of the British with Japanese-style quality circles.

Resonant management development

Finally, management development in this context should be closely linked with organizational and economic development. The development of individual managers, at the same time, should be enhanced by high-powered instruction, reading and discussion on comparative philosophies. The philosophies we have focused upon in this research are individually oriented *pragmatism*, organizationally centred *rationalism*, industrially based *wholism* and communally oriented *humanism*. Management will thereby be led to refine its intuitively based insights, tinged with a feeling for a society as a whole. This leads us on to culture.

Level 4—'Images' of organization

4/1 EXPLICIT CULTURE
How can the spirit of origination with which our greatest art and artifacts, music and literature are imbued inspire our business community?

In search of excellence

In our particular journey into European management we have only proceeded tentatively beyond the layer of 'ideas', at level 3. The world of culturally laden 'images' makes up the fourth and deepest level of not analysis but pure synthesis. The most recent example of such symbolic influence on management is that passion for excellence that Peters and Waterman (1982) have originated, with many a customer-care and total quality programme following in its wake. The fact that we Europeans may be taking that image of 'excellent' management on board out of its American context seems to pass many of us by.

In fact excellence, within the European tradition, is manifested most clearly within the arts, rather than in business. Whereas the empirical tradition has given rise to excellence most notably in drama and literature, the idealistic one is most noted for its orchestral music. While the rationalist philosophy has created, most markedly, art and architecture, the humanistic tradition is acclaimed, in Italy and Spain at least, for it dance and opera.

The unique quality of Europe

To outline what is involved at this symbolic level without proceeding substantively hereafter, we shall draw on the work of that extraordinary Spanish diplomat, academician, writer and institution builder, Salvador de Madariaga (1886–1978). For, in the first half of this century, de Madariaga was not only a Spanish ambassador and then Professor of Literature at Oxford, but he also wrote his unique *Portrait of Europe* (1968) while establishing his 'College of Europe' in Bruges. De Madariaga based his European portrait in general, as well as his appreciation of 'Englishman, Frenchman, Spaniard' in particular, upon the comparative literature of the constituent European nations (de Madariaga, 1922). These he first contrasted with their Continental neighbours. For de Madariaga, whereas in Africa the stress is on the roots and in Asia it is on the foliage, in Europe the focus is on the stem. The roots are the obscure part of the tree of life, garnered and pooled by the vast commonality of our ancestors. The foliage, light and airy, is strong in Asia from where Europe has drawn its great religions.

Europe is strongest in the stem, the one individualized part of the tree, in which the structure stands out as a well-defined unit of life, the conscious mind and will. While Asia yearns towards heavenly things and Africa remains sub-earthly, Europe dispenses its being into myriad separate human stems; and prefers to express its genius in terms of individuals. Significant differences of variety within a relatively narrow field of unity, for de Madariaga, account for the typically European gift of quality. The essence of quality for the European is uniqueness. Someone, something, has quality when he or she or it can be distinguished from the rest.

The variety of Europe, on the one hand, gives to each of its 'characters' in their inner conversation enough definiteness and richness for the discussion to be lively. The unity of Europe, on the other, preserves enough common ground and sufficiently reduces the barriers between the inner voices for the discussion to be stimulating and fertile. It is this perennial argument going on in the inner recesses of the European being which has determined the remarkable evolution of the European intellect. For the intellect, like all forms of life, is stimulated by exercise. Sad to say, hitherto such lively intellectual debate between European countries and cultures has not taken place among its management schools. Rather, American management concepts have dominated the academic scene, narrowing the basis for individual distinctiveness.

Intellectual quality and individual distinction, then, are naturally interrelated. They must be tasted or directly felt, de Madariaga claims, in order to be known. Unity the stem, variety the branches, quality the flower, taste the aroma, such is the symbolic tree of the spirit of Europe. In this cultural realm, therefore, it is aesthetically based intuitions, combined with feelings, that need to be drawn upon.

4/2 ARCHETYPAL MANAGEMENT
How can management tap the spirit of Europe as a whole, and hence the hearts and minds of its people, both within the business community and without?

The spirit of nations
As we have now seen, de Madariaga portrays Europe as a continent of quality rather than quantity, rich in shades and tensions. Within it people have acquired not only neat individual but also neat national outlines. These, in turn, are so clearly defined that they can be conveyed in one word—symbols. Specifically, an Englishman is an 'island', for whom a word is a 'tool'; a Frenchman is an 'crystal', for whom a word is a 'blueprint'; a German is a 'river', for whom a word is an 'encyclopedia' of the idea it expresses; and an Italian is a 'foil', for whom a word is an exquisite 'morsel'.

The archetypal energy field
The archetypal field has first to be uncovered for managers, through such interpreters as Salvador de Madariaga and the African adventurer, novelist and soul-mate of Jung, Laurens Van Der Post (1978). Then these need to be converted into a European business context. In effect, Jung's psychological types, as reflected managerially by Myers Briggs, are a rational form of archetypal expression (Fig. 4.1).

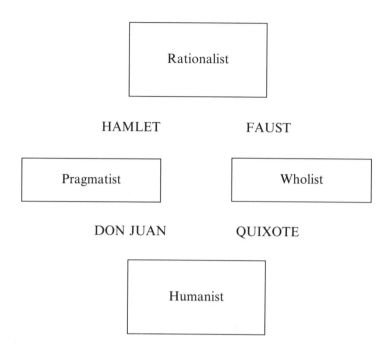

Fig. 4.1   Archetypal forms and psychological types

Our key developmental task at this final layer is therefore to enable managers to journey back and forth between archetypal and rational, empirical and ideal forms, both within the European business community and in the marketplace. Because of its Renaissance traditions, Italy may well be the most fertile ground for such originative activities in which deep feeling combined with profound intuition is of the archetypal essence. In effect, a truly transformative business community, deeply grounded in European soil, would be able to turn its archetypal images into everyday industrial and commercial effect, as Alberti's plastic and political artists! Finally, in order to establish such a business community alternating between outer-directed and inner-directed layers Europe would need to be operating at all the levels—one to four—or its innovations would never see the light of day. Whereas surface attributes can function without the depths, albeit duly removed from their sources of origination, the imaginative depths cannot be realized without passing through the surface. It is now time to conclude.

Conclusion

The European manager–organization–association–community that combines realism with idealism, reason with humanity, will span four levels of being. Each of these, moreover, will involve both outer- and inner-directed layers of activity. This, as we shall see, has significant implications for management and organizational development.

REVIEWING THE LEVELS OF EUROPEAN MANAGEMENT

The four levels in their turn have the following characters and trajectories:

- *Attribute*-based level 1 is directed at the individual manager and his other team. It involves him or her responding to and thereafter exploiting the varied behaviours and attitudes that can be explicitly observed or implicitly recognized among individual Europeans.
- *Model*-based level 2 is directed at senior management, individually, and at the Board, collectively. It involves them both in perceiving and also conceiving diverse institutional frameworks and organizational concepts, within the constituent European nations.
- *Idea*-based level 3 is directed at what Porter (1990) has termed a 'business cluster', or at what the French call a *filière*, via the German style of communitarian *Aufsichtsrat*. It involves such a grouping in both appreciating the significance of and in also regenerating industrial and economic policies. These, in their turn, are set in the context of the philosophies of diverse European language groups.
- *Image*-based level 4 is directed at business-in-society, within a regional, national or international network. It involves that communal body, on the one hand, in being immersed in the 'humanities' of a particular society, and, on the other, in actively transforming it. Explicit cultural forms and implicit archetypal ones form the communal 'lingua franca' at this particular stage.

IMPLICATIONS FOR MANAGEMENT AND ORGANIZATION DEVELOPMENT

The specific implications for the development of managers, their organizations, their whole industries and business communities are finally as follows:

- The activation of *individual managers' attributes*, whereby each can manage adeptly across cultures requires both behavioural change through exposure to diverse regions and countries (including language training) and attitudinal change through appropriate simulations and role plays (backed up by suitable instrumentation and measurement).
- The perception of *models of organization and management*, on the one hand, is enhanced by appropriate case material, both live and

documented—in book and case form. Their conception, on the other, is enhanced by didactively based teaching, provided by original management thinkers from each European country, together with the seminal books each has written.

- The development of *economic and philosophical ideas* about an industry, an economy and a society requires an exposure to all walks of life, in a particular language group, as well as the assimilation of its seminal economic and philosophical ideas through lectures and readings. The regeneration of an industry or of an economy requires a combination of attitudinal change, model rebuilding and philosophical exploration.

- The transformation of *business-in-society* requires both an affinity with the indigenous art and culture, mediated through appropriate interpreters, and an ability to use archetypal images in order to create organizational forms that are built upon archetypal foundations with a view to subsequently winning over indigenously rooted hearts and minds.

Not surprisingly European management has some way to go before it comes of age. However, we do hope that in this particular book we will set out some of the important milestones along the way. We start with Anglo-Saxon pragmatism.

Part II

Pragmatism—Experiential

5

Free enterprise

Companies in the past have tended to expect their employees to conform to the wishes of the company. This is less and less practicable as a philosophy of operation, and I believe absolutely that in the future it will be the company that conforms to the individual that attracts and motivates the best people.

John Harvey-Jones, *Making it Happen*

The pragmatic space

Pragmatism, as a philosophical main stem rooted in individual self-consciousness is often linked to both empiricism and individualism. Such a pragmatic approach to business is particularly strong in the Anglo-Saxon world, but is also in evidence in the Benelux countries and Scandinavia (Fig. 5.1). From that potent source has sprung the free market (economically), the competitively inclined enterprise (commercially), and the independent-minded entrepreneur (psychologically). The combined fruits are profitable commercial and personal growth. While commercial growth is outer directed, personal growth is inner directed.

The present-day apostle of pragmatism, experimentation and individualism in management is, of course, Tom Peters in America. However, the American pragmatic approach within the organization has been imbued with other philosophical streams, particularly the rationalist one against which Peters so strongly reacts. For a purer form of managerial pragmatism we shall turn to England, and ultimately to its greatest management thinker, Reg Revans.

PRAGMATISM IN TIME

Within a historical perspective the entrepreneur, rooted in Victorian traditions of self-help, is now being transformed into a modern manager engaging in individual self-development. In that context the self-assertive entrepreneur is being supplanted by the self-actualizing manager. Jan

61

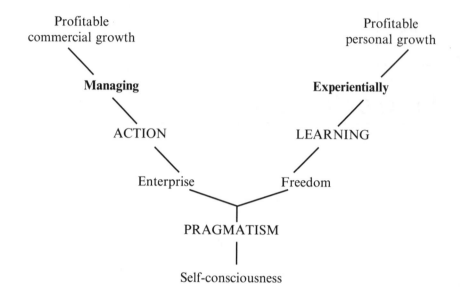

Fig. 5.1 The pragmatic tree

Carlzon and John Harvey-Jones is a case in point. Similarly, the independent firm, having been grounded in classical free enterprise, is now beginning to emerge as a learning company. Whereas in this chapter we shall be outlining the empirically based images and ideas—the roots and main stem—in Chapters 6 and 7 we shall be concerned with more specific models and attributes—the pragmatic branches and fruits.

Images of self—the roots of empiricism

THE ARCHETYPAL SELF

To be or not to be
In seeking to balance individual freedom and social discipline the European manager has to establish harmony between will and mind, management and organization. According to the Austrian philosopher and economist, Rudolph Steiner (1972), the development of individual self-consciousness in the UK was foreshadowed by the Magna Charta in 1215. England has therefore been its purest representative in the world, though the faculty has unfolded in Europe and, to a greater or lesser extent, all over the world.

In the pursuit of individual freedom we become fully conscious of our own ego. The consummation of a Shakespearean tragedy is always a supreme act of self-recognition, forced on the hero by the inexorable drive of external events. It is the terrible shock of contact with the material world, the necessity for grappling, alone and unaided, with its evils that brings us face to face with our true selves. Such self-consciousness stays not only to contemplate the ego we have discovered but to pour forth devotion to the external world which it is our mission not only to perceive but also to redeem. This mood of self, with its twofold nature, has been peculiarly English (Faulkner Jones, 1932).

Self in world

English self-consciousness finds its expression in and through physical activity. The most striking manifestation of this has been the rapid development in the last few centuries of the physical sciences. Industrial civilization, moreover, first developed in England, arose out of them. At the same time, the average English manager is inclined to overestimate not only the importance of the material plane but also the strength and independence of his or her own ego: 'What must be felt and recognized in English literature is not intellectual brilliance, not the apotheosis of human passions, but the subtle, manifold expression of that new element on earth—human individuality' (Faulkner Jones, 1932). Again we are reminded of Harvey-Jones's style of leadership.

For the self-conscious individual not only becomes aware of himself or herself but also has the power to recognize the ego as it appears in others. Shakespeare, for example, was able to experience many other individualities, ranging from Hamlet to Ophelia, Othello to Desdemona. For Tom Peters it is the power to get close to the individual customer that ultimately counts.

THE UNDERLYING CULTURE

Natural involvement

According to Rudolph Steiner, we are being driven by the course of evolution, into closer contact with matter. Through his 'extra-empirical' bent, 'the English writer awakens loving interest in the outer world, transforming it into something higher' (Faulkner Jones, 1932). The empirically oriented writer, like the pragmatically oriented manager, works primarlily from sense observation. He or she builds up a feeling for the world from a detailed knowledge of the separate parts that make up the whole. The English poet rarely uses the word 'nature', but observes with remarkable accuracy each flower, bird and tree until a tender intimacy develops. For the Anglo-Saxon manager, again, closer points of contact with other employees, and customers, necessitate progressive de-layering of organizations.

Close to life

The pragmatic world view, then, keeps as close as possible to life. From life it borrows its complexity, its elasticity, its illogicality, its delicate shading. It does not worry about form. Whereas thinking implies a separation from things thought, experience is a stream of life which bathes the individual at every moment in a well of practicality. When the outcome is that of inspiration, the neglect of form allows a greater freedom on the part of the creative spirit. That spirit is enhanced when allied to a deep sense of social service: 'A kind of internal inspiration seems then to guide the work, like the instinct that guides the root towards the richer layer of earth' (de Madariaga, 1968). Reg Revans, as we shall see, is a typical case in point.

Having briefly reviewed the cultural roots, let us now investigate that pragmatic main stem. In fact this has underpinned the development of business and management in the modern era, at least until the 1960s when Japan and Germany came into their own. We shall start with Francis Bacon, the person who invented scientific method in the sixteenth century.

Learning and enterprise—the main stem of pragmatism

PRAGMATIC PHILOSOPHY

Pragmatism can be traced back for our purposes to the inductively based scientific investigations in the seventeenth century of Queen Elizabeth's Lord Chancellor, Francis Bacon (1561–1626). Its immediate economic derivatives are those of Adam Smith's eighteenth-century free enterprise and Samuel Smiles's nineteenth-century self-help. Finally, a twentieth-century social philosopher and management thinker has fused together enterprise and learning, self-help and self-development. This originator of 'action learning' is Reg Revans, England's Cambridge physicist and most original management thinker.

Francis Bacon—the advancement of learning

The exponent of a new philosophy in the latter part of the sixteenth century, Bacon was born into a world that, as today, was becoming part of a new European and global order. England had detached itself from feudal Europe and was becoming a nation state with a national Church. Power was being transferred from the Church to the laity, perhaps in the same way as power today is shifting from unionized labour towards professionally based knowledge workers. In the so-called 'device' of 1592, Bacon analysed the problem which confronted his age. The learning of the day bore little relation to the productive processes of industry. That proclamation has a familiar ring to it some four hundred years later!

The story of Francis Bacon is that of a life devoted to one great idea. The idea gripped him as a boy, grew with the varied experiences of his life and occupied him on his deathbed. The idea is now commonplace, partly realized, partly tarnished, still often misunderstood. But in his day it was a novelty. It was simply, according to Bacon's biographer Benjamin Farrington (1973), that knowledge should bear fruit in work and that science should be applicable to industry. 'May God the Creator,' Bacon urged, 'protect and guide this work both in its ascent to glory and in its descent to the service of man.' The ascent to glory is the inductive process leading to the highest axioms. The descent to the service of man in the deductive process by which science is applied to works. These, for Farrington, are the two most important moments of the Baconian scientific process. The ascent we may describe as learning and the descent as innovation.

Only learned men, Bacon maintained in his *The Advancement of Learning*, find business as agreeable to health of mind as exercise is to health of body (page 15). Man, Bacon insisted, must find out the facts about the universe. He must maintain the great continuity and transmission of learning through universities dedicated not to the dry husks of ancient learning alone but to research upon the natural world of the present. Then and only then would the invisible world drawn from man's mind become a genuine reality. Lamentably, 'Elizabethan craftsmen or seafarers sometimes made discoveries', Bacon noted, 'but the experiments of calloused hands were often scorned by gentlemen' (page 23). For Bacon, artisan and scribe, action and learning, need to be inextricably intertwined. This was certainly not so for his predecessors.

Touching the popular mind

Truth for the medieval schoolmen rested upon the belief that reality lay in the world of ideas largely independent of our sense perceptions. Francis Bacon presented quite another 'engine', as he termed it, for the attainment of truth. He opposed this engine of *inductive logic* to the old way of thinking. In essence, his argument was as follows. People must refrain from deducing general principles for which they have no real evidence in nature. Instead, they must dismiss much of what they think they know and begin anew patiently to collect facts from nature. They must never stray far from reality until it is possible, through close observation, to deduce more general laws. 'The real problem for Bacon', according to his American biographer, the scientist and philosopher Loren Eisler (1962), 'was to break with the dead hand of the traditional past, to free latent intellectual talent, to arrest and touch with hope the popular mind.' Though he sought to combine the discoveries of the practical craftsman with the insights of the philosopher, Bacon saw more clearly than any of the other Renaissance writers the development of the experimental method itself. Science, for him, was therefore inherently democratic.

Bacon therefore eliminated reliance upon the rare elusive genius as a safe road into the future. It involved too much risk and chance to rely upon such men alone. Instead, Bacon placed his hope for Utopia in the education of plain Tom Jones and Dick Thickhead, as did Harvey-Jones 400 years later. Bacon had an enormous trust in the capacities of the human mind, even though no one had defined better than he its idols and distortions. Perhaps Bacon imposed too much hope on the common man. He, the Lord Chancellor, was willing to build his empire of hope from common clay. It is not, Bacon explained, the pleasure of curiosity nor ambition or fame that are the true ends of learning. Rather, it is a restitution in man of the sovereignty and power which he had in the first state of creation.

Combining reason and will

Francis Bacon regarded learning as composed of two parts. First there is existing knowledge, organized and disseminated through books and other forms of communication. Second, there is the discovery of new knowledge through experience, indeed through experiment. In the first event or occurence after the fall of man, Bacon argues, we see an image of the two estates, the contemplative and the active. They are presented in the two persons of Abel and Cain, and in the two simplest and most primitive trades of life, that of the shepherd and that of the husbandman: 'The knowledge, which respecteth the faculties of mind, is of two kinds: the one representing understanding and reason, and the other his will, appetite and action; whereof the former produceth position or degree, the latter action and execution.' While, for example, we might turn to Michael Porter's *Competitive strategy* for position and degree, we would look to John Harvey-Jones to *make it happen*, through appetite and will. The two were hitherto disconnected.

The great instauration—creating a learning society

To remedy this situation Bacon suggested in the 'device' that royal assistance was required. A library of books ancient and modern in all tongues should be collected. There should be botanical gardens and a zoo on the grandest scale, fully accessible to observation. A museum should contain and classify inanimate natural objects and the products of man's ingenuity and skill. A laboratory should be equipped with all materials required for experimental research. Bacon calls such societal learning or relearning, 'instauration', that is, a restoration or renewal. He takes 31 ancient fables of the Greeks and draws from them his own political and scientific views. The title page tells us that the book is 'The Great Instauration' Francis of Verulam, Lord Chancellor of England.

Bacon tried to make of man an actively anticipatory rather than a reminiscent or 'present' creature. To anticipate, however, the human being must be made conscious of his own culture. Education must assume a role unguessed in his time and imperfectly realized in ours. It must neither denigrate nor worship the past. It must learn from it. Bacon is not content to subsist in the natural world as it exists, nor to drift aimlessly in history. The focal point for all his thinking is action not system building.

> The organizing principle of all his vast erudition was the aim of extending, not man's power of argument, but his power of action. But the special character of his enterprise was his insistence that a reform in practice depended on a reform in thought. Progress in power and progress in knowledge are two aspects of the same thing. Works were the test of truth rather than having value above it.
> (Eisler, 1962, page 58)

Bacon, like a typically 'Western' manager, was a pragmatist. Aristotle's logic was an aid to thinking; its goal was logical consistency. Bacon's logic was a guide to action; its test was whether it worked. The same applied to Adam Smith's free market economics.

The market mechanism

FREE MARKET POLICY

Theory: Adam Smith—promoting free enterprise
Adam Smith (1723–90) was a Professor of Moral Philosophy at Glasgow University in the late eighteenth century. The naturalist school of philosophy to which both Bacon and Smith belonged had an unbroken tradition from the later Greek Stoics onwards. It received a great stimulus in the Renaissance and the Reformation, and showed itself in a modified form in Hobbes and Locke. It then came to full flower in the latter part of the seventeenth century.

In spite of their sharp distinctions from the Stoics, Francis Bacon and Adam Smith—according to the British economic historian Eric Roll (1953)—can be regarded as representative of a single stream of naturalist thought. Its essence is a reliance on what is natural as against what is contrived. For Smith only complete competition was consistent with natural liberty. Only such competition could ensure that everyone obtained the full rewards for their efforts and added their full contributions to the common good. Human conduct, according to Adam Smith, was naturally activated by six motives. These were self-love, sympathy, the desire to be free, a sense of propriety, a habit of labour and the propensity to truck, barter and exchange one thing for another. Given these springs of conduct, each person was naturally the best judge of his or her own interest and should therefore be left to pursue their task in their own way.

According to Smith, if left to himself man would not only attain his own best advantage he would also further the common good. Each individual was led by an invisible hand to promote the interest of society. The medievalists had called for good works; the reformers for faith. The classicists demanded neither, their concern being this world rather than the other. Instead, Smith drove home the demand for *laissez faire*, a system of natural liberty, as the best means of bringing about the wealth of nations. In such a system individuals could pursue their own self-interest, but, regardless of their intentions, a providential order would tend to turn the pursuit of self-interest into an instrument serving the interest of society.

Labour theory of value

Let us now pursue the argument. In Smith's own words:

> The annual labour fund of every nation must be regulated by two different circumstances. First it is regulated by the skill, dexterity and judgment with which its labour is generally applied; and secondly by the proportion of those who are engaged in useful labour, and those who are not.
>
> (*The Wealth of Nations*, page 1)

The division of that labour, Smith argues, is not the effect of a conscious plan. Rather

> it is the necessary, though very slow and gradual consequence of a certain propensity in human nature. This has in view the propensity to truck, barter and exchange one thing for another.

Almost every other race of animals, Smith continues, when grown to maturity is entirely independent and in its natural state has occasion for the assistance of no other living creature. But man has constant occasion for the help of his fellow creatures, and it is in vain for him to expect it from their benevolence only:

He will be more likely to prevail if he can interest their self-love in his favour, and show them that it is for their own advantage to do for him what he requires of them. It is not from the benevolence of the butcher, the brewer or the baker that we expect our dinner but from their regard to their own interest.

(page 12)

Among men, Smith maintains, 'the most dissimilar geniuses are of use to each other'. Every man thus lives by exchanging, or becomes in some measure a mercant, and the society itself grows to be what is properly a commercial society (page 13). The spirit of self-help, underlying Smith's *Wealth of Nations*, was spelt out one hundred years later by his English compatriot, Samuel Smiles.

The pursuit of self-help

PRACTICE: SAMUEL SMILES—PROMOTING SELF HELP

Mutual improvement societies

For Samuel Smiles (1812–1904) free enterprise, as an institutionally based firm, was fuelled by self-help, in its personal form. *Self-Help* was published in 1859, the same year as Charles Darwin's *The Origin of Species* and John Stuart Mill's essay *On Liberty*. Smiles built the book on a series of talks he had given to young artisans who had formed an evening school in Leeds for mutual improvement. It was a time when little was expected of government but much was expected of individuals. The cults of self-help and self-improvement were well spread, representing the value of achievement over that of birth. There were in 1860 over 200,000 members of mechanics' institutes and mutual improvement societies, lyceums and libraries. Adult education took place at most of them. There were three million members, moreover, of friendly and provident societies.

What Smiles applauded was not so much success itself as the moral character that lies behind it. In tune with the religious professions of the age, he celebrated patience, courage, endeavour and the perseverance with which worthy objectives were pursued. He praised individualism, unlike his Scottish predecessor, Adam Smith, not solely as a means to worldly gain but also as the path to independence and self-fulfilment.

Help from within

For Samuel Smiles the spirit of self-help is the root of all genuine growth in the individual. Moreover, exhibited in the lives of many, it constitutes the true source of national vigour and strength. Help from without, he said, is inevitably enfeebling in its effect, but help from within invariably invigorates:

> Indeed the worth and strength of a State depends far less upon the form of its institutions than upon the character of its men. For the nation is only an aggregate of individual conditions. Therefore civilization itself is but a question of the personal improvement of the men, women and children of whom society is composed.

National progress, he added, is the sum of individual industry, energy and uprightness: 'It follows that the highest patriotism and philanthropy consist not so much in altering laws and modifying institutions as in helping and stimulating men to elevate and improve themselves by their own free and independent individual action' (page 19). It may be of comparatively little consequence how persons are governed from without. Everything depends, for Smiles, on how they govern themselves from within, including the careful utilization of their energies. The solid foundations of liberty must rest upon individual character.

Education through life

The spirit of self-help, according to Smiles, as exhibited in the energetic action of individuals has at all times been a marked feature in the English character. Schools, academies and colleges give but the merest beginnings of a culture. Far more influential is the life education daily given in people's homes, in the streets, behind counters, in workshops, at the loom and the plough, in counting houses and factories, and in the busy haunts of men. A man perfects himself by work more than by reading. It is life rather than literature, action rather than study, and character rather than biography, which tends perpetually to renovate mankind.

The career of industry, Smiles therefore indicates, which the nation has pursued has also proved its best education. No bread eaten by man is so sweet as that earned by his own labour, whether bodily or mental. The duty of work is written on the muscles of the limbs, the mechanism of the hand, the nerves and lobes of the brain. In the school of labour is taught the best practical wisdom.

SERVANT OF THE MARKETPLACE

Contracting out

In the nineteenth century Samuel Smiles managed to combine enterprise and learning under the guise of self-help. Modern capitalism in the twentieth century, on the other hand, loses the connection between self-assertiveness (enterprise) and self-development (learning). It is this loss of connection which, as we shall see, has recently led classically free-market economics astray.

The British economist Andrew Shonfield made the following observation in the mid-1960s 'It is noticeable that some of the nations which made the most complete and successful adaptation to the political problems of the earlier era of capitalism seem to be stuck with especially inefficient political machinery when they apply themselves to new problems' (Shonfield, 1965). This is outstandingly true, Shonfield argues, of the Anglo-Saxon countries. Britain and the USA, both holding to common law tradition, were brilliantly inventive in using their legal systems to create an environment in which a great reserve of previously suppressed business initiative was liberated. They concentrated the main weight of their effort on the protection and enlargement of private property, just as Ronald Reagan and Margaret Thatcher did in the 1980s. The arrangement governing society were turned into a series of contracts between owners of various things, including owners of their own labour, about the terms on which such property was to be used. The system was harsh, but its product, Shonfield maintains, was a degree of personal liberty rarely, if ever, realized before.

Traders above all
The British, for Shonfield as for Napoleon before him, have seen themselves as traders above all. Such a pragmatic individual is thought of as being no more than a servant of the market, responding, just like a merchant, to a series of transient opportunities: 'The notion of a supplier with a long term production policy, with a product that is distinctive and special, is not something readily absorbed into the thinking of British capitalism' (page 119).

In Britain—unlike, for example, in France, Holland or Sweden—the State is not visualized as the carrier of an overriding national interest. It is rather seen as one among several entities which compete with one another on behalf of their individual and differing interests. As a result, personal liberty is probably more secure than in a more interventionist setting. Yet the State's inhibitions also make it less inclined to pursue, as in Germany and Scandinavia, positive social goals. Witness the stand Britain is taking today against the EC's social policies!

For classical economies as preached by Adam Smith—the picture of a perfect market, unimpeded by the influence of any public authority, with a vast multiplicity of buyers and sellers, none of them strong enough to impose a desired direction on events—'The market place, the small independent trader, and the noninterventionist public authority were indissolubly associated with political freedom' (Shonfield, 1965, page 71). The resulting economic emphasis has led to what we might term a 'pragmatic imbalance'.

The pragmatic imbalance

OUTER DIRECTED – INNER DIRECTED

Having reviewed the pragmatic domain, from its implicit cultural form to its explicit economic function, we should be in a position to locate it within the European whole. For it is the economic outlook which, in theory if not also in practice, has predominated. Moreover, when the Eastern Europeans today call for a 'free market economy' it is this Anglo-Saxon brand of modern capitalism that they inadvertently seek, notwithstanding its limitations.

In effect, as we have seen, the pragmatic world view—with its dual conditions of enterprise and learning—has been only partially adopted in recent times. For the enterprising expression of individual liberty, reflected in Adam Smith's promotion of the 'free market', has eclipsed the learning variety promoted by Francis Bacon. While pragmatism of the outer-directed variety enhances market awareness, individualism of the inner-directed kind reinforces self-awareness.

REG REVANS—ACTION LEARNING

Francis Bacon was a seminal influence in British science and technology, Adam Smith in political economy, and Samuel Smiles in education. Yet the three have been seen to be somewhat far apart. In fact it has been only very recently that Reg Revans, Britain's most original management thinker, has brought together the notions of free enterprise, self-help and individual learning.

It is one's perception of a problem, Revans maintains, one's evaluation of what is to be gained by solving it and one's estimate of the processes at hand to resolve it that together provide the springs for human action. Moreover, at the present rate of technological change the problems to be solved differ from one day to the next. It follows that everyone in the organization, from those who frame the policies to those who manipulate the ultimate details of technique, must be endowed to the greatest possible extent with the means of learning. We now turn from the main stem of pragmatic philosophy and market economy to first, the institutional and second, the managerial offshoots. In the process we shall draw most particularly on Handy's *Gods of Management* and on Revans's action learning.

Summary

THE ADVANCEMENT OF INDIVIDUAL LEARNING
- The focal point for all knowledge is action, not system building.
- Knowledge should bear fruit in works, so that science becomes applicable to industry.
- Pragmatists refrain from using general principles and draw inferences from collecting facts and observing nature.
- We should escape from the dead hand of the traditional past, free latent talent, and tap the individual will.

THE PURSUIT OF FREE ENTERPRISE
- Only complete competition is seen to be consistent with natural liberty.
- Only such free competition can bring about full reward for personal effort and fully contribute to the common good.
- Entrepreneurs are activated by a desire to be free, a sense of propriety, and the propensity to exchange.
- Each such person is naturally deemed the best judge of his or her own interest, and should therefore be left to pursue a task in their own way.

THE EXERCISE OF SELF-HELP
- The spirit of self-help is the root of all genuine growth in the individual.
- Exhibited in the lives of many, self-help constitutes the true source of national vigour and strength.
- Help from without is inevitably enfeebling in its effect, but help from within invariably invigorates.
- Civilization itself is but a question of the personal improvement of the individual men, women and children of whom society is composed.

COMPETITIVE ECONOMIC POLICY
Pragmatically based, competitive economic policies are oriented towards the establishment of a free market, leading to a free society.

ESTABLISHING A FREE MARKET
- Classical economics gives us the picture of a perfect market, unimpeded by the influence of any public authority with a great multiplicity of small buyers and sellers, none of them strong enough to impose a desired direction on events.
- Competitive nations see themselves as traders in that their producers are seen to be no more than servants of the market, responding to transient opportunities.

- The concept of a supplier with a long-term production policy is not something readily absorbed into free market thinking.

CREATING A FREE SOCIETY

- The marketplace, the small independent trader, and the non-interventionist public authority are associated with political freedom.
- The State in a competitive country is visualized as one among several which compete with one another on behalf of the individual.
- The competitive way, therefore, makes for a State which embarks on any venture with an intense awareness of its own limitations.
- Personal liberty is then more secure but the State's inhibitions also make it less assured in its pursuit of positive goals.

6

Pragmatism in European management

As indicated in Chapter 5, the pragmatically based approach to business and management is centred upon the individual person and upon the autonomous enterprise. At the same time, as with the other philosophical domains, there is a clear division between outer- and inner-directed approaches. Whereas the former, in this pragmatic instance, is focused on self-help and action, the latter is oriented towards self-development and learning. Indeed, as we shall soon see, it is Revans's concept of 'action learning' which serves to link the 'old' pragmatic world-view of enterprise, leadership and commercial growth with the 'new' experiental perspective on learning, empowerment and personal growth (Fig. 6.1).

Character-building institutions
As mentioned in Chapter 5, for Shonfield (1965) unadulterated individualism in economics and business, as in management and organization, inhibits the effectiveness of institutions. Independence, in fact, is favoured over both dependence and interdependence. Similarly, an inductively based world view inhibits the development of structures and functions. This is one of the reasons the British have a reputation for 'muddling through'. As managers they also invariably submit to the greater conceptual power of the Americans, whose managerial—as opposed to business—thinking draws upon a combination of philosophical systems.

Unlike countries such as France, Germany, Holland and Sweden, the Anglo-Saxon nations tend to leave business and management alone, to get on with pursuing their own destiny. When a Socialist government or a trade union does exert an influence, more often than not it acts as an antagonist against business rather than as a protagonist. Similarly, the public and private sectors, unlike in France or Japan, are notoriously

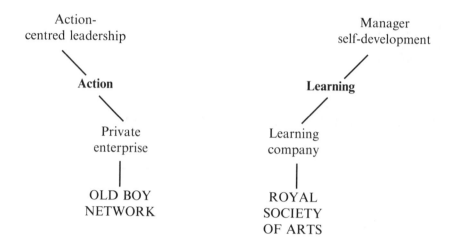

Fig. 6.1 The pragmatic branches

distant from one another. Finally, institutional collaboration as manifested in trade associations, chambers of commerce or training organizations are far less of a combined force than they are in Germany, Holland or Scandinavia.

However, there are three autonomous institutions, each of which plays a distinctive part in the business and managerial destiny of the United Kingdom. Emerging directly from a pragmatically oriented world view, these are the 'Old Boy Network', the so-called 'Industrial Society' and the 'Royal Society of Arts',

THE 'OLD BOY NETWORK'

It comes as no surprise that a pragmatically oriented culture should value experience and personal connections with men (and, more recently, women) of 'standing'. However, there is more to the English 'old boy network', as a structural outcome of a pragmatically based world view, than immediately meets the eye. After all, the old adage 'it's not what you know but who you know' could just as well apply in a family-centred, humanistic culture as in an individualistically oriented one. So what is England's distinctiveness in this experiential respect, how is its institutional make-up affected and what are the implications for pragmatically oriented organizational frameworks elsewhere?

The old school tie

Pragmatically oriented societies, where precedent transcends logic, are inevitably bound by tradition. Such tradition, of which the 'class system' in Britain is a particularly strong manifestation, in fact belies rationality. A theoretically established order, de Madariaga (1922) affirms, would be in direct opposition to the instinctive nature of the English hierarchy. The class system is therefore 'a kind of living archive of past deeds'. A dominant feature of the English class system in general and the old school tie in particular is the public school. In it the English boy is carefully moulded to type and it is leadership 'character' rather than cleverness in management to which this type accords. The public school, in effect, substitutes itself for the family as a character-moulding agency. To that extent, the Battle of Waterloo was won on 'the playing fields of Eton' rather than in the classrooms of any Grande Ecole.

Alongside the leadership character and brand of exclusiveness that is associated with the old school tie is a gift for spontaneous organization within the old boy network. This cuts across the formal organization to which the pragmatist is so mentally ill attuned. As a merchant banker or legal adviser, the pragmatist is at the same time practical and vague because he or she believes that thought, embodied in institutional bureaucracy, is rigid. Hence the British government's and the Danish people's reactions to the Brussels bureaucracy. Conversely, life, embodied in the spontaneous group, is mobile.

The group, once defined, acquires its own self-control. Its strong tendency towards social discipline is a wholly spontaneous force, without any intervention from the external order. Its members ensure that their faculties and individual tendencies are subordinated to the action which is expected of them. For de Madariaga (1922):

> It is a sort of mutual vigilance which keeps ever alive the complicated system of collective tendencies of the Englishman. The individual lives in an atmosphere which is not free, but on the contrary is crossed by a network of tendencies. These are divided into zones of different densities, ruled by laws and obligations which, owing to their natural character, attain a particular efficiency. The individual thus watched by his own social self becomes obsessed by a continuous presence of self-consciousness (page 25).

The 'club' culture

Perhaps the best-known management thinker in Britain, Professor Charles Handy of the London Business School, Irish born and also a classical scholar, has characterized the old boy network as a *club culture*. Interestingly enough, one of his most recent books was entitled *The Age of Unreason* (1990), though his seminal work remains *The Gods of Management* (1980). Drawing metaphorically from the Greek gods he sketches four predominating organizational forms:

Zeus, the head of the Gods, famed for his impulses and the power of his presence inhabits one of them. Apollo, fond of rules and order, inhabits another. Athena is the goddess, protectress, as I see her, of problem solvers. Dionysius, for me, is the supreme individualist (*The Gods of Management*, 1980, page 17)

In the 'club' culture where Zeus reigns supreme, Handy argues, people or information as well as money can be

> the object of his collector's instincts, knowing intuitively as he does that these commodities are at least as powerful. To this end he will invest considerable time in creating and maintaining networks, potential sources of useful people, information or even cash.

Zeus likes uncertainty, because uncertainty implies freedom to manoeuvre, through politics, people and networks (page 59). In England, there are a proliferation of both social and recreational clubs—hence club culture—wherein such networking and spontaneous organization takes place. But it would be a mistake to view this organizational form, so characteristic of a merchant bank, in isolation.

The Oxbridge phenomenon

The breeding grounds of Britain's elite, Oxford and Cambridge, encapsulate the pragmatically based outlook each with its shades of particular difference. The University of Oxford, bastion of the Tory Party and the City of London, is renowned for its classical education. The relationship between the pragmatic world view and a classical education is an intriguing one, Charles Handy being one of its stereotypes.

For it is not the classical forms, as in France or Italy, that are venerated but the heroic journeys described in Homer and Virgil, combined with the flavour and nuance of their great poetry. The combined poet and adventurer, historically personified by Lord Byron or by Lawrence of Arabia, is generic to the English spirit. Cambridge University, like Oxford, is well known for its individualized tutorial system but also, and unlike its illustrious conterpart, has a reputation for breeding eccentrics. Its famous graduates in recent times range from the economist John Maynard Keynes to Reg Revans, each of whom is a total original in his or her own right.

Handy, in effect, differentiating between the power-centred (club), role-centure, task-centred and person-centred organizations, inadvertently outlines the dominant institutional forms within a pragmatically oriented society. Interestingly enough, only the role-centred one is functionally and structurally bound, and thus culturally alien to a pragmatic people. The other three all cater for varieties of individual self-assertiveness (club-centred), self-development (task-centred) and self-expression (person-centred).

So the role- and rule-centred bureaucracy, for all its obvious usefulness in maintaining routine operations, is looked upon with some disparagement. For pragmatism favours individual improvisation and spontaneous organization over rigidly contrived organizational forms. According to Handy,

> individuals in the role culture are part of the machine, the interchangeable human parts of Henry Ford's dream. The role, the set of duties, is fixed. The individual is he or she that is slotted into it.
>
> (*The Gods of Management*, page 59)

It is not surprising, then, that the bureaucratic success stories in British business are products of Jewish family culture, as in the case of Marks & Spencer and Sainsbury, or else are of Anglo-Dutch parentage, as in Shell and Unilever. Finally, ICI, Britain's largest manufacturer, is of Germanic and Swedish origins.

THE INDUSTRIAL MISNOMER

Individual–task–group

Large-scale industrial as opposed to a commercially or professionally based management would seem to require the kind of preconceived organizational order that is anathema to the pragmatic world view. Interestingly enough, there is an institution in Britain, called the 'Industrial Society', which has gained considerable visibility in the last twenty years or so. Yet, not surprisingly, it has achieved its main reputation, together with Professor John Adair of the University of Surrey, for championing the cause of the individual leader.

Adair's (1964) particular concept of action-centred leadership combining individual–task–group has become a hallmark of the 'Industrial Society'. In fact the institution had little to do with industrialization as embodied in physical production *per se*. Rather, in the Anglo-Saxon world today, as depersonalized management principles have become ever less popular among practitioners of the managerial art, personalized leadership is in ever-greater demand.

Character building and teamwork

The marrying together of individual, task and group is part of the well-ingrained emphasis upon teamwork. Part and parcel of the character-building activity, so intrinsic to public school education, is the development of that capacity inbred through 'the playing fields of Eton'. Such teamwork, though, as in rugby football with teams of 13 or 15 players, is much more easily promoted in the small group than in the large organization. Charles Handy makes this point in advancing his case for a 'new Apollo', to displace the old bureaucracy. John Harvey-Jones just such a 'new Apollo', for such leaders like to break down their organizations into smaller units:

> Small, in this context, is not so much beautiful as essential. Without the appropriate scale, Apollo loses his human face, our Dionysian (individualistic) instincts are denied, and the old symptoms of resistance to Apollo emerge. When Dionysius is denied his claims and pressures dominate. Once placated, our other cultural instincts can come to the fore. Apollonians, treated as individuals, can devote themselves to predictability, Athenians to planning; knowing that each is necessary to the other (Handy, 1980).

In fact, Handy's Athenians, those knowledge workers who much prefer networks to hierarchies, are naturally inclined towards project groups, many brains making for better solutions. Therefore whereas a typical Dionysian is Clive Sinclair, Athenians are less individually renowned.

The mechanics' institutes

The Athenians' love of problem solving, at the same time, provides the key to their pragmatic desire to make things, to make things happen, and to 're-create'. Moreover, it arises not out of a desire to better order the world but rather to manipulate it, to play with it, and occasionally to re-create it. The British lover of metals, for example, can be traced back not only to the Celts but also to the Norse god Thor, a 'smith'.

The mechanics' institutes mentioned in Chapter 5 were a nineteenth-century example of a spontaneous organization, within which the working people of Britain duly applied themselves to their love of metals. Unfortunately, the technical colleges and polytechnics that have followed them in the twentieth century are only a pale shadow of the former institutes' glory. Unpopular, maladapted Apollo has taken over from the fertile blend of Athena, Dionysius and Zeus that served to spearhead the English Industrial Revolution. At the same time, the British industrial psyche remains scarred by the image of those 'satanic mills' contained within the bleak urban landscape that was the unwanted product of the enterprise of Zeus.

ORGANIZATIONS AS VILLAGE COMMUNITIES

The pride of England from an aesthetic point of view is not contained in any of its great cities—as in the case of Paris in France or Barcelona in Spain—but in its beautifully compact villages. In fact what is so striking about the English countryside, duly likened to pragmatic thought structures, is its patchwork form, combining unconventional order with conventional disorder. The basic principle of an English garden is that it must be carefully planned to look as unplanned as possible. There must be no formal symmetry. The object is to make the garden appear as if it were part of the natural landscape and not an imposed artificial pattern. Nature must be seen to be given its head, just as the unconventional Richard Branson blends in with his country's natural landscape.

In Handy's terms individual variety—Zeus, Athena Dionysius— must be encouraged by organizational order—Apollo—rather than be suppressed by it. To support his case, Handy uses the appropriate metaphor of the village.

> The village, with its villagers, must replace the Greek temple (Apollo) as the centrepiece of the organization. Villages are small and personal. Their people have names and characters and personalities. What more appropriate concept on which to base our institutions of the future than the ancient organic social unit whose flexibility and strength sustained human society through millennia. Common purpose, informality, leadership, individuality, honesty, initiative. All good motherhood words. Words that indicate art rather than science are the materials of management in the village.
>
> (*The Gods of Management*, page 20)

THE LEARNING SOCIETY

Education for capability
Handy has in fact recently been serving as chairman of that longstanding British institution, the Royal Society of Arts. Interestingly enough, the RSA has not rationally divided itself into component art forms. Neither has it promoted the humanities nor served some philosophical ideal. Rather, and true to pragmatic form, its function has been to promote not only arts and artifacts but also commerce and industry!

In fact, in recent years, it has championed the cause of education for capability as opposed to the pursuit of knowledge for its own sake. Interestingly enough, the RSA has been challenging the knowledge-centred State in its secondary schools. For these have not been inbued with the pragmatic tradition of the advancement of learning, whereby the accumulation of knowledge is linked with the production of works. This happens in the UK only at primary school!

The gifted amateur
The amalgamation of art and artifact with commercial acumen that is within the RSA heritage can be linked with the Oxbridge tradition. Within this, classics is merged with business. For many centuries, in fact,

inductively oriented pragmatism whereby the individual learns from life has given rise to the gifted amateur. Whereas, as we shall see, the rationalist is 'trained for life', the empiricist learns from and through it. Whereas a vocationally based apprenticeship forms part of a developmental, Germanic tradition, the gifted amateur arises from the experientially based one.

Perhaps the best-known case was William Caxton (*c.* 1422–*c.* 1491), who brought the printing press to England from Bruges in 1476. Caxton was an early and prominent example of a well-known type, the individualistic Englishman following his own hobbies. As a successful merchant he made enough money over a period of 30 years to devote his later life to the literary pursuits he loved. He began by translating French books into English. While so engaged he fell in love with the mystery of movable printing type. In 1474 and 1475 he produced abroad one of his own translations, the first books to be printed in English. Then in 1476 he set up his printing press in Westminster, and for the 14 remaining years of his life printed a hundred books. His success as a translator, printer and publisher did much to lay the foundations of literary English. Together with the cult of the gifted amateur, venturing into unexplored vocational territories, is that of the British explorer.

The urge for exploration
The RSA, like the scientifically and geographically oriented royal societies formed in England in the nineteenth century, have promoted the activities of scientific, natural and commercial explorers. That urge for exploration, so strongly ingrained within the pragmatically formed self, is connected with the particular European madness that de Madariaga (1968) attributes to the English:

> Daring to venture out into the oceans and unlimited plains of the spirit which the intellect is unable to charter, the three mad peoples of Europe nourish the three most intelligent, the French, the Germans and the Italians. Without them the Russians, the English and the Spaniards would have remained incapable of moulding their lava into durable shapes. Without these mad peoples, in their turn, the three people of the intellect would have remained empty moulds (page 27).

Professionals, in Handy's British eyes, in being free to express themselves and to be true to themselves represent Dionysian virtues with a due touch of eccentricity, or madness! Such individualistic professionals in Britain put a mark on their jobs. Their work is not an anonymous act, even though it conforms to a set of standards common to their profession. Freedom also implies that one is owned by no person or organization, even though one may lend the organization one's skills! In effect, Handy makes the case for membership, as opposed to employment, so that one belongs to an organization as to a village. One cannot be sacked from one's village, although life may be made fairly unpleasant by neighbours, but one can leave or choose not to join.

Manager self-development

RESEARCHING WITHIN

Reg Revans has spent the past 50 years trying to raise managers' and the nation's consciousness of their unique origins and destiny. In the process he has run management development programmes in Belgium, Britain, America, Australia, India and Egypt. Revans has continually maintained that the salvation of individual countries and their enterprises is not to be found by observers scouring the world—particularly today the American or Japanese worlds—in the hope of finding some miracle. Their salvation rather, their 'Kingdom of God' is to be found within their own shores and within the wills of their own people. At the level of the individual firm, Revans argues, it is not unreasonable to suggest that an essential part of any research and development policy is the study of human effort. From this are created the saleable products of the enterprise.

IDENTIFYING WITH LEARNING

In this respect Revans sees the social innovation, the rationally based division of labour, for which Adam Smith bears so much responsibility. The main contribution that people have to make to a collective task, he says, is their own time. If they feel that the management which determines both what their tasks are to be and the ways in which they should do them is remote—and perhaps neither very competent nor particularly sympathetic—they are bound to regard their employment as an insult to their self-respect.

> The fundamental questions of adaptation today lie in the field of human learning. Human beings learn only when they want to learn, and only when they identify with the persons for whom, or from whom, they want to do so.
> (Revans, 1967, p. 469)

What might be called the smoothness of the horizontal flow of work and the willingness of people to do the work are inextricably mixed. Hence for Revans, the division of industrial problems into relations between processes and between people is an illusion. There is one field of difficulty alone. Human relations in the factory depend upon the extent to which people perceive their work to be economically and effectively arranged. Where this is not so, discontent will arise. The over-organized factory impairs freedom of thought and decision. The under-organized one fritters away the hours of life that all of us, who deplore wasting time, can live only once. That is pragmatism for you!

FORMING LEARNING-BASED GROUPS

It is the task of management, Revans maintains, to distribute authority in such a way as to give all employees the level of problems they can settle on their own or by consulting other people. It is in the big organization that the centre of decision and the periphery of action face the greatest risk of mutual misunderstanding.

Learning must demand not only information about the latest shift of policy. It must demand power to get the knowledge needed to see one's part in what is going on. In particular, one needs to know the effect of one's behaviour upon those with whom one works.

Revans has taken a leaf from Adam Smith's book insofar as he has focused on the importance of learning-based exchange in the creation of wealth. At the same time, and in direct contrast to his illustrious predecessor, he has accentuated the value of combining forces. For Revans this is best achieved within small 'action learning' groups rather than in large-scale business consortia.

The fact is that Reg Revans, living three hundred years after Adam Smith, has witnessed a revolution not only in the physical sciences but also, and more importantly for our purposes, in social studies. Real progress is found to consist, Revans argues through Arnold Toynbee's *Study of History* (1968), in a process defined as 'etherealization'. This involves overcoming material obstacles, which serves to release the energies of society. People now respond to challenges that are internal rather than external, spiritual rather than material. In this respect Revans's view is not dissimilar from that of Francis Bacon. However, it draws on recent work in experiential psychology which has emerged from the pragmatic-empirical tradition.

MANAGING EXPERIENTIALLY

According to Revans, one of the outstanding needs in the education of managers is a frame of reference for describing, communicating and evaluating the subjective consciousness of personal action. The language of the management academy, he says, is a code of depersonalized abstractions, such as economic theory and network analysis, taught by experts. There are, he says, or simply can be, no professionals to instruct us on what to do or even upon how to do it, for the method of the lesson is also its content. Knowledge is the consequence of action, and to know is the same as to do. Thus self-knowledge, the key to mastery in an uncertain world, is the same as self-development. Revans locates the manager as the individual he or she is and must always remain, at the centre of the activity that engages him.

> A real decision, firstly, is always that of a particular person, with his own ends not to be neglected. He has his own fears to amplify his problems, his own hopes a mirage to amplify his resources, and his own prejudices, often called experience, to colour the data in which he works. A choice of goals, secondly, so much bound up with decision theory, is yet distinct from it. The ends for which one strives, deliberately or subconsciously, as an individual or with others, are but partly determined by the calculations of economic strategy. For behind them jostle the egocentric drives of the individual. Thirdly, there is the relevance of information, that product of which the raw material is data and the manufacturing process the personal sensitivities of the individual. Fourthly, the theory of systems describes the web in which the wordline of a particular manager is entangled. The assessment of probability is, fifthly, that farrago of mathematical statistics and simple guesswork by which we attempt to assess our forgotten experience, our present wishfulness and our future hope. And, sixthly, the learning process integrates everything that one has so far become, and one's hope for future improvement.
>
> (Revans, 1965, page 48)

In combining subjective awareness with objective method, therefore, a manager cannot change the system of which he or she is in command—at least in any new sense—unless the individual is changed in the process. The logical structure of both, for Revans, are in correspondence.

The change in the system we call action; that in the self we call learning. Learning, he says, to act effectively is also learning how to learn effectively. Revans, in fact, is revisiting and reconstituting the philosophies of both Francis Bacon and John Locke, in managerial mode.

According to Locke's theory, man comes into the world with his mind a blank tablet (*tabula rasa*) as void of ideas as of knowledge. It is the senses which first 'convey into the mind several distinct perceptions of things'. This source of ideas Locke designated as 'sensation'. The second source is 'the perception of the operations of our mind within us, as it is employed about the ideas it has got. Such operations furnish the understanding with another set of ideas, which could not be had from things without'. This second and only other source of ideas Locke designated as 'reflection'. Knowledge, in other words, is the product of experience in both an outer (sensation) and an inner (reflection) sense (Coates *et al.*, 1965). Therein lie the seeds of pragmatically based learning, which, for Revans, must exceed the rate of change.

ENHANCING PRODUCTIVITY THROUGH LEARNING

When the rate of change is high, Revans argues, if it is to be met with equanimity then the learning must be rapid. Those who cannot keep up with what is new will lose control of their surroundings, while those who take innovation in their stride will profit by being able to turn it to their advantage. In times of convulsion the advantage lies with those who are able to learn. Those who have consciously learnt how to learn have in particular learned to recognize the difference between two things. First, there is the acquisition of knowledge already known to other persons, which Revans calls 'programmed'. It has already been (or could be) written down. Secondly, there is the exploration of managers' own manifest ignorance, so as to clearly identify what questions they need to ask if they are to master the unknown that lies ahead. Revans denotes the overall capacity to learn as L, the former ability to acquire programmed knowledge as P and the latter power to identify such discriminating questions as $L = f(P,Q)$. Such a learning formula, with its two kinds of knowledge, harks back to both Bacon and Locke.

BECOMING AN ACTION LEARNER

In the final analysis, and on the one hand, Revans's action learning renews Francis Bacon's 'instauration', in contemporary scientific guise. On the other hand, it reconstitutes Adam Smith's wealth of nations, duly informed by today's experientially based psychology: 'It is a virtue of action learning, that like truth itself, it is a seamless garment; with its help all parties alike, manager and workman, should tackle their common foe, the external problem' (Revans, 1980, page 240). In that sense, outer-directed competition between man and his wily competitors is replaced by the inner-directed struggle between man and the thorny problems he faces.

In that way Revans's road to managerial as opposed to personality based capitalism is not paved with a rationally based, Ford-style division of labour. Rather, it is founded upon a scientifically based approach to problem solving. Similiarly, his path to cooperative endeavour is paved not with institutionally based strategic alliances but with reciprocal exchange in small groups.

More specifically, in Revans's modern extension of both Bacon's great seventeenth-century instauration and Smiles's Victorian practice of 'self-help':

- The reinterpretation of knowledge is, in effect, a social process, carried on among two or more learners in purposefully structured small groups. By the apparent incongruity of their exchanges, they frequently cause each other to examine many ideas afresh.

- Within the context of such a social process managers learn with and from each other by mutual support, advice and criticism during their attacks on real problems. They alternate between active project management and reflective review, in small groups, of themselves and their activities.
- Within such action learning sets, finally, there are no chiefs or Indians but only 'comrades in adversity' and a set facilitator. Each manager may therefore in seeking to enrich and enlarge his or her own subjective self through 'spiritual barter' reciprocally help to enrich and enlarge the subjective selves of his or her colleagues.

Revans, standing on the shoulders of his predecessors Bacon, Smith and Smiles, has interwoven the advancement of learning among managers with their mutual support among 'comrades in adversity'.

It is also worth noting that Revans focused most of his attention, in Britain at least, on nurses and coalminers, duly reinforcing his identification with the man and woman in the street. Finally, Revans was also honouring the individualistic, pragmatic tradition, albeit reinforced by mutual interest, whereby people stood together but each on their own two feet.

Self-in-action

ACTION-CENTRED LEADERSHIP

An individualistic culture like the Anglo-Saxon one is bound to focus upon leadership as a primary subject of management concern. In fact, in the course of the 1980s there was a renewed focus on personality-based leadership in the managerial literature as opposed to impersonally based management.

Interestingly enough, moreover, whereas in America the focus has been upon the inspirational aspects of leadership, in Britain action-centred leadership has taken root. Pragmatism has made its duly 'sense/thought'-oriented mark over humanism's 'intuition/feeling'—oriented one. This focus on leadership, finally, remains outer directed towards free enterprise, whereas the signs of our times are increasingly inner directed towards the advancement of learning.

MANAGER SELF-DEVELOPMENT

While Francis Bacon was Chancellor of England and originator of scientific method in the time of Queen Elizabeth I, Reg Revans was a Cambridge physicist who applied scientific method to management in the time of Queen Elizabeth II. While Bacon studied the classics while attending to his country's affairs, Revans studied the Bible while attending to the coal board's productivity problems. Like the best of pragmatists, they not only learnt from their own lives but also enabled others to learn from theirs.

We now need to turn from the concept of experiential management in general to pragmatic managerial attributes in particular. As our pragmatic guide, in this latter respect, we shall turn from the Englishman Reg Revans to the Irishman Charles Handy.

Summary

PRAGMATIC INSTITUTIONAL FRAMEWORKS

The old boy network
- Leadership character rather than cleverness in management is what counts.
- The public school rather than the family is the character-moulding agency.
- Spontaneous organization, as embodied in the old boy network, transcends formal organization, as reflected in bureaucracy.
- Personal freedom is collectively channelled not by any formal rules but by social expectations, reflected both in the task and through peers.

The 'cottage' industry
- Competitive battles, like the one fought at Waterloo, are won on the playing fields of Eton rather than, for example, in the classrooms of the 'Grande Ecole'.
- Duly set in the context of the village community, where small is beautiful, everyone has his or her garden, and such a garden is planned to look as unplanned as possible.
- 'Cottage' industry is embodied not in large-scale organization but in action-centred leadership.
- This is backed up by teamwork, serving to bind together the individual, the task and the small group.

The learning society
- Whereas professional managers are systematically trained, the gifted amateur learns from life, whereby
- Art and artifact is merged with commercial acumen, so that competition without (commercial performance) is matched by competition within (personal excellence).

- The urge for exploration is extended from outer realms of business enterprise into inner ones of personal learning whereby
- The pragmatist becomes his or her own person, and the experiential manager becomes similarly free to express, and to be true to, his or her self.

PRAGMATIC MANAGEMENT MODELS

Action-centred leadership

- The contemporary English economist, Norman Macrae, was the first management thinker to coin the term 'intrapreneur'—an entrepreneur operating in a large-scale organization.
- The former military man John Adair, through his 'action-centred leadership', combined individual–task–group in establishing a hallmark of Britain's 'Industrial Society'.
- Portraying power, role-, task-, and person-centred managers, the classical scholar turned management educator, Charles Handy, compares and contrasts managerial individualities.
- Eccentric management scientist, Stafford Beer, in his *Design for Freedom*, describes ways and means of creating organizational variety to cater for individual differences.

Action-centred learning within

- Action learning is a means of development requiring its subject, through responsible involvement in some real, complex, stressful problem, to achieve personal change by
- Successful phases of actively experimenting, deductively theorizing, reflectively observing and concretely experiencing.
- The learning achieved therefore is not so much an acquaintance with new factual knowledge as it is the reinterpretation of the subject's existing knowledge.

Action-central learning without

- Reg Revans's action learning is aimed at enabling every enterprise to make better use of its resources by engendering within it a social process of learning
- Based on learning with and through others—in small learning sets of 'comrades in adversity'—engaging in mutual exchange of information, opinion and advice.
- The underlying structures of successful achievement, of learning, of intelligent counselling, and of scientific method are—for Revans—the same.

7

The experiential manager

Outer and inner directed

John Harvey-Jones, in *Making Things Happen*, personifies action-centred leadership and also manager self-development, respectively. Whereas one is outer directed, primarily aimed at commercial growth, the other is more inner directed, placing greater store on personal growth. Both approaches, however, emphasize experience over thought, as the key to effective management. Harvey-Jones, in Charles Handy's terms as we shall see, alternated between the four 'Gods of Management' that characterized British people (Fig. 7.1).

The manager as an individual

THE GODS OF MANAGEMENT

From the fourteen Greek gods that reigned on Mount Olympus, Charles Handy selected the four—Zeus, Apollo, Athena and Dionysius—that he considered important for managers. In effect, those he selected turned out to be predominantly in a pragmatically oriented society. There are three individualists: Zeus the entrepreneur, Athena the problem solver, and Dionysius, the free spirit; while there is only the one organization man, Apollo the analytical manager. Each, moreover, has his or her particular approach to thinking and learning, influencing and changing, motivating and rewarding people.

Zeus the entrepreneur

Entrepreneurs move quickly to a possible solution and then test it. A logical step-by-step analysis is not their way. They like to deal with a jumble of events, relying on 'soft', impressionistic data. They *learn by trial and error* and *by and from personal example*. Heirs to succession are

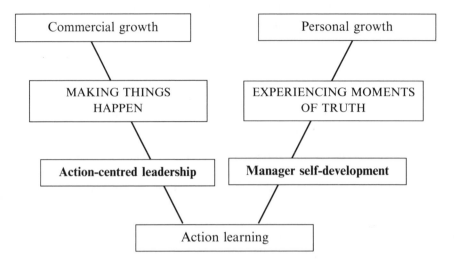

Fig. 7.1 The experiential manager

tested in the organizational proving grounds. Such entrepreneurs learn from the successes and failures of both themselves and others rather than from theories in books.

For entrepreneurs *it is track record that counts*. Ownership or resources, on the one hand, and personal charisma, on the other, are telling influences. From these power bases Zeus creates change by changing people. Individuals are the link pieces in the influence chain. Results speak louder than reasons, especially from credible operators. 'Who said that?' is a more pertinent question than 'What was said?' Entrepreneurs thrive in a world full of personalities and power.

Entrepreneurs *look for power over people and events*. They like to see things happen as a result of their personal actions. To this end, they will invest considerable energy into developing and maintaining personal networks. Such enterprising managers like uncertainty, because *uncertainty implies freedom to manoeuvre*. Money is a thermometer of success; politics, people and networks are a way of life.

Athena the problem solver
Athenians are *problem solvers*. Fundamental to such problem solving is the *desire and ability to work with others in teams*. Learning is by continual exploration and discovery of the hypothesis–test–re/hypothesis variety. Such Athenian managers would do Revans proud! Athenian cultures tend

to think of individuals as resourceful rather than as human resources, regarding them as people responsible for their own ultimate destinies.

Athenians bow to expertise. To command such a 'task culture' one has to earn people's respect for one's task competence. *Obedience is replaced by agreement*, directives by persuasion, vertical direction by horizontal participation. The first Athenian step in an influencing process is to change the definition of the focal problem or task. Change the problem and you can change the direction of activity.

Athenians *like variety* and get bored by certainty. They *seek professional self-advancement* rather than hierarchical promotion. Athenians prefer the task to be defined rather than the role, wanting to maintain discretion over the means to any end. Such learners, then, respond to payment by results, to group assignments and to what Handy terms 'defined uncertainty', that is, the solution of identified challenges. They thrive in concultancy-based organizations, research departments, or communications. They get restless in steady states and indecisive in crises.

Dionysius the individualist
Dionysians defy rigid classification. To be a Dionysian, Handy maintains, is to believe that *you have nothing much to learn from any one person, only from life*. Dionysians therefore prefer to learn by immersion in new experiences. They want opportunities but demand the right to choose between them. It is hard to influence Dionysians since they *do not perceive themselves as working for the organization*. It is their very unpredictability that gives them the freedom they seek. Dionysian cultures are therefore managed on a one-to-one basis. The 'leader' interacts with each person individually, meetings being held only for the dissemination of information or to ask for ideas on a situation of common interest.

Like Zeus characters, Dionysians *want to make a difference to the world*, but it does not have to be through power or people or resources. It does not even have to be noticed. Truly Dionysian professions, like law and architecture, forbid any form of advertising. Dionysians are loners who gather together in an organization only for convenience. They can be tolerated within organizations only if they have great talent.

Apollo the analytical
Apollo, within a pragmatically oriented society, is culturally somewhat ill attuned. In fact, for Handy (1985)

> most organizations will have a Zeus-cum-Athena at the apex, with individuals who have the power to ignore amongst themselves the rules they set for others.

The mechanisms of Apollo are thus often confined to the lower and middle regions (page 50).

As we shall see in the chapters that follow, a limited view of organizational rationality reflects Handy's pragmatic bias.

For Handy, Apollonian thinking is *logical, sequential, analytical*. Such managers like to proceed methodically from problem definition to solution. Intelligence is a matter of convergent thinking. Leaning is strongly connected with training, leading to the acquisition of knowledge and skills. Activities, in fact, can be broken down into sets of required knowledge, skills and experience.

For Apollo, power is connected more with one's role and position than with personal charisma. Such a *role carries particular rights and responsibilities*. Whereas in an Apollonian culture the manager has authority, by virtue of his or her position, in a Zeus one the manager is seen to be an authority in his or her own personal right. To change Apollonian organizations one must change either the roles and responsibilities or the rules and procedures. Changing an individual has a minor impact compared with altering the structure or systems.

Apollo *values order and predictability*. Things need to fit into place, with contracts precise and honoured, roles prescribed and adhered to. Duty and obligation are all-important. Apollo pursues certainty as avidly as Zeus shuns it. He or she seeks formal authority and status, and pursues long-term career security.

A plea for appropriateness
In the final analysis Handy makes a plea for appropriateness in managerial behaviour.

> If harmony is health, the healthy organization is one that uses appropriate methods and assumptions of influence in a particular culture. Thus, for example, persuasion is effective in a Zeus culture if it comes from a member of the club; in an Apollo culture, it is accompanied by the requisite authority (page 63).

The interesting point here is that Handy's so-called 'cultures' are corporately rather than ethically or nationally based. In fact all four of his Greek gods, with Apollo something of an odd one out, are pragmatically, experientially and individualistically oriented.

Conclusion

PRAGMATISM FOUND AND LOST

We now come to some intriguing conclusions along the pragmatic way. The first of our findings is the positive one. Pragmatically oriented societies in Europe have a richly laden empirically based philosophy to draw on, with respect to individual and organizational enterprise and learning. Francis Bacon's advancement of learning, derived from the nature of science; Adam Smith's free enterprise, underpinned by natural law; Samuel Smiles's self-help, linking self-culture to human nature; and Reg Revans's action learning all serve as natural extensions of pragmatic, empirical and experiential traditions.

The second conclusion, regarding Britain—if not also the Benelux countries and Scandinavia—is overwhelmingly negative. European pragmatically based management thought has not yet been consciously and wholeheartedly drawn upon. It has freed up enterprise, thereby paying heed to the outer pragmatic core represented by Smith and Smiles and Bacon, but it has largely ignored Bacon and Revans. In favouring Phil Crosby over Reg Revans in its commitment to total quality, and Tom Peters over Charles Handy in its search for excellence, the business community is in fact rejecting the inner core of its European empirically based heritage.

On the one hand, 'Total Quality Commitment' and 'Extraordinary Customer Care' have little to do with the traditions of Europe. On the other, the attainment of managerial unity within cultural diversity and the advancement of inductively based learning in interactive groups has everything to do with ourselves.

PRAGMATISM IN A EUROPEAN CONTEXT

Part–whole

Why have Europe's managers failed to live up to their pragmatically based potential? Why have they not wholeheartedly transformed entrepreneurial self-help into managerial self-development, thereby advancing learning? Why have they not transformed autonomous enterprises into veritable learning organizations?

Interestingly enough, the failure to work pragmatism/empiricism through its logical conclusion in a managerial context is due to a lack of pan-European influence. For if a part is to realize itself as a whole it needs to play its part in the whole. While Britain philosophers and scientists, for example, have been cross-fertilizing with their European counterparts for centuries, not so its management thinkers.

Pragmatism–rationalism

To gain power and influence, experientially based management practices need to be conceptualized and converted into principles and procedures. Such processes are more rationalist than pragmatic in nature. Revans's ideas, for example, while powerfully original and colourfully depicted, are seldom clearly articulated. As a result, Britain, as well as Holland and Scandinavia, has bought in duly articulated managerial principles from outside Europe, primarily from America. Instead they should have been working with the rationalists—as Adam Smith did with the French economist Jean Baptiste Say—to codify their own managerially based inductions.

Pragmatism–rationalism–wholism

To turn a clearcut concept grounded in particular soils into a robust idea with due versatility requires a rich historical setting. Concepts need to be shaped by context, both in space and time. At a macro level Adam Smith's free market was adapted, both in theory and practice, to a series of European contexts. We have France's *dirigisme*, Germany's social market, and, more recently, central Italy's socio-economic network. However, at a micro level these contextual adaptations have remained, at best, implicit rather than explicit. Cooperation between pragmatism and wholism at the level of the firm has been supplanted by competition between capitalism and communism at the level of the economy at large.

Pragmatism–rationalism–wholism–humanism

Finally, turning a versatile idea into a universal one takes more than contextual adaptation. It requires a profound appreciation for the general human condition, both actual and potential. A 'Renaissance man' such as Leonardo da Vinci, so much steeped in the Italian cultural tradition, has not found his way into business. The European, humanistic tradition has remained outside the business realm. The gulf between a European business executive and civilization remains as wide as that between da Vinci and Agnelli, which is why Aurelio Peccei and the 'Club of Rome' has struggled to make an impact on business.

We now turn from pragmatism to rationalism, from one generic factor of production to another.

Summary

Self-assertiveness
- Conflict and competition is used constructively.
- Deviance is not threatening.
- There is a general willingness to take calculated risks.
- Rules and regulations are there to be broken.

Self-discipline
- This is oriented towards self-interest through performance and productivity.
- Personal and financial growth is the task at hand.
- Personal independence and achievement is valued over and above organizational interdependence and social balance.
- Excelling, that is, being the best, is preferred to 'levelling', that is, being the same as others.

Self-development
- Personal autonomy is highly valued so that close supervision is disliked.
- Individual learning and creativity is valued so that employees are not afraid to disagree with the boss.
- Managers are expected to consult before making decisions, drawing on, and out, individual differences.
- Self-development, and the development of others, is pursued to further individual and organizational learning.

Self-expression
- Overriding importance is attached to freedom of expression.
- Involvement with the company is of a 'calculative' as opposed to 'moral' nature.
- Individual initiative is encouraged.
- Individuals aspire towards personal leadership and variety as opposed to depersonalized management and conformity.

Part III

Rationalism—Professional

8

Rationalism in European business

The Frenchman Henri Fayol called for the introduction of formal management training rather than relying upon sink-or-swim approaches in the 1920's. Such training would lead people to function better in the home, in the church, in the military and politics, as well as in industry.

James Stoner, Management, 1982

The rational space
Pragmatism rooted in individualism gives rise to the individual manager and the market economy. Moreover, it supports free enterprise, and can be identified with experiential management. In contrast, there is rationalism as a second philosophical underpinning of European management. Often linked with 'scientific' management, it is founded upon a deep appreciation of form. Depersonalized management and organization replace personalized leadership and enterprise. As rationally designated branches, moreover, noble work and intellectual virtuosity displace leadership and learning as its foliage. Finally, industrial expansion and social equilibrium supplant commercial and personal growth as outcomes.

In the management literature, hitherto, a European brand of rationalism has been most clearly personified by Henri Fayol in France. Furthermore, to the extent that an American brand of 'scientific management' has prevailed, so such rationality has been distorted by the pragmatic 'Western' soil in which it has been planted. We now have the task of redressing the balance. In so doing we shall be drawing on Gallic rather than Anglo-Saxon culture, most especially in France, but also in parts of Belgium and Switzerland.

RATIONALISM IN TIME
Over time, the administrator, reaching back towards military, civil and clerical as well as industrial heritage, has been viewed as a modern

manager. Similarly, the rationally based institution, having been established as a functionally standardized bureaucracy, is newly emerging as a complex organization. As such, it contains structurally evolving strata of growing complexity. To that extent, the functional elements—production, marketing, finance, personnel—that underpin business performance are supplanted by structurally based ones—increasingly complex strata of physical, economic and social organization.

The shift from pragmatically based behaviourism to rationally based cognition affects both individual and institution. Depersonalized management functions and objectified organizational structures displace personalized leadership and person-centred power and influence (Fig. 8.1).

This fundamental change in outlook is required as an organization develops from a small-scale enterprise into a middle-sized institution. In that context the United States took the lead at the turn of the century, transforming many of their business enterprises into 'scientifically managed' organizations. However, lacking the prolifically rational grounds that may be found, for example, in France and Switzerland, the Americans have distorted the 'scientism'. Functional autonomy has supplanted structural integration, both within the organization and without. Such an imbalance lives on to this day. In other words, an intricate form of European rational management has yet to make its conceptual mark against the American 'melted-down' variety.

Images of mind—the roots of rationalism

ARCHETYPE OF REASON

In Europe the power of mind was first conveyed with devastating effect through the art and philosophy of ancient Greece (de Madariaga, 1968, page 24). More immediately accessible today, though, is the art of France. The image of Rodin's 'thinker' is perhaps the best known artistic expression of René Descartes' world view—'I think therefore I am'. While the pragmatist presents thoughts with a blurred outline the rationalist defines the object in mind with the neatest possible edge. While the pragmatist takes from the object of which he or she thinks all that is considered useful at the moment, the rationalist looks at a person or object systematically and with premeditation. Whereas the essential and the self-evident for the one—for example, John Harvey-Jones—is the act, for the other—for instance, Henri Fayol—it is the idea. Just as the experientially oriented person seeks from thought and feeling a practical result, a rational person seeks from them an intellectual experience. While England's William Shakespeare lays bare that essence of a particular individual which distinguishes him or her from all others,

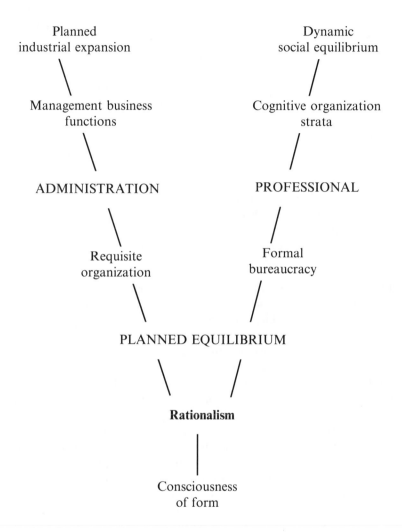

Fig. 8.1   The rational tree

France's Jean Baptiste Molière begins from the ideal figure. Rationalist playwrights tend to generalize what they observe in the various individualities around them, as Fayol did for management. Molière's miser, for example, represents a synthesis of all the traits exhibited by all misers.

The multifarious activities which are met in a pragmatically oriented culture by the free and spontaneous growth of private initiative must, therefore, in a rationally organized one, rely on the leadership of the

State: 'The movements of their collective life must be pre-arranged, laid down beforehand by some foreseeing mind well trained to imagine moves on the chess board of possibilities' (de Madariaga, 1922, page 134). Instead of coming nearer to life, the intellectual tends instinctively to draw apart from that which he or she wants to understand. Moreover, everything for the intellectual is limited by hard-and-fast plans and can only change by sudden recrystallizations into equally set forms.

A CULTURE OF FORMS

It might be said that civilization is the art of forms, a kind of intimate sense for forms. The French possess this sense to an incomparable degree, in all dimensions of life. Therein lies the characteristic eloquence of the high-flying French manager. For form, in the eyes of a complete rationalist, is not merely outward elegance, ornament, grace. It is rather a kind of inward elegance which results from the true balance of the parts, their harmonious arrangement and the clearness and beauty of the whole (de Madariaga, 1922, page 70).

Beauty is attractive to the intellectual, in both art and mathematics, because it is an abstact idea, the practical manifestations of which are agreeable and pleasurable. Even the most basic aspects of daily life, like food and drink, possess their idealized forms. In such a rational culture custom is of lesser importance than law. The framework of society, in effect, is constantly thought out, deduced from general laws. Equality is a geometrical plane made up of human points. It is beautifully level! The political evolution of a rationalistic France, for example, is in contrast to that of a country like England. In England the constitution evolves slowly and pragmatically. In France the political mould of the country is broken now and then into a new mould and a new cast is made. France is the specialist in constitutions of all nations, as it has been a specialist in managerial form and function. Written constitutions follow each other through sharp turns or revolutions in the life of that country to a greater extent than in the rest of Europe. Why should that be?

The structural idea—the main stem of rationalism

BACKGROUND

Rationalism in modern Europe can be most clearly traced back to the deductively based philosophy of René Descartes (1596–1650) in the seventeenth century. It was subsequently duly extended by the structural-functionalists thereafter. Its immediate economic derivative is *dirigisme*, preconceived by the Physiocrats in the eighteenth century and extended by the French socialists in the nineteenth. Finally, management thinkers who have taken respectively functional and structural leads have been the French industrial engineer Henri Fayol and the Canadian organizational psychologist Elliot Jaques.

RATIONALIST PHILOSOPHY

René Descartes—'I think therefore I am'

Descartes, like his English counterpart Francis Bacon, believed that science should divest the world of mystery, and should fill the gaps in our understanding with real knowledge:

> Though he clung to the concept of substance, Descartes tried to characterize it in such a way that it lost its old mysteriousness. For Descartes the soul is nothing but thinking (Kolakowski, 1972).

However, Descartes parted company from Bacon insofar as he believed that empiricism was not to be trusted. In his view, the existence of the material world was not self-evident on the basis of direct perception. According to Descartes, fundamental laws of the universe could be discovered independently of experience, by careful analysis. Hence the French predilection for planning. People, in their thinking nature, stood apart from the world, in its physical nature. In the same way as mind and body were things apart for Descartes, so experience based on the physical senses—sensing—stood apart from thinking. Experientially based perceptions, of oneself or of one's world, were to be mistrusted.

Structuralism—the quest for mind

Following in the footsteps of Descartes, and contrary to the behavioural orientation, the rationally based quest for mind has been a perennial European concern. Accompanying this quest has been a belief in the uniqueness of a person's cognitive processes, the importance of language and the appropriateness of a structural approach to understanding behaviour and society. The French structuralists favoured an interplay between perplexing data and broad but precisely formulated theoretical frameworks. They welcomed the judicious application of biology, mathematics and other disciplines to socio-scientific problems (Gardner, 1974, page 38). One of the most prominent structuralists in recent times, has been the Swiss psychologist Jean Piaget (1896–1980).

Piaget sought to prove that human knowledge has specific, ascertainable, structural properties. He proposed three broad stages of human development and claimed that a small number of logical-mathematical formulations embraces the nature of each. Elliot Jaques, as a management thinker, takes on where Piaget left off, as we shall see in the next chapter.

Piaget, additionally, reasoned that an organism's intelligence was embodied in a series of structures with latent tendencies for development. These could be brought out by appropriate interaction with the environment. The organism was not a passive reflector but rather possessed active potentialities which could unfold to a greater or lesser extent. All depend upon the nature of their interaction with the environment. Piaget thereby ties thought to action, and sees the level of thought as a direct reflection of the actions of which the person is capable. His guiding picture of the individual attaining knowledge depicts a seeking, exploring individual continually acting and coordinating his or her actions until they eventually coalesce into structures.

We now turn from rationally based philosophy and psychology to rationally oriented economics. This leads us to the eighteenth-century Physiocrats and the nineteenth-century French socialists.

Dirigisme

DIRIGISTE ECONOMIC POLICY

The Physiocrats

France's eighteenth-century Physiocrats brought to the economic order the same rational outlook that Descartes brought to the natural one. For example, both the Physiocrats and the Scottish empiricist David Hume (1711–1776) were attached to economic individualism and liberalism. However, the philosophies on which their attachment was based were entirely different. The views of the Physiocrats were based on a preconceived order of the world, harmonious, immutable and beneficial. To Hume the point of departure was the nature of man rather than that of the world:

> The Physiocrats were rationalists who set out to find self-evident truths in the light of reason rather than with the help of experience. Hume, on the other hand, was an empiricist who practised the method of observation, relying on introspection and the lessons of history.
>
> (Spiegel, 1971, page 86)

While these rationalists sought theoretical sources of insight the empiricist looked for practical ones.

For *François Quesnay* (1694–1774) the most prominent Physiocrat, the moral law calls for adherence to a natural order which 'self-evidently is the most advantageous for mankind'. The justice of this order is derived from its utility, and its immutable attributes are the natural rights to individual freedom and private property. Hume, however, was no believer in natural rights. Instead of the dogmatic utilitarianism of the Physiocrats he supported an empirical one. Private property deserves endorsement because it is socially useful under existing conditions. The same discrepancy of focus between the rational order perceived by Jacques Delors and the level playing field sought by John Major prevails today.

The French socialists

Although the nineteenth-century French socialists diverged somewhat in their political and economic perspectives, their basic reliance on rationality remained a common denominator. In that respect they followed both a structuralist and a Physiocratic trajectory.

Claude Henri de Rouvroy, Comte de Saint-Simon (1760–1825), was a nobleman with a chequered career as a soldier, wealthy speculator and poverty-stricken pamphleteer. He was a tireless advocate of industrial development, full production and the primacy of economics over politics. To place science and technology at the service of the State, he assigned, in an early version of his proposals, a commanding position to scientists and engineers. In later versions the emphasis shifted to bankers and businessmen, who as members of a sort of planning board were to constitute a managerial elite and assume the direction of the economy.

Charles Fourier (1772–1837) wanted to reorganize society in a manner that would be conducive to social harmony and, at the same time, permit the gratification of fundamental psychological needs. These needs, arising from the immutable nature of a person, were stifled in the commercial society of nineteenth-century France. Therefore Fourier recommended the voluntary formation of cooperative associations. each called a 'phalanx' and made up of 400 families. These were large enough to offer a variety of specialized occupations but not too large for the cultivation of personal relationships. Work would acquire the features of play or sport, and since each individual would be a member of a large number of different teams, interests and loyalties would be diffused throughout the community. The vision of Fourier was in many respects the opposite of Saint-Simon's. Saint-Simon, closer to the Germanic world view, worshipped production and work. Fourier, closer to the Anglo-Saxons, valued a person's innate passions for variety, adventure and friendly association with fellow-beings. But they both envisaged rationally structured organizations of one kind or another.

Pierre Joseph Proudhon (1809–65) was in fact the first social reformer to call himself an anarchist. He espoused a loosely knit 'federalism' among local and regional communities and a system of 'mutualism' which called for reciprocal rights and duties. These were grounded not in the compulsion of law but in freely entered contractual arrangements. Proudhon saw life enmeshed in a series of contradictions, problems to which there were no ready solutions other than 'balance' or 'equilibrium'.

One moral idea underlies the whole of Proudhon's thought: the idea of justice. Justice is the same as reciprocity, equality, equilibrium. Social life, nature itself even, contains immovable contradictions. Proudhon's search is for the discovery of the right idea which would abolish contradictions. That idea is the concept of justice as an equilibrium of opposing forces. The political order of the ideal society should also reflect the equilibrium of forces or, as Proudhon calls it, the social mutualism. The state must disappear. Between Saint-Simon and Proudhon, in-dustrial expansion and social equilibrium, lies the field of tension that is contained within rationalism.

The state as entrepreneur

'DIRIGISME' IN CONTEXT

Rational influence

In the event, the State has not disappeared. Although Europe today is far removed from State socialism in the traditional Marxist sense, State planning—as in France or Sweden—plays a significant part in business and economic life. For British economist Andrew Shonfield (1965), the effective conduct of a nation's life, as far as the rationally disposed French are concerned, must depend on the concentration of power in the hands of a small number of exceptionally able people. The design and efficiency of the machinery of government then determines the degree of practical success achieved. The long view and the wide experience, systematically analysed by persons of authority, are the intellectual foundations of the system. The design and efficiency of the machine of government then determines the degree of success achieved by the economy as a whole, incorporating both public and private enterprise.

Public enterprise

The State as entrepreneur in a rationally oriented economy is taken very seriously. There is in all this an ingrained mistrust of the natural play of forces of a free economy. Instead there is a profound conviction that it is better to produce synthetically, as in a laboratory, the theoretical conditions of a competitive market than to ride the shocks and hazards of real competition:

The official in the Commissariat tends to see 'his' industry in intimate terms, as that of a day to day counsellor—part industrial consultant, part banker, part plain bully. His job is to maintain a constant pressure on industry, by any tactical means that happen to be available, to keep it moving in some desired direction (Shonfield, 1965, page 137).

The officials of the Plan seem to live in each other's pockets. The celebrated coherence which is the mark of French planning appears to be achieved by a system of communication that resembles a university common room.

The rational economic model then has two basic aims. First, it is geared towards stability, that is harmony and protection for all citizens. Second, it is focused on expansion and planned development, so that each country should not be left behind in the internationally competitive race. Since it is assumed that individual enterprise in France, at least, can very seldom be trusted to satisfy these objectives the achievement of these aims requires the state to invervene directly and at all levels. 'L'état' therefore must rule and make harmonious the entrepreneurial system. It must stimulate and favour different groups within it according to the priorities of the common aims. It must be satisfied, however, with applying very general pressures and relying, for the more practical problems, on the individual entrepreneurs. While the State alone pressures for change it must rely on the entrepreneurial class to realize it (Crozier, 1968, page 28).

Such a *dirigiste*, rationally oriented society, as we shall now see, is bound to place great emphasis on education of the mind—as opposed to the cultivation of will or character. As such, the managerial cadre becomes part of an intellectual elite.

Structural/functional models—institutional frameworks

A RATIONALLY BASED EDUCATIONAL SYSTEM

A cadre with a mission

'Cadre' in French is a noun meaning a 'frame'. It corresponds to 'manager' in English. Cadres have become the social group to emulate, a rationally oriented society's trend setters. There is a quasi-divine mission associated with their function. The French seem to regard their managers as the moral as well as the economic saviours of their nation. In that sense they can be differentiated from the Anglo-Saxon business leaders, the Germanic industrialists and the Italian impresarios.

For almost two centuries, the top engineering Grandes Ecoles, spear-headed by l'école polytechnique, have groomed their alumni to take up positions as 'les cadres de la nation'—the nation's organizers in spheres as diverse as business, politics and public service. The intensity and duration of the Grande Ecole training equips the would-be manager or administrator with an ability to cope with pressure, a lengthy span of concentration and an analytical mind.

Managing with mathematics

Much of the best and worst in the French national spirit according to management analysts Lawrence and Barsoux (1990), can be imputed to the concept of education as inspired academic pedagogy, confined to the classroom. Its role is to transmit knowledge and to train intellects, not to develop the full individual:

> Where America extols money, West Germany work and Great Britain blood, France has nailed its flag to the post of cleverness. It is achievement in the educational field which determines inclusion among the decision makers of France (page 30).

In keeping with the desire for objectivity, in France mathematics is the central feature of a rational culture's selection methods in education. From secondary school onwards priority is given to the mastery of mathematical tools and to the quality of logical inference. The whole edifice seems founded on abstract principles which are only tenuously linked to the development of well-adjusted personalities. Maths is deemed a faithful indicator of the ability to synthesize and to engage in complex abstract reasoning, qualities which are highly prized in all spheres of professional life.

Isolated into strata

The rationally based educational system in France is bureaucratic, first, in its organizational structure, which is highly centralized and impersonal. Second, it is bureaucratic in its pedagogy since the act of teaching and the human relationships it involves imply an unusually wide gap between the teacher and the student. This corresponds to and prepares for the strata isolation of the bureaucratic system. It is also bureaucratic in the content of the teaching, which is rather more abstract and divorced from the requirements of actual life than in other industrial countries. There is a very strong pattern of opposition between the teacher, who soars above his pupils and delivers the truth in an unquestioned, uninterrupted way, and the 'delinquent community' of the pupils. They can resist the strong pressure of the system only by resorting to an implicit negative solidarity and occasional anarchistic revolts, the famous 'chahuts'—uproars

(Crozier, 1968, page 240). So we find that there are isolated individuals unable to unite for constructive activities, and the absence of face-to-face relationships between the subordinates (children) and a distant authority (teacher). Moreover, impersonal rules give the only standard measurement of achievement.

THE POLITICO-ADMINISTRATIVE SYSTEM

Rational administration

Stratification is not exclusive to education in France. In the rationally based French political and administrative system, according to Crozier, decisions are made through the working of three different subsystems. All three are simultaneously closely interdependent and very far apart operationally.

The administrative subsystem operates through a complex web of public agencies deeply influenced by the bureaucratic traits of the rational model. As a result, the people with the power to decide remain far above the pressures of those who are affected by their decisions. Problems of coordination therefore arise.

A rational approach to policy making

The policy-making subsystem has behaved in a similarly rational way. The French political class has fought and debated endlessly, but on abstract principles and not on bargaining realities. It has consented to compromise, Crozier maintains only at the last minute, when the force of circumstance could be evoked.

These drawbacks have assumed greater importance with the acceleration of change and with the general social evolution. Both make it more difficult to accept the exclusion of several groups and serve to increase the frustration of the citizens. The functions of State affect the latter increasingly without a comparative improvement in the possibilities of citizen participation.

THE PATTERN OF INDUSTRIAL RELATIONS

In France, centralization and State intervention have comprised the standard, rationally based solution to the problem of communcation between management and workers. This has made for much misunderstanding. Instead of bargaining with the employers, the working class directs all the muscle power it can muster at the State, that is, the rational society's 'brain'. It is the State that will impose on the employers the necessary reforms by the way of impersonal, mandatory rules. Reforms will thus come from the political world and not through compromises directly negotiated by the interested parties. The rationally based labour movement therefore must be politically oriented because of the importance of the State in the strategy of the social struggle. But this political orientation makes for weakness, because it imposes bureaucratic centralization and prevents the rank and file from participating directly and consciously. To fill the gap it is necessary to resort to a radical ideology which is the only way to maintain the coherence of the movement. Such an ideology is assumed to give some rationale to the cumbersome tactics and the many manipulations of the local groups.

As a whole, the French labour movement can be viewed as one manifestation of the rational model. It prefers finally to submit to impersonal rules and to appeal to a superior authority than to fight and compromise in its own right. To the extent that this applies to industrial relations in other parts of Europe, so rationalism might prevail over pragmatism or, as we shall see, over wholism or humanism.

BUREAUCRACY AND CHANGE

In reviewing the overall dynamics of the rationally circumscribed society Crozier identifies, three main patterns appear as decisive. First, there are alternating periods of routine and crisis. In fact, crisis is necessary to break up the routine order. Second, there is a will and passion for planning, ordering and equalizing all situations. Third, there is a tension between the negative and conservative behaviour of all formal groupings and the effervescence and intellectual, irresponsible creativity of individuals.

First, to obtain a limited reform within a rationally based system one is invariably obliged to attack the whole rational entity, which is thus constantly called into question. Reform can therefore only be brought about by sweeping revolution. Second, whenever a change occurs that enhances the situation of some persons or groups within a system, all peers of these persons or groups exert a similar pressure to preserve their distance from them. Third, the creativeness of the individual is the natural counterpart to the predominance of routine and is a necessary preparation for the crisis period. Since groups are considered to have difficulties in constructive cooperative action, the initiative must be left to individuals, and it takes the form of intellectual expression.

The preservation of individual autonomy and creativity may be considered as one of the latent functions of the routine–crisis cycle. Its negative phase, routine, protects individuals against arbitrary decisions and leads them to criticize the existing order and to invent a crisis for the positive phase of the cycle. Such crisis offers exciting possibilities of action to a few people while taking on, for others, the appearance of a *force majeure*. Change thus finally comes without having to resort to the dependence relationships implied by a gradual, reasonable and conscious adjustment. Rationalism, in such a case, is intermeshed with pragmatism.

Pragmatic–rational polarity

SUSTAINED POLARITY

In the history of capitalism, Shonfield (1965) maintains, Britain and France, European embodiments of pragmatism and rationalism, supply the convenience of sustained polarity. It is remarkable how two nations, geographically so close, so interested in a neighbour's way of doing things, so proud of their capacity to learn from outsiders, should yet have been so little influenced by each other's experiences. The sharp contrast in national style and practice has not been noticeably modified over the centuries. Whereas pragmatic individualism scores when it is necessary to get a business started, rational organization comes into its own at the next stage of commercial or economic development. Whereas in the first instance the individual enterprise has vigour and thrust, while government intervention is often sluggish or ill timed, in the second case the opposite tends to occur.

It would seem, therefore, that in economic life rationalist and pragmatist should join forces in the same way as Newton brought to bear inductive and deductive logic in his grand synthesis. All too often business mergers across cultures fail to bring about the kind of philosophical and cultural as well as technical and commercial synergy to which we are alluding here. Moreover, as we have now seen, the rational world view is very different from and thereby complementary to the pragmatically based one.

There is a rational thread that runs all the way through, from René Descartes to *dirigiste* economic planning, albeit that it twists and turns along the way. Unlike the pragmatists who are ultimately concerned with behavioural processes and outcomes—whether free enterprise or action learning—the rationalists orient themselves towards mental ones. Whether charting the corporate mind, the structure of bureaucracy, the natural economic order, or even the mental processes underlying the human soul, their cognitive orientation remains pre-eminent.

RATIONALLY BASED INSTITUTIONS IN CONTEXT

Bureaucratic rationality, according to Crozier (1965), has produced a new and increasingly elaborate model of routine activities, to be carried out on an egalitarian and impersonal basis. However, and as will be highlighted in Chapter 8, this has meant no competition and cooperation at the group level. State and group quasi-monopolies have imposed the one best way. The procedure makes planning difficult, because planning ahead implies organizational experimentation and a cooperative attitude among individuals. Planned growth implies greater trust in human motivations, fostering initiative at all levels, more cooperation between individuals and more competition between groups.

Modern organization man, Crozier adds, is groping for a new culture, open to all and thus a mass culture, yet lively and creative enough to encourage each individual to participate with the best of himself:

> It is not surprising that France, whose bureaucratic and bourgeois system permitted the blossoming of one of the most elaborate individual structures of the pre-industrial era, should remain attached to it somewhat longer than other nations. But we can hope that when change comes, as it now does, the challenge offered to French ingenuity may be met by a positive contribution to the new humanism that must develop in the context of the new organizational reality.
>
> (Crozier, 1965, page 314)

For such a new organizational reality we turn to Elliot Jaques.

Summary

RATIONAL SOCIAL PHILOSOPHY

Structuralism—the quest for mind
- Contrary to the behavioural orientation of the individualists, the quest for mind has been a perennial concern of the rationalists.
- Accompanying this quest has been a belief in the uniqueness of a persons cognitive processes.
- Whereas the image of a person as a struggling biological organism with strong drives governing his or her behaviour, has held sway in behaviourally oriented social science.
- Structuralism threatens this outlook, attributing to the individual innate mental structuring and functioning, the subject playing an active role in constructing knowledge.

Planning—the quest for order
- The eighteenth-century economic rationalists brought to the economic order the same ordered outlook that rational philosophers brought to the natural one.
- These economists set out to find self-evident truths in the light of reason rather than with the help of experience.
- Whereas, for them, in the marketplace the free play of individual forces is frustrated, resulting in economic conflict rather than harmony.

- In their rationally planned world that ideal and immutable providential order and harmonious individualism reaches its full flowering.

RATIONAL ECONOMIC POLICY

Dirigisme
- The effective conduct of a nation's life depends on the concentration of power in the hands of a small number of exceptionally able people.
- The design and efficiency of the machinery of government determines the degree of practical success achieved—the State as entrepreneur is taken very seriously.
- There is in all this an ingrained mistrust of the natural play of forces of a free economy.
- There is also a conviction that it is better to produce synthetically the theoretical conditions of a competitive market than to ride the shocks and hazards of real competition.

Public/private coordination
- Economic achievement is more sharply focused than other advanced countries on high-tech products and government-sponsored projects.
- To be a public sector firm in a coordinated economy means to partake in the power and glory of the State—it is image enhancing, not image demeaning.
- Planners thereby develop and promote an intricate network of commitments on the part of private firms, all in return for favours from the State.
- Its job is to maintain a constant pressure on industry—as part industrial consultant, part banker, part plain bully—to keep it moving in some desired direction.

9

Function and structure

Until now, rationally based European management has been eclipsed by the so-called 'scientific' Americans, Henry Ford and Frederick Taylor. That having been said, two European management thinkers—Henri Fayol in the past and Elliot Jaques in the present—have gained worldwide reputations. Like Ford and Taylor before them, they have focused on the large-scale organization that transcends the more pragmatically based enterprise.

As indicated in Chapter 8, such a rationally based approach to business leads to depersonalized management and bureaucratized organization. Moreover, whereas the outer-directed approach to industrial organization is functional in orientation, the inner-directed one is structurally oriented. Whereas the former is oriented towards standardized management principles and formal business functions, the latter is focused upon structurally evolving strata of 'requisite' organization (Fig. 9.1).

Industrial administration

Henri Fayol (1841–1925) started out as a French mining engineer in the latter part of the nineteenth century, before turning to general management. In fact, though his book on industrial administration was published in France in 1916, the first English translation came out in 1949. In it Fayol emphasized the universality of administrative activity.

FUNCTIONAL MANAGEMENT

Fayol divided industrial administration into the five elements that we know so well today (see Pugh *et al.*, 1971), those being:

- To *forecast and plan* (in French, *prévoir*), that is, to examine the future and draw up a plan of action. The essence of planning, for Fayol, is to allow for the optimum use of resources. Interestingly enough, in 1916, Fayol also argued for a National Plan in France.

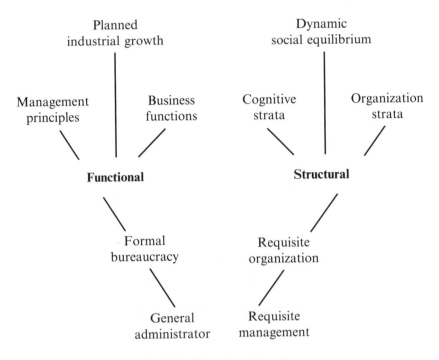

Fig. 9.1   The rational branches

- To *organize*, building up the material and human structure of the organization. Central to this is a procedure through which plans are efficiently prepared and carried out.
- An organization, for Fayol, must start with a plan, a definition of its goals. It must then produce an organization structure appropriate to its goals. Third, the organization must be put in motion, which involves the *command* element, thereby maintaining activity among its personnel.
- Command refers to the relationship between a manager and his or her subordinates in the immediate task area. But organizations have a variety of tasks to perform, so *coordination* is necessary, binding together, unifying and harmonizing all activity.
- Finally there is *control*, logically the final element. Through control a manager checks that the other four are performing properly, seeing that everything occurs in conformity with established rules and expressed commands.

THE FUNCTIONS OF ORGANIZATION

Apart from the functional elements of management outlined above, Fayol identified a comprehensive set of thirteen organizational principles, including:

- *Division of work*: specialization allows the individual to build up expertise and thereby be more productive.
- *Authority*: the right to issue commands, along with which must go the equivalent responsibility for its exercise.
- *Discipline*: which is two-sided; employees only obey orders if management play their part by providing good leadership.
- *Unity of command*: each employee should have only one boss.
- *Subordination of individual interest to general interest*: management must see that the goals of the firm are always paramount.
- *Remuneration*: payment is an important motivator.
- *Centralization or decentralization* is a matter of degree, depending on the condition of the business and the quality of the personnel.
- *Scalar chain*: an hierarchy is necessary for unity of direction but lateral communication is also fundamental.
- *Order*: both material and social order are necessary. The former minimizes loss of time and useless handling of materials. The latter is achieved through organization and selection.
- *Equity*: in running a business a combination of kindliness and justice is needed.
- *Stability of tenure*: is essential due to the time and expense involved in training good management.
- *Initiative*: allowing all personnel to show initiative is a source of strength to the organization.
- *Esprit de corps*: management must foster the morale of its employees and maintain harmonious relations.

As we can see Fayol set the tone for many formal organization structures since to follow. While the German sociologist Max Weber has been given the credit for delineating the structure and functioning of bureaucracy, as we shall see, Weber in fact lamented its very existence. Fayol was a more wholehearted supporter of bureaucracy, and his successor, Elliot Jaques, is even more explicitly so. Moreover, Jaques, as we shall see, displays an intricate, rationally based appreciation of both organizational and managerial functioning and structuring. In so doing he crosses the divide from externalized, standardized bureaucratic functions to inner internalized 'requisite' structures.

Bureaucracy in management and organization

'REQUISITE' BUREAUCRACY

Two current management theorists in the French rationist mode are Elliot Jaques and Michel Crozier. In this chapter we describe the work of the former, and in the next chapter, that of the latter. The argument that

Jaques (1976) pursues is that, contrary to general opinion, bureaucracies *per se* are neither centralizing nor localizing powers, neither humanizing nor dehumanizing. They are dependent institutions, social instruments, taking their initial objectives and characteristics from the associations which employ them. The bureaucracies that dehumanize are those which have outgrown their organization structure or have never had an adequate structure, or are too rigidly controlled from the centre.

Some types of structure facilitate normal relationships between individuals, making it easy for them to link into immediate social relationships, with feelings of trust and confidence. Jaques calls such structures 'requisite' or socially connecting. They are 'requisite' in the sense of being called for in the nature of things including human nature. They are socially connecting in the sense of linking a person to society, and giving him or her a hold upon it.

Other types of structure make it difficult or impossible for individuals to have normal relationships of confidence or trust. They force social interactions into a mould calling for forms of behaviour which arouse suspicion, envy, hostile rivalry and anxiety, and put brakes on social relationships. Mutually antagonistic groups and societies form. Jaques calls such institutions antirequisite or alienating. They run counter to a person's normal nature, and separate individuals from their society. His rationally based bureaucracy is different.

BUREAUCRACY IN INDUSTRIAL SOCIETY

Ubiquitous organization
Until the onset of the Industrial Revolution the bureaucratic hierarchy was almost exclusively confined to the governmental and religious sectors of society. One of the outstanding features of twentieth-century industrial societies is the concentration of nearly all the working population into employment in bureaucratic organizations for a wage or salary. There is little purpose in arguing in favour of this process of bureaucratization, according to Jaques, or even decrying it, for bureaucracy is merely the instrument of a deeper social process. The simple fact is that if we decide to proceed with the development of industrialized societies, then bureaucracies on a large scale are here to stay.

Fortunately, he says, the progress of civilization does not depend on changing the nature of people; there is more than enough goodness in human nature to make a better society possible. If further progress is to be made it will be because of the discovery and creation of more humane institutions. The well or ill functioning of an institution is not just a matter of 'personalities'. Its primary source lies buried in the structure of the organization itself. Because bureaucratic institutions are ubiquitous in industrial society, their possible organizational form is a matter of importance to the establishment of a good society. Such institutions have their characteristic role relationships.

Role and social structure

The concepts of role relationships and social structure are central to Jaques's argument. The design of institutions is the theme and functional roles and role relationships are the building blocks of which the institutions are to be constructed. In a most general sense a role may be defined as a knot in a social net of role relationships. A role stands not on its own feet but in relation to other roles with a connection between them.

Role relationships thus constitute a field within which behaviour occurs. The persons occupying the roles are part of the total field. Roles, finally, have two major properties: first, their detachability from the person who occupies them; second, their stability.

There are two main levels at which Jaques's concept of social structure may be used. The first is the system of connected roles. The observable, practical relations may be termed the surface structure. The second meaning applies to underlying systems or wholes which can give explanatory meaning to the world of observation. Unlike the pragmatically based approach to organization and management, which is focused upon a personality-shaping role, Jaques's rational outlook is focused on role-shaping personality. Role, in its turn, is shaped by function.

FREEDOM AND DISCRETION

For Jaques, the functioning of social institutions depends on more than having the right individuals. To begin with, it is based on having the right social structures. As far as bureaucratic systems are concerned, it is impossible to describe or define what is meant by the right person until the nature of the task has been defined and the organization designed and constructed to enable the work to be done. Different situations therefore require different sorts of leadership.

The need for managerial leadership of any kind is a reflection of the fact that the employment relationship is requisitely a social exchange. It is not just a matter, therefore, of the manager saying 'Do this, it's what you're paid for!' Rather, for Jaques (1991) it is requisitely a matter of

> I want this task done and I am assigning it to you; I am accountable for assessing the outcome and for keeping a running appraisal of your competence; if you do well, I shall arrange for you to be rewarded within the limits of the resources

allocated to me, and I shall also see to it that you are considered by those higher up for advancement; I believe that I will act justly towards you, but if you feel that I do not then you have access to an appeal procedure. You must finally adhere to the rules and regulations that bind us both, but within those limits you have the freedom to exercise your own discretion in carrying out tasks without undue interference from me.

Moreover, employees in such a 'requisite' bureaucracy have their rights.

The rights of the individual

According to Jaques, there are four basic rights, that must requisitely be taken for granted if bureaucracy is to be humane and creative. They involve the right to *employment and opportunity*; to *participation* in the control of policy changes in the employing organization; to *equitable reward*; and to *individual appeal* against decisions which are felt to be unfair or unjust.

The technical problem of an enlightened society is to create a production technology which is not only economic but which also provides a balance of work roles. These should be suited to the spread of talent and ability of the population at any given time. Unemployment is 'non-requisite' for the insecurity it brings and the wastage of human capacity it entails. Requisite procedures and the avoidance of societal imbalance call for a continually buoyant economy and full employment.

Socialist planning makes this possible—but the cost is the loss of opportunity for individual entrepreneurial initiatives and risk. Capitalist societies gain the freedom for more or less individual enterprise but manipulate the employment situation. The requisite solution requires getting the best of both worlds.

FUNCTIONING OF BUREAUCRATIC SYSTEMS

For Jaques, the translation of the objects of an enterprise into actual work requires the assigning of specific tasks to be carried out by employees of the enterprise. Tasks that are directly concerned with the objects and operational activities of the enterprise are termed *operational*. They can be distinguished from all other types of task concerned with supporting and facilitating the discharge of the operational tasks. These are referred to as *support* tasks. Operational tasks are those which constitute the content of the business (public and private) transactions. The three major operational tasks are the *development* of goods and services (D); *provision* of these (M); and their *selling* (S). All three are necessary to constitute a full operational transaction.

D exchanges energy in the form of new knowledge and ideas; *M* exchanges energy in the form of raw materials brought in and services delivered; *S* exchanges energy in the form of active negotiation with the client and market environment. It is essential that these systems should be organized in terms of these operational transactions.

Horizontal relationships

As Jaques sees it, the widespread desire to get rid of the bureaucratic hierarchy because it is allegedly autocratic finds expression in the continual search for more 'democratic' or 'organic' forms of work organization. Each new group structure, be it autonomous work group or matrix, is thereby hailed as a victory for cooperative over bureaucratic organization, signalling the imminent demise of bureaucracy.

In fact, Jaques argues, these are simply various arrangements of laterally related roles into working groups. As such, they are exceedingly important in their own right, being essential components of effectively functioning bureaucratic systems. So-called functionally autonomous work groups, for example, in his terms, are stratum-1 groups of workers encouraged by their stratum-2 section manager to work together in a collateral relationship. Similarly, groups put together in matrix fashion for special projects form integral parts of the functioning of bureaucratic systems. Managers or co-managers remain accountable for the performance of their subordinates. Such performance varies according to the organizational strata involved.

'REQUISITE' MANAGEMENT AND ORGANIZATION

Organizational strata

Bureaucracies are hierarchical systems. They contain a range of different levels, reflected in different levels of work. Jaques's definition of level of work is given in the form of a measuring instrument based upon the maximum of time spans during which people are required to exercise discretion:

> Evidence suggests, as a first proposition, that there is a universally distributed depth structure of levels of bureaucratic organization, whereby natural lines of stratification exist at 3-month, 12-month, 2-year, 5-year, 10-year and even higher levels still. The second proposition is that the existence of the stratified depth-structure of bureaucratic hierarchies is the reflection in social organization of the existence of discontinuity and stratification in the nature of human capacity. The capacity is referred to as work-capacity, which is further analysed in terms of a person's level of abstraction. A multi-modal distribution of capacity is postulated. The third proposition is that the rate of growth of the

work-capacity of individuals follows predictable paths. Maturational shifts in the quality of an individual's capacity occur as he moves across the boundary from one level of abstraction to another

(Jaques, 1976, page 100)

What Jaques postulates is the existence of a universal bureaucratic depth stucture, composed of organizational strata with boundaries at levels of work represented by time spans of 3 months to 20 years. These strata are real in the geological sense, with observable boundaries and discontinuity. They are not mere shadings and gradations. Requisite organization of bureaucracy must be designed accordingly.

In other words, strata of organization need to be built up that are 'requisite' for the complexity of the task in hand. The complexity of a task lies in the number, variety, rate of change and degree of interweaving of the variables involved in it. Jaques identifies seven such levels, or strata, of organization:

1. These are shop or office floor level activities, requiring a person to proceed along a prescribed linear path, getting continual feedback in order to do so—for example, drilling holes with a jack hammer, typing a letter.
2. These kinds of task are found at first-line managerial level; the individual must anticipate potential problems through accumulating significant data—for example, design a new jig for a machining process, working out the design as the job proceeds.
3. Increasingly complex situations require alternative plans to be constructed before starting out, one to be chosen and serially progressed to completion. This involves heading a project team, for example, to create a new software program, having initially to select between alternatives with varying times, costs, specifications.
4. These comprise a number of interacting programmes which need to be planned and progressed in relation to each other. Trade-offs must be made between tasks to make progress along the composite route. New venturing, for instance, requires a combination of overlapping product development, market analysis, product engineering and commercial assessment, with mutual adjustment along the way.
5. These are the kinds of tasks faced by presidents of strategic business units in large corporations. Practical on-the-spot judgements must be used to deal with a field of ambiguous conceptual variables, and to make decisions envisaging second- and third-order consequences. This involves driving half a dozen critical tasks to achieve a seven-year plan, continually picking up important areas of impact and likely

consequences of change, keeping profitability at a reasonable level while maintaining customer goodwill, high employee morale, and a growing asset base.

6. At this level executives must build up a picture of likely critical events worldwide. This entails international networking to accumulate information about potentially significant developments that could affect the business and its business units, forestalling adverse events and sustaining a friendly environment for corporate trade.

7. At this level CEOs work out strategic alternatives for worldwide operation, using complex conceptual information concerned with culture, values and the business of nations and international trade well into the twenty-first century.

Because, in the final analysis, each category of task complexity has a coresponding category of cognitive complexity in human beings, complexity in work can be matched with complexity in people in the same organizational layer.

These propositions can be applied not only to the design of organizational structure for bureaucracies but also to coping with changes in these systems induced by the developing capacities of their employees. If the propositions are valid and reliable, Jaques argues, they will show that the relationship between bureaucracy and individuality is not an unresolvable conflict to be softened by uncomfortable compromise. Rather, it is a dilemma that can be dealt with by creative interaction between social institution and individual.

'Requisite' management and leadership

Effective leadership for rationally minded Jaques (1991) is indistinguishable from 'requisite' management. It demands four straightforward and basic conditions (page 295). First, a person must have the necessary competence to carry the particular role, including strongly valuing it. Second, that person must be free from any severely debilitating psychological characteristics that interfere with interpersonal relationships. Third, the organizational conditions must be requisite, that is, conforming to the properties of hierarchical organizations and human nature. Fourth, each person must be encouraged to use his or her natural style, namely to allow the full and free expression of his or her natural self.

Central to Jaques's concept of 'requisite' management, are the manager's powers of cognition. In that sense Jaques is a direct disciple of Piaget. However, he is also concerned with values, knowledge and skill, wisdom and temperament. Ever inclined to use mathematical formulae, for Jaques:

Current actual capacity (CAC) = $fCP.V.K/S.Wi(-T)$
where
CP = cognitive capacity, that is, mastery of complexity,
V = values, interests, priorities,
K/S = skilled use of relevant knowledge,
Wi = wisdom about people and things,
$(-T)$= the absence of serious personality/temperament defects.

For Jaques, the concept of cognitive processing lies at the heart of any possibility of understanding the nature of competence at work. Cognitive processes are the mental processes by means of which a person is able to organize information to make it available for doing work. This processing enables the individual to deal with information complexity. When a person's cognitive processing is equal to the complexity, he or she is comfortable. Cognitive power is the potential strength of cognitive processes in a person, and is therefore the maximum level of task complexity that someone can handle at any given point in his or her development. Just as we find that the greater a person's cognitive power, the greater is the mass of information that can be coped with, so we find that the greater the person's cognitive power, the longer is that person's time horizon. Not only do cognitive processes come in greater or lesser degress of complexity, they also proceed in discontinuous jumps. Each of these steps is characterized by a change in the very nature of the cognitive process, just as materials change in state from crystalline to vapour as they are heated. A fundamental point is that as we mature we progress through developmental stages, moving from one type of cognitive processing to the next more complex one. But for Jaques there is more to management than cognition.

Values–knowledge–wisdom–temperament
Jaques's experience is that everyone will put their best effort into doing what they value. People, he says, are spontaneously energetic with respect to things that interest them. The issue is not to encourage output by incentives but to provide conditions in which the work itself has its inherent value. Such work allows the individual to release and direct his or her energy and imagination.

According to Jaques, we learn from our experience, from teaching and from practice. We store our learning in the forms of knowledge and skill in the use and application of that knowledge. By knowledge we refer to objective facts, including procedures, which can be stated in words, formulae, models or other symbols that one can learn. By skill Jaques refers to the application of facts and procedures that have been learnt through practice to the point that they can be used without thinking.

Action without sound theory, Jaques finally believes, can be counterproductive. Unsound theories distort our experience, narrow our vision and leave us none the wiser about the effects of our actions on others. Action without sound theory is folly. Wisdom can be developed in people, especially by good mentoring by a more senior person.

For rationally minded Jaques, though, in the final analysis, focus upon personality traits is misguided. Emotional make-up has little effect upon the person's in-role leadership work unless these qualities are at unacceptable or abnormal extremes: 'Our argument is that the personality variable figures in managerial leadership in a negative rather than a positive way' (Jaques, 1991, page 83). Take note, within this objectively rational world view, of the mistrust of raw, subjective personality.

Many people would argue that it is precisely by understanding and attending to the special emotional needs and personality styles of each individual that a 'leader' can best motivate a follower. But that can result in the 'difficult' personalities getting special attention compared with their more collaborative colleagues. For Jaques, this is not what managerial hierarchies should be about. Managerial hierarchies are not seller–buyer situations or families. It is simply not acceptable, Jaques argues, for individuals to behave in ways that are disruptive of working relationships. At the same time, people are in need of development.

Fostering the development of individuals
The development of individuals involves taking note of the rate of growth of their potential and trying to provide work opportunities consistent with it. Second, they should be given the opportunity to consider their values, gain the necessary skilled knowledge, reinforce their wisdom and take the necessary steps to get rid of any seriously abnormal personality quirks they may have. Mentoring, in relation to the former, is the process whereby a manager-once-removed (MoR) helps the individual to understand his or her potential and how it might be applied to achieve full career and organizational growth. There are four major approaches to development.

Coaching is the process through which a manager helps subordinates to understand the full range of their roles and then points out the subordinate's strengths and weaknesses. *Teaching* involves the imparting of knowledge to individuals by lectures, discussion and practice. *Training* is a process of helping individuals to develop or enhance their skill in the use of knowledge through practice, either on the job or in a learning simulation. *Skill* enables individuals to use their knowledge in problem-solving activities without having to think, thus freeing discretion and judgement.

Whereas an individual's aspiration towards equilibrium between work capacity and level of work is absolute, that between level of work and payment is relative. In the case of pay, each person's aspirations appear to be geared to a sense of fairness of economic reward relative to others. In the case of work, however, each person's level of aspiration is geared to his or her deepest feelings of reality and freedom.

The construction of adequate grading and progression systems, therefore, is an essential mechanism for making individual freedom real. If his or her level of work in time-span terms is shorter than time-span capacity, the individual will be deprived of the opportunity to test his or her capacity at full stretch. The individual will therefore be unable to maintain his or her relationship with reality over as wide a spectrum as possible. Conversely, if his or her level of work is longer than his or her current work capacity, a person's freedom will be destroyed. That person's relationship to reality will be disorganized, and the deepest anxieties aroused. Notwithstanding all this, individuals and organizations are always in a state of flux.

Evolving strata

GROWTH OF BUREAUCRATIC SYSTEMS

For Jaques, bureaucratic systems are internally live and changing, as the occupants of the systems join, develop, change and leave. There is a continual ebb and flow, with stable periods and critical change periods. At the same time, different parts of the system change at different rates, as do the individual members of these parts of the system.

It is precisely by identifying such differences in individuals that a society can accomplish two important social ends. First, it can arrange social procedures to make it possible for everyone to gain a level of work and career consistent with his or her work capacity. Second, it can bring political power and legislative control to bear to ensure that bureaucracy is managed in a manner consistent with the political outlook of the society. Thus whether or not bureaucratic organization would lead to economic elitism would be a political decision.

Size of organization, Jaques maintains, tends commonly to be regarded as a function of size of market, the nature of the economy, the type of technology and other such external factors. They are necessary but not sufficient. For Jaques, ultimately, the distribution of sizes of bureaucracy will be determined by the distribution in level of work capacity of those available to manage the bureaucracies.

There is a kind of Archimedes' principle at work whereby bureaucratic systems grow to the level of work capacity of their chief executives. Conversely, chief executives stimulate bureaucratic systems to grow to the level consistent with their work capacity. In citing the existence of up to seven strata of organization, preconditioned by executive work capacity, Jaques is following in the structural footsteps of Jean Piaget.

EVOLVING STRATA OF ORGANIZATION

As the strata of operation ascend from the practicality of the operational world to the abstraction of general management, the total field is available now to the manager only in conceptual form. It appears

> in histograms of performance, drawings of product families and other such conceptual models. He must now have that sense of security in his abilities to let go to some extent of the concrete outside world, and to rely upon an interplay between data of immediate experience and data culled from mental constructs. The manager or administrator must learn how to work from an office, not in complete detachment but with sufficiently frequent contact with the various parts of his domain to keep lively examples in mind of the activity of the situation he is dealing with *in abstracto*.
>
> (Jaques, 1991, page 176)

Elliot Jaques, in the final analysis, stands firmly on the foundations of French structural-functionalism. Within his general theory of bureaucracy he is pursuing Gardner's 'quest for mind', that perennial concern of the rationlist philosophers, in an organizational context. In so doing he takes bureaucracy out of its mechanistic confines and gives it an organic facelift. He also, with his developmental outlook on organizational strata, moves the managerial debate towards the Germanic, wholist *weltanschauung*, to which we shall turn in Chapter 11. Before then, however, we need to review the rationally based management attributes.

Summary

Functions of management
- Nineteenth-century French industrial engineer, Henri Fayol, provided a coherent, theoretical analysis of the functions of management and activities of industrial organization.
- Divided managerial activities into the deductively based functions of planning and organizing, command, coordination and control.
- At the same time focused structurally on division of work, authority and discipline, unity of command, centralization and decentralization, equity and order.

- Finally, focused industrially on production, sales, financial and personnel management.

Formal bureaucracy

- Whereas rational management is functionally led, bureaucracy is positioned closer to the structuralists.
- For such professional managers bureaucracies *per se* are neither humanizing nor dehumanizing.
- They are dependent institutions; social instruments, taking their initial objectives and characteristics from the associations which employ them.
- They can be rationally designed and managed with due regard for the constructive qualities of human beings and for the societal qualities of a liberal democracy.

Requisite organization

CP the necessary level of cognitive complexity to match the task complexity of the specific managerial role

V a strong enough sense of value for the managerial work, and for the leadership of others

K/S appropriate knowledge combined with experienced practice, involving skilled use of that knowledge

Wi the necessary wisdom about people and things

(–T) the absence of abnormal temperament, disrupting ability to work with others

Strata of organization

1. *Reactive* (shop floor activity) Direct action in immediate situation—proceed along a prescribed, linear path—e.g. typing or drilling.
2. *Responsive* (practical supervision) Anticipate potential problems by accumulating necessary information—e.g. designing a new jig for machining process, working out the design as the job proceeds.
3. *Adaptive* (project planning and control) Require alternative plans to be constructed before starting, one to be chosen and serially progressed to completion—e.g. heading a project team to create a new software programme.
4. *Transactional* (business management) Trade-offs must be made between related tasks, competing for resources, e.g. in new venturing between overlapping product development, product engineering and commerical activities.
5. *Pro-active* (strategic management) Driving forward half a dozen critical tasks to achieve, e.g. a five year plan, continually picking up important areas of impact and likely consequences of change.

6. *Interactive* (environmental management) Forming a picture of potentially significant developments worldwide that could affect the business, forestalling adverse events and building up a friendly environment for trade.

7. *Transformative* (visionary management) CEO's work out strategic alternatives for worldwide operation, using complex ideas concerned with culture, values and the business of nations well into the twenty-first century.

10

The rational European manager

Rational managerial attributes

Rational managerial attributes are connected with intellectual virtuosity and organizational meritocracy, from an externalized perspective. Similarly, they are associated with the nobility of work and the logic of honour, from an internalized one. The expected outcome or product of such managerial attributes is a combination of industrial expansion and social equilibrium. As we can see, the overall attitude is very different from that of the pragmatically oriented manager. It is more like that of Jacques Delors or Alfred Sloane than that of Margaret Thatcher or Lee Iacocca. The breeding ground for such rationally based 'professional management' is the Grande Ecole rather than the English public school or the German *Gymnasium* (Fig. 10.1).

Lawrence and Barsoux (1990), in their well-known book *Management in France*, explain convincingly that

> France has come closer than any other nation to turning management into a separate profession, with its own entry requirements and regulations. Managerial status in France is not part of a graded continuum but rather a quantum leap involving a change in legal status (for example in terms of pension entitlement) as well as subtle change in outlook and self-perception (page 17)

According to these two researchers, management in France is considered a state of mind rather than a set of techniques; the successful development of executives depends on creating a distinctive shared identity, a sense of belonging to the French managerial class.

Managers in the 'Hexagone', therefore, see their work in the first place as an intellectual task. The bias is for intellect rather than action. The interpersonal aspect, which plays such a significant role in the Anglo-Saxon approach to management, is far less significant for a typical French manager. This goes hand in hand with a capacity for quantitative

129

Fig. 10.1   The fruits of rationality

expression and the numerate discussion of strategy formulation. One of the managers interviewed by Lawrence and Barsoux expressed this aptly when he said, 'in France we won't make decisions unless we have confidence in the figures'. Even if we assume that he might have overstated his point, this belief in numbers differs distinctly from the attitude to figures in other cultural settings.

Let us first take the case of the German CEO, whose company not too long ago made a successful acquisition in the USA, costing several billion dollars. When he was asked how much quantitative analysis had been done beforehand, he answered, 'I need very few figures; it is in the first place my experience which tells me whether there is a strategic fit and whether the price is right'. When he made this remark he rubbed his thumb against the tips of his fingers to indicate what *Fingerspitzengefühl* (or intuition) means to him in such situations. Against this backdrop a remark of Jacques Calvet, the chief executive of Peugeot SA (PSA), the owner of Peugeot and Citroën, recently made in an article is particularly telling: 'I have a fault from which I suffer greatly. I am too logical, not sufficiently oriented by intuition' (Fisher, 1992). Moreover, Calvet is commonly considered the archetypical product of the French educational system.

Despite these features, some of which have to be seen as dysfunctional, the French elite is widely admired both within France and without, particularly on the technical side of business. Many French companies are leaders in their respective industries: Michelin in tyre making, L'Air Liquide in industrial gases, L'Oréal in cosmetics, Carrefour in retailing, to name only a few. This elite has indeed internationalized French industry substantially in recent years. What, then, are the rational attributes that have served to bring this about?

THE NOBILITY OF WORK

The American subordinate works for someone who specifies precisely what is wanted from him or her. Conversely, managers and engineers in a rationally oriented culture, as Philippe D'Iribarne (1990) sees it, tend to create their own system of values for themselves. Each establishes his or her own interpretation of his responsibilities. The accent is therefore not on being accountable to someone, in the Anglo-Saxon sense, but on considering what needs to be done. At the same time, D'Iribarne maintains, each person's actions are not framed by precise rules and procedures. In fact there is a lot of room for manoeuvre. When rules and procedures have been duly put in place each person interprets them in his or her own way, without feeling tied by what is written. There exists a considerable gap between the official and the unofficial, the latter being alluded to with a certain discomfort.

This particular rationally based approach, whereby one is associated with one's duties rather than with the rules themselves, is very different for D'Iribarne from the pragmatic context. This sense of obligation is not contractually inscribed or explicitly agreed upon. It is attached, rather, to the particular role, or function, or trade or profession to which one's group belongs. The expression 'to properly do one's work' is heard again and again. A vibrant sense of self-esteem is attached to this realization of one's obligations. Along with this immersion in the role, and unlike the adversarial relationships between management and trade unions on a national level, there is a great deal of moderation and mutual adjustment at plant level. A works foreman may consider himself to be like a nurse, nurturing children. Therefore, the existence of obligations appropriate to each station, the value accorded to moderation and the power of arbitration held by legitimated authorities leads to a quality of cooperation which should not be disdained. However, as Crozier (1964) has identified, there are dysfunctional aspects.

There exists an element of suspicion between the different groups. Such rivalry is exacerbated by the affect of strata in rational society, one kind of work being deemed more noble than the other. Social prestige—*noblesse*—is important.

On a sectoral scale the noble domains are those with a high capital intensity in which the problems of manufacture are secondary to those of conception. These include aviation, space, nuclear energy, telecommunications. The essential criterion in determining prestige seems to be the degree of immateriality of the task. Electronics therefore has a high element of abstraction and therefore of purity and nobility, which places it way ahead of mechanical engineering with its brute force! In the commercial arena, for example, dealing with immaterial flow of funds is more prestigious than dealing with tangibles. The more ethereal specialities like marketing or communications are deemed more uplifting than the utilitarian functions like purchasing or production. This leads us on to D'Iribarne's noted concept of 'the logic of honour'.

LA LOGIQUE D'HONNEUR

In a rational society which claims to have abolished inequality, the distinction between what is noble and what is lowly, between what is pure and impure, still plays a fundamental role. Reference from the past to the sacredness of the clergyman's work or to the ennobling nature of activity has been transplanted into a wider organizational context. Such sacredness, moreover, is connected with honour.

Within a society controlled by honour, according to the eighteenth-century French philosopher Baron de Montesquieu (1689–1755), what a person owes to him- or herself is always less than that which he or she owes to others. In that context the limited scope of contract or of rules is established. For a person of honour the result of the activity is not as important as the beauty of its exercise. For Montesquieu, moreover, a prince should never prescribe an action that dishonours a man, because that would render such a man unable to serve him. He who commands must also respect the duties that honourable conduct demands of him.

In a pragmatically based society contractual relationships are regarded as an ideal form of relation. Such a transactional approach to management can serve to get the best out of people. Management by Objectives (MBO) is a typical case. However, such an approach is unlikely to have universal appeal and will not work well, according to D'Iribarne, in a rationally inclined culture. Such a culture tends to regard authority as residing in the role, not the person. This contrasts with the Anglo-Saxon view that authority is vested in the individual's personal, moral or charismatic authority. In the rational mind this lesser investment of the self is a means of preserving personal choice, independence and individual dignity. The contractual approach likens hierarchical relations to those between producer and consumer.

However, in rational society, duties are largely fixed by the customary practices established by a professional group. The prospect of superior and subordinate contracting together to establish a working relationship would therefore not go down well. Similarly, the superior would be expected to behave in a way that was honourable, in terms of his or her own station. In the European context a professional administrator must draw on the intensity of the devotion that the individual has for work, through which he or she gains a sense of honour. Individuals being managed must not begin to feel that their independence is being encroached upon or that they are being rendered servile.

A rationally oriented European culture deploys the regime of honour, of station. It serves to distinguish in this way between nobility and debility, obligation from privilege. Nobody is allowed to bend the common law, but everyone is rightfully devoted to what is part of his or her communal responsibility. The sense of honour is there, moreover, to defend a person's noble interest against vulgarity. Moderation and the rendering of service are the order of the day whereas excess and servility are ruled out. One's sense of duty, for d'Iribarne, is modelled upon the particular society in which one lives or works. In the Anglo-Saxon world, according to D'Iribarne, the respect is for contract. In Holland and Germany respect is for integration with the community. In rationally oriented France, finally, respect is associated with intellect and honour.

Intellect and stratification

INTELLECTUAL VIRTUOSITY
The rationally trained 'Grande Ecole' graduate engineer, according to Lawrence and Barsoux, is first and foremost the product of a mind-stretching system. It is the system which nurtured him or her for leadership positions in industry. Individuals assume the values, outlook and poise of the 'ruling class' from an early age. The Attali brothers, who were respective heads of Air France and the European Bank for Reconstruction and Development, are typical cases in point. They may not be *au fait* with the technicalities and jargon of management but they have the social wherewithal and psychological authority to take up positions of power. The seal of approval from a prestigious engineering school endorses its holder's capacity for rapid learning and intellectual virtuosity. In addition, the schools bestow on their students the social wherewithal and an influential alumni network. At 'l'école de polytechnique' all graduates, high and low, call each other 'camarade'. Alumni associations run career services offering jobs to new graduates and restless old boys alike.

Trained for life
Moreover, those who have attended these schools are deemed 'formée à vie', trained for life, further training being rendered superfluous. There is a deep-rooted belief in France, if not also in Switzerland, that administrators are born, not made. In most countries educational pedigree is simply an entry ticket into a company. But in rationally oriented France, Lawrence and Barsoux (1990) maintain, it is an employment passport which often constitutes an assurance for life. The

net result is that 'Grande Ecole' graduates are generally not inclined to risk their talents in an entrepreneurial way to stimulate new business. They deploy them, instead, to gain authority in bureaucratic hierarchies.

It is in the latter half of their career, moreover, that the effects of attending the 'right' school come to fruition. It is then that some individuals move into the positions of power that put a premium on such qualities as distinguished appearance, good manners, tact and taste. So while companies ostensibly drop educational credentials as criteria for selection, they replace them with credentials which elevate members of the same population. Because, moreover, the rationally schooled graduate is virtually guaranteed an illustrious career, he or she can concentrate on doing a good job. In other words, he does not have to devote an inordinate amount of time to self-publicity.

As a direct result by Anglo-Saxon standards managerial job advertisements are seen to involve little emphasis on drive and initiative. Typically they refer to more cerebral qualities. A rational culture seems to focus on qualities of reception—analysis, synthesis, agility of mind—at the expense of qualities of emission—charisma, pugnacity, capacity to communicate and motivate.

Predictable career progression

Professional aspirations tend to be couched in terms of intellectual satisfaction or increased independence rather than more money, power or prestige. This toned-down view of careerism may be related to the rather predictable nature of career progression, and the fact that one's education holds sway over all other possible variables. Moreover, mobility is envisaged as a last resort, involving the loss of protection afforded by length of service.

The high ratings of blue-chip companies are therefore largely related to security of employment within the company itself, or the security of the employment they confer on those who pass through them. Colgate-Palmolive, for example, is renowned for its high turnover of cadres, but those who acquire its 'etiquette' label emerge with a valuable 'carte de visite', that is, a calling card. Ultimately, though, at least until quite recently, the 'rational dream' of parents was to see their offspring enter State service. Mid-career transfers, at the same time, from the public to the private sector, are considered rewarding.

Public–private partnership

In a rational society added value may be obtained from entering public service and using one's privileged knowledge of its workings as a springboard for a second career in industry. Therein professional administrators don their golden slippers, coloquially referred to as 'pantouflage'. There is a steady osmotic flow from the public to the private sector, usually taking place in a person's mid-thirties. By this time the cadre has ample public sector experience to offer as well as an appreciation of career limitations in public service. Yet they have sufficient drive left to make an impact in the private sector. Customer firms often save posts for those who have placed State orders with them. Former civil servants possess an intimate knowledge of State rules and regulations. Even if they cannot use personal contacts they are conversant with the way political and governmental networks operate. At the same time, they are definitely not risk-taking entrepreneurs.

It is ironical that the nation that introduced the word 'entrepreneur' (Jean-Baptiste Say in 1800) should have been traditionally so weak in that domain. According to David Landes, the bourgeois family values hampered economic growth in the nineteenth and early twentieth centuries by emphasizing social success over individual profit or industrial expansion. Innovation and success in business were held in low esteem and risk taking was shunned for fear of bankruptcy.

The largest public and private groups alike—because management is seen to be generic to organizational life rather than particular to individual sectors—are headed by products of 'la haute administration'. As former civil servants they are responsible for building bridges between the comapny and the State. It would seem, moreover, that the State has taken over responsibility for training individuals to assume leadership positions.

Esprit de planification

What is inevitably valued in a rational society is abstractness as a concomitant of intellectuality. Thus finance has a high standing because it is associated with mathematics and cleverness while production is a victim of its perceived lack of intellectual challenge. For the rationalist it is the person who, by virtue of his or her intellectual prowess, can adapt to any situation. The tradition of generalist engineers who foresaw France's early industrial expansion in the latter half of the nineteenth century still taints rationally based corporate perceptions. It is the generalists who are perceived to make it to the top.

The best decisions are made, in effect, when one is able to be at some distance from reality. On a national scale this willingness to defer to a greater design can be seen in the rationally based system of *planification indicative*. The manifestation of formal intelligence and educated cleverness is shown in a variety of ways. It is seen in the higher numeracy of rational managers and in the numerate dimension of strategy formulation.

It shows in the *esprit de planification*, in the readiness to systematize and doggedly to correct. For the professional administrator, in fact, eductional capital is by far the most precious form of currency. Thus inherited privilege is turned into merited privilege.

Management formality

The rational European seems to adhere to a classical conception of management which favours methodically planned activity punctuated by formal meetings. The cadre is a meeting specialist in much the same way as his or her pragmatically oriented counterpart may be considered an adept troubleshooter. Meetings also provide the cadre with a stage on which to display his or her oratory skill.

The formal meeting, therefore, is a sort of microcosm of organizational life where status can be enchanced by skilful advocacy and stylish expression or else lost by poor eloquence. Formality shows in the quality of executive prose, in the treatment of written communication as an end as well as a means, in a penchant for formulation and a capacity for inference. It also shows, of course, in technical virtuosity and in a talent for conceptual design.

The agenda to a meeting is known in advance as are the people attending and the proceedings are formalized. This reduces uncertainty. Rationally disposed managers like to have a 'territory' to call their own, and the impregnability of this sanctuary tends to increase with organizational status. The pattern of interpersonal relations, in that context, is formal, avoiding face-to-face relationships. This has historical connections.

STRATIFICATION AND EGALITARIANISM

Avoiding face-to-face relationships

For Michel Crozier (1964) the privileges and particularisms of France's 'ancien régime' have gone, but the same patterns have persisted. There is still individual isolation and lack of constructive cooperative activities on the one side, strata isolation and lack of communication between people of different rank, on the other. According to Lawrence and Barsoux, in fact, the rational manager believes that friendship obliges, provides a lever for favours, exposes the 'friend' to manipulation, and makes him or her dependent. In order to get round this perceived dependence and manipulation they have therefore concocted a system of authority relations based on ritual which minimizes the personality input, the need for personal interaction.

The rational manager, in the spirit of Descartes, separates his or her inner self from outer activities. The pattern of isolation and lack of initiative of the individual, the protective role of the strata, and the tradition of apathy in public affairs, according to Crozier (1968), results in a particular pattern of interpersonal relations. It revolves around a basic difficulty in facing conflict, in confronting authority relationships, and in developing acceptable leadership at the level of the primary group.

Authority and independence
Group members showing initiative risk being deserted by their colleagues and being deeply humiliated. Apathy is a rational response if people want to avoid conflict and escape dependency: 'Strata isolation, focusing on rank and status, and the impossibility of forming groups across strata, all stem from the same cultural conditions predetermining the possible scope of authority relations' (Crozier, page 34). Meanwhile, authority and independence can be reconciled within a bureaucratic system. Specifically, impersonal rules and centralization make it possible to reconcile an absolutist conception of authority with independence in relationships. On the one hand, the rational manager cannot bear, according to Crozier, the omnipotent authority which he or she feels is indispensable if any kind of cooperative activity is to succeed. On the other, such employees are prepared to entrust one person with absolute authority, provided he or she is remote and cannot act directly upon them. Rationally oriented corporate management has the peculiarity of placing in the hands of an individual—the *Président-Directeur Général*—what in most countries is shared out. The PDG is what the Anglo-Saxons call chairman and managing director, rolled into one. His or her role is in even sharper contrast to that of the *primus inter pares* German *Vorstandsvorsitzender*, a chairman of the executive committee.

The paradoxical weakness of power
People on top of a rationally based organization theoretically have a great deal of power and often much more than they would have in other, more authoritarian, societies. But these powers, Crozier explains in contrast to Hofstede, are not very useful. People on top, he says, can only act in an impersonal way and cannot interfere with the subordinate strata. They also cannot, at this extreme point of view, provide real leadership on a daily basis. If they want change they must go through the long and difficult ordeal of crisis. Thus, although they are supposedly all-powerful because they are at the apex of the whole centralized system, they are actually considerably weakened. The pattern of resistance of the different isolated strata means that they can use their power only in truly exceptional circumstances.

Certain rationally based values precondition these prevailing patterns, specifically those of harmony, security and independence. Professional administrators dislike disorder, conflict, everything that might bring uncontrolled relationships. They cannot move in ambiguous, potentially disruptive situations. Rationally based successes are therefore conspicuous at the two ends of the organizational scale. First, through individual activity, a person is in complete control of his or her own endeavour. Second, through large-scale routine operations, a bureaucratic system of organization protects the individual from human interference.

Intrinsic controls

According to Philippe D'Iribarne (1990), however, there is no precise rational model, in that obvious sense. Following the underlying logic of French rationality, he says, hierarchical relationships serve to delineate people's station, their traditions, their rights and obligations, rather than their contractual position. They constitute a holding idea for a jumble of possibilities, depending on the particular superior or subordinate involved.

In a rationally ordered society one does not find the same contractual relationships between management and worker as set down by negotiations with the trade unions, as in pragmatically oriented Britain or America. The power that superiors have is dependent on the state of the company and the performance of the unit in question. If there is a crisis, their power is great; if the unit is performing adequately, their power is minimal.

In a rationally based organization, moreover, the notion 'to know one's job' entails not only its technical aspects but also the purposes and obligations intrinsically involved. The person who 'does his or her job' thereby conforms to all these requirements. The 'control' function is therefore very different in Europe from that in America. Rationally based control, in this intrinsically European context, is a matter of reconciling oneself, and one's work, with one's conscience.

The functional executive

FROM FORM TO FUNCTION

In conclusion, and as we have seen, there is a progression, in the best of all rational worlds, from an innate sensitivity for form towards planned industrial growth and social equilibrium. Along the way economic *dirigisme* emerges in contrast to the free market. Depersonalized role competence overtakes personalized leadership, and the nobility of intellectually based work surpasses the versatility of wilfully based enterprise.

In a European context France as a whole embodies such rationality, in its purest form, though there are significant regional differences in orientation within the country. At the same time, apart from the fact that the European continent as a whole has prided itself historically on its intellectual prowess, there are areas of relative strength and weakness. Generally, the northern and central Europeans are likely to have a stronger rational orientation than the western (active), southern (emotive) and eastern (intuitive) peoples.

FROM BUREAUCRACY TO 'REQUISITE' ORGANIZATION
Most pragmatically oriented management analysts, like Hofstede and indeed Tom Peters, fail to grasp the structural essence of a rationally based bureaucracy, as in fact Philippe d'Iribarne and Elliot Jaques have done. Most bureaucracies around the world, from America to Argentina, are only partially grounded in rationality. They are impure! As such, they lack the egalitarian features that accompany the stratification, the structural subtleties that accompany functionalism.

Moreover, as in the pragmatic case, the rational organization is evolving, in this case, from effectiveness to requisiteness. In the process there is a shift of emphasis, from the outer to the inner directed, from management principles and business functions to cognitive capacity and organizational strata. This change of emphasis befits our movement towards an information age. Whereas, for the pragmatist, the shift in individual orientation is from self-help to self-development, in the rational case it is from intellectual virtuosity to cognitive capacity. Similarly, whereas the shift in institutional focus, in the first instance, is from free enterprise to the learning company (Lessem, 1993), in the second case it is from formalized bureaucracy to requisite organization.

RATIONAL STRENGTHS AND WEAKNESSES
Rationality comes into its own not in the creation of but in the maintenance and development of an enterprise. France's entrepreneurial base, for example, is weak, because of the comparative lack of 'self'-centredness in the culture. Similarly, in a rationally based society the power of the centre, most particularly the State, is strong, whereas the influence of the periphery is weak. As a result, large-scale enterprises will dominate over small, and government will have considerable say in the running of business affairs.

From the point of view of individual and organizational learning, moreover, the rationalist will feel at home with conceptualization and with formal organization. In the same way, the empiricist is inclined towards experimentation and towards improvisation. In the final analysis, whereas the rational person relates self to organization, the pragmatist relates the organization to self. We now turn from European pragmatism and rationalism to 'wholism'.

Summary

Professional integrity
- The professional emphasis is not on being accountable to someone but on considering what needs to be done.
- Control in the coordinated system, is a matter of reconciling oneself and one's work with one's conscience.
- Hierarchical relationships serve to delineate people's stations, their traditions, their rights and obligations, rather than their contractual positions.
- Unlike the adversarial relationships between management and trade unions on a national level, there is a great deal of moderation and mutual adjustment at plant level.

The logic of honour
- In a rational society the distinction between what is noble and what is lowly plays a fundamental role.
- Reference from the past to the sacredness of the clergyman's work or to the ennobling nature of activity has been transplanted into a wider organizational context.
- A professional manager must draw on the intensity of the devotion that the individual has for his or her work through which such a person gains a sense of honour.
- The individual being managed must not feel that his or her independence is encroached upon or that he or she is servile.

The nobility of abstraction
- On a social scale the noble domains are those with a high capital intensity in which the problems of manufacture are secondary to those of conception, such as aviation, space.
- The essential criterion in determining prestige seems to be the degree of immateriality of the task—electronics is superior to mechanical engineering with its brute force.
- In the commercial function, dealing with immaterial flow of funds is more prestigious than dealing with tangibles.

- In that context the limited scope of contract or of rules is established—for a person of honour the result of the activity is not as important as the beauty of its exercise.

Prevailing harmony
- Certain values precondition the prevailing patterns—the values of harmony, security and independence, combined with the difficulty of tolerating ambiguous situations.
- Rationalists dislike disorder, conflict, everything that might bring uncontrolled relationships—they cannot move in ambiguous, potentially disruptive situations.
- Rationally based successes are therefore likely to occur at the two ends of the scale—individual exploration and collective routine.
- Individual explorations where a person is in complete control of his or her own endeavour, and routine operations where a bureaucratic system protects the individual from human interference.

The submerged self
- The graduate elite are virtually guaranteed illustrious careers, and can therefore concentrate on doing a good job without having to devote much time to self-publicity.
- In the professional manager's mind this lesser investment of self is seen as a means of preserving personal choice and independence.
- Rationalists believe that friendship obliges, provides a lever for favours, exposes the 'friends' to manipulation, and makes them dependent.
- In order to avoid this perceived dependence and manipulation, professionals have concocted a system of authority relations which minimizes social interactions.

Avoidance of relationships
- Impersonal rules make it possible to reconcile an absolutist authority with individual independence.
- Sectoral isolation, focusing on rank and status, inhibits forming groups across strata.
- The resulting protective role of the strata results in a basic difficulty in facing conflict.
- This causes problems in confronting authority relationships, and in developing acceptable leadership at the level of the primary group.

Part IV

Wholism—Developmental

11

Closed and open systems

... the attitude of Bertelsmann publishers was in accordance with the task to be accomplished. These men were certainly not concerned only about money ... Rather, their work was aimed at the well-being and the needs of the people of their time. Their efforts were dedicated to the readers of their publications, the citizens of our city, and the employees of the company.

Reinhard Mohn, Chairman of Bertelsmann's Supervisory Board

Wholism in European business

WHOLISM IN PLACE

Rationalism has given rise to depersonalized management and to dependent bureaucracy. Pragmatism yielded the personalized entrepreneur and independent enterprise. What, then, of wholism, and its kindred philosophy, idealism (Fig. 11.1).

For many people 'idealism' represents the very antithesis of business enterprise in which it would seem 'realism', above all, should prevail. Yet Germany, where the core of 'wholistic' philosophy has been developed, is currently the most successful of the European economies. Why should this be?

Wholism, as a philosophical main stem, is rooted in the collective consciousness espoused by the Swiss psychologist, Carl Jung. Such idealism is often associated with 'wholism' or *gestalt* philosophy, and with a systemic or a developmental *weltanschauung*. From that source has sprung the social market, economically, and managerially, a particular two-tier corporate governance system: the interdependently minded supervisory boards as well as the boards of management. The combined fruits are industrial wealth and social welfare. A business personality who embodies such an approach is Bertelsmann's chairman, Reinhard Mohn. Countries other than Germany which have elements of such a wholistic approach are Holland and Sweden, within the EC, and Japan, outside it.

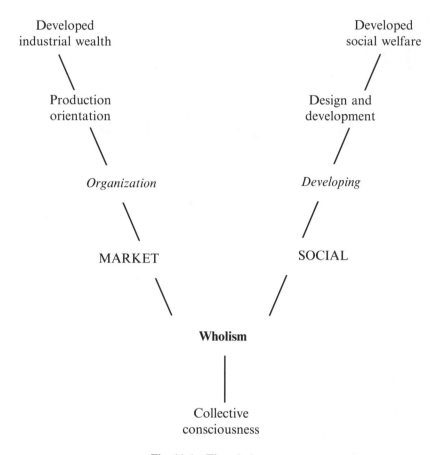

Fig. 11.1 The whole tree

WHOLISM IN TIME

Within a historical perspective, nineteenth-century 'idealism', or wholism in economics and management, was reflected in a collectivism, socialism or communism that spread, in varying degrees, across Europe. Though in each European country such a philosophy developed its own national flavour, the seminal European influence was that of Karl Marx, who was in turn deeply influenced by G.W.F. Hegel. Notably Marxism had little influence on the internal organization of the firm. Its impact was upon the economic and social environment around it. While, on the one hand, nationalization, or indeed subsequently privatization, had little effect on the internal management of private enterprise, on the other, the cooperative enterprise has exercised limited influence in Europe.

In fact, the influence of 'wholism' on the business organization itself has been most visible in recent years in Japan, rather than in America, the management laboratory of the world. From a theoretical standpoint, without question, the 'Idealism', compared with pragmatism and rationalism, has been the one philosophy most neglected by the American academic management establishment. A European group, however, that has developed the 'wholistic' standpoint and applied it to the firm itself is the Nationale Pedagogical Institute (NPI) in Holland. The NPI has spearheaded this approach, that is, from differentiated to integrated management and organization, over the past twenty years. In so doing it has been inspired by the idealism of the German philosopher–playwright Johann Wolfgang von Goethe, and by the Austrian philosopher–economist Rudolph Steiner.

The 'wholistically' founded institution, once a differentiated mechanism within a closed system, that is, a business 'cartel', is now beginning to emerge as an integrated organism within an open system, as a business 'constellation'. Such an open systems perspective, for example, led NEC's President Koji Kobayashi to combine computers with telecommunications. To that extent, the differentiated elements—production, marketing, finance, personnel—that underpin performance are being supplanted by integrated ones—resources, information, processes and relations. Whereas in this chapter we shall be exploring idealistically rooted images and ideas—the roots and main stem—in Chapters 12 and 13 we shall be concerned with more specific models and attributes. Wholism, then, is rooted in the central part of Europe

Images of the whole—the roots of idealism

THE ARCHETYPAL CENTRE

The heart of Europe
Germany, for de Madariaga, lies at the core of Europe, at the centre of her body and the apex of her mind. From the vast sea of Russia, he writes, the European spirit sets in motion towards the West, passing through the rapids of Poland, to flow later in the mighty river of the German soul. From the Black Sea another current brings to its core the dark Balkan passions, to which Hungary imparts a vigorous rhythm. These two currents, meeting in Vienna, endowed the world with the treasures of Mozart, Beethoven and Schubert. To the extent that management based in Berlin, Prague or Vienna review the Russian source, and establish, symbolically and literally, a new east–west connection, they will be renewing the European Economic Community.

The spirit of becoming

Germany is located, Madariaga believes, between Europe's conscious and unconscious being. Idealists live within themselves and it is there, in their inner laboratories, that they draw their plans and prepares their deeds, As a people whose way of living has long been one of wandering tribes, Germans look at life as something ever in flux, never to be caught and shaped in hard-and-fast moulds. Their seemingly rational orientation towards social discipline, therefore, is only used as an outer container for the fluidity of their inner emotions.

Time, in the wholist context, is the bed of the river of history, whereby people and societies are seen to live in a continuous becoming. There is a world of difference between the well-articulated sets of practical arguments in a French Descartes and the stream of dialectics which flows from a Kant or a Hegel. In other words, a thing for the 'wholist' is not done; it becomes done. The German language, therefore, reduces to a minimum the instant we call the present, merging it into instants before and after:

> Hence the avoidance of 'sein', to be, which the German discards for 'werden', to become. He does this precisely in order to express that sense of fluidity, which is the deepest feature of German life.
>
> (de Madariaga, 1968, page 82)

Such an affinity with flow, duly embodied in Hegelian philosophy, is equally strong with the Japanese.

A DEVELOPMENTAL CULTURE

Fluidity of form

Both the pragmatists and the wholists, de Madariaga maintains, are somewhat deficient in the sense of form but for different reasons. In the former it is due to their predominant interest in action. The latter, on the contrary, neglect form to take refuge in their inner being. The deficiency of form in the pragmatist manifests itself as complication, accumulation, improvisation; in the wholist as dealing with the world of the fluid and nebulous. Life, which for the rationalist is like a string of clearly defined crystals, for the wholist is like a river.

The River of Collective Life

The pragmatists are akin to earth, the rationalists to air, the humanists to fire and the wholists to water. The natural motion of water is along the ground, as low as possible; while the natural motion of fire is upwards against all there is to block the way of the ascending flames.

The Germans, in the final analysis, feel in touch with their source through the continuous flow of the river of their collective life. In contrast, the fiery Spaniards feel the beginning of things in the native and pristine impetus of the fire that rises within them. Anarchist, disobedient Spain longs for the gregarious ways of obedient Germany. The Germans, de Madariaga argues, too gregarious and nationalistic for the health of Europe, would benefit from an alliance with the most individualistic and universal of all Europeans.

The idea of development—the main stem of wholism
Whereas pragmatists and rationalists have between them continually straddled the divide between sensation and thought, wholists have positioned themselves between reason and intuition. Whereas the most famous philosophical representative of the former is probably Immanuel Kant, a pre-eminent representative of the latter is Goethe.

However, probably the most distinctive brand of idealism can be traced back to Leibniz's concept of harmonic conjunction in the eighteenth century. It was duly extended in the nineteenth by both Hegel's historical dialectic and Marx's dialectical materialism. Finally, the management thinkers who have taken respectively historicist and dialectical leads are the German sociologist Max Weber, and the Dutch organizational psychologist Bernard Lievegoed.

IDEALIST PHILOSOPHY

Reason and intuition
Arguably the two best-known historical representatives of 'wholism', apart from Hegel himself, are the philosopher Kant (1724–1804) and the playwright Goethe (1749–1832). Whereas Kant was oriented towards reason, and Goethe towards intuition, each held the other in positive mutual regard.

While Kant, like Descartes, demanded that mathematics should enter into every part of the theory of nature, Goethe energetically rejected any such notion. Physics, for Goethe, must be divorced from mathematics. It must be completely independent, and try to penetrate with all its loving, reverent, pious force into nature and its holy life, quite regardless of what mathematics accomplishes and does. For Kant, science rests on experience, observation, mathematical deduction (Cassirer, 1963, page 64), not upon intuition. The greatest discoverer is distinguished from the laborious imitator only by degree. Nature and art, truth and beauty remain divorced.

For Goethe, there is no sharp division between the truth and beauty. For him the beautiful is a manifestation of secret natural laws, which without its appearance would have remained forever hidden from view. Laws of nature and laws of beauty cannot be set off from each other in their origin or their meaning: 'He for whom nature begins to reveal her open secret feels an irresistible longing for her most worthy interpreter, art' (Eckerman, 1930). Goethe, therefore, recognized no sharp boundary between intuition and theory. Merely looking at a thing, says Goethe, can tell us nothing. Each look leads us to an inspection, each inspection to a reflection, each reflection to a synthesis. Analysis and synthesis are two inseparable acts of living. They cooperate with one another, like inhaling and exhaling.

Systematic–systemic

In the recognition of universal and natural laws Kant and Goethe are completely at one. But their ways of establishing and justifying their basic assumptions are quite different. Kant follows his logico-analytical path. He begins with the analysis of the principle of causality. Experience, for him, is no aggregate of sense impressions, but a system. Such a system must rest on objectively valid and necessary principles.

Understanding is, for Kant, the faculty of rules and the empirical rules of nature are only particular instances and applications of the *a priori* rules of understanding. In this way the special laws of nature become specifications of the universal laws of understanding. Kant declares that nature is the existence of things, insofar as it is determined in accordance with natural laws. Goethe cannot stop with such a nature, *natura naturata*. As artist and scientist he desired to penetrate into *natura naturans*. The idea of metamorphosis becomes his guide. In this great process of the inner productivity of nature Goethe does not think like Kant in terms of relations; he can only think in intuitive forms.

We see in the works of the old German architecture, Goethe said,

> the flower of an extraordinary state of things. Whoever comes immediately close to such a flower, will only stare at it with astonishment; but he who sees into the secret inner life of the plant, into the stirring of its powers, and observes how the flower gradually unfolds itself, sees the matter with quite different eyes. He knows what he sees.
>
> (Cassirer, 1963, page 53)

Freedom then, for Goethe, consists not in refusing to recognize anything above us but in respecting something which is above us; for by respecting it we raise ourselves to it, and by our very acknowledgement prove that we bear within ourselves what is higher, and we are worthy to be on a level with it. In this respect there is a harmonic relationship between Goethe, Leibniz and Hegel.

Whereas Kant and Goethe are probably the best known of the 'wholists', Leibniz, the 'Aufklärer school' and Hegel established an important philosophical backdrop for Marx and Weber, whom we will shortly be rediscovering.

HISTORICISM AND THE DEVELOPMENTAL—LEIBNIZ AND THE 'AUFKLARERS'

Leibnizian philosophy had provided eighteenth-century thinkers with a powerful set of metaphors for dealing with change and individuality. One of these, *harmonic conjunction*, expressing a major goal of Leibnizian thought, aimed to combine unity with diversity without submerging one into the other. The life process, Leibniz said, involves the development of a specific something (*ein Etwas*) that while changing still remains individual and true to its nature. From this proposition the 'Aufklärer school' (1740–90) drew the conclusion that there was an intimate tie between past, present and future that science could not dissolve.

These German 'Aufklärers' directed their research at developmental and structural relations, and to synthesizing them. Increasingly the 'Aufklärers' located the motor element of history in the actions of a person's spirit (Reill, 1975). Historical development, moreover, became the story of our attempt to achieve harmony. Wholist aestheticians, in fact, defined perfection as the achievement of harmony between inner and outer life. Here aesthetic and historical ideals met and mutually reinforced each other. A system of events offered a skeleton, or structure, within which the historian might work, but it remained lifeless. It allowed one to survey the whole, to discriminate but not to integrate. It gave knowledge, not understanding. Intuitive comprehension subsumed conceptualization and raised it to a higher level of understanding. Historical understanding was an active apprehension of the individual and the whole. It was not simply a process of conscious rational thought, though rational analysis was necessary. Historicism operates on a dualistic principle in that it attempts to mediate between conflicting ideas such as change and continuity, individuality and communal being, freedom and necessity, value and causality.

The 'Aufklärer', finally, saw change in terms of the tension between the dead and living forces of society. In this view tradition is transformed but not destroyed. Each new historical creation contains a strong admixture of whatever preceded it. Historical understanding, furthermore, had to be nourished by action, by continual application of historical reason to situations. The dialectics of change, in fact, lead us inevitably on to G.W.F. Hegel (1770–1831), who played such an enormously important part in developmental thinking.

HISTORICAL DIALECTICS—THE PHILOSOPHY OF HEGEL

Germans are Hegelians, according to Nietzsche, even if there had never been a Hegel. In contrast to the Latins, they instinctively ascribe to evolution a deeper meaning and higher value than they ascribe to what is:

> The German is by nature not content with the immediate aspect of phenomena. He gets behind appearance and thinks there is scarcely any justification for the concept of being.
>
> (Roll, 1953, page 222)

For Hegel, progress in scientific understanding is neither an accumulation of facts upon an observational base nor is it characterized by the arbitrary, and non-accumulative replacement of theories: 'Hegel's approach to the study of science can be described as developmental, whereby theoretical transformations are comprehended in terms of a wider system of human interests (Lamb, 1980, page 108).

Goethe derived the forms of development and life of mankind from the observation of nature. For both, whereas they saw that originally work satisfied the immediate needs of the individual, it subsequently became abstract and universal. For no one produced, ultimately, what he himself needed. It therefore became impossible for a man to satisfy his needs except by collaborating in the total satisfaction of everyone's needs. Need and work, raised to the level of the whole, constituted in themselves—for Hegel and for Goethe—an immense system of solidarity and mutual dependence.

In this process of productive work, moreover, there develops 'culture', theoretical as well as practical. Work is culturally educative in that it accustoms people to being busy in general and to having regard to the will of others. It teaches objective physical activity and universally applicable skills. It disciplines man and, for Hegel, raises him to the universal level of spirit. Moreover, Hegel maintains, individual reality is self-reflected reality of the universal. Thus the individual man is a particular instance of universal humanity, the essence of which is spirit.

We now turn from general philosophy to economic policy, starting by comparing and contrasting Romantic with classical economists.

HISTORICIST ECONOMIC POLICY

Romanticism

Interestingly enough, in eighteenth-century Germany there was a school of economic philosophy that had more in common with Japanese economic thought today than with Adam Smith's free enterprise then. Adam Müller (1779–1829) stressed altruism and religion in opposition to what he regarded as Smith's egoism and materialism. The State, he thought, must be regarded as an organism. The individuals who were the cells could not be thought of outside the totality of the State.

The State, moreover, must concern itself not only with tangible things but with the totality of material and non-material goods. The real object of political economy, according to Müller, is a double one. First, it involved the greatest multiplication of all the utility of persons, things and goods. Second, it entailed the production and intensification of that product of all products, the economic and social union of the great community or the national household. We shall see how this historical view is reflected in the Ordo-Liberal economics of our day.

The factors of production are not land, labour and capital but nature, people and the past. The last includes all capital—physical and spiritual—which has been built up in the course of time and is now available to help in production. Economists, says Müller, have tended to ignore 'spiritual capital'. The fund of experience which past exertion has made available is put in motion by language, speech and writing; and it is the duty of scholarship to preserve and increase it. All these elements collaborate in all production. They are now contained within the term 'human' or 'intellectual' capital.

What makes writers like Müller into a historical school is the overwhelming importance they assign to history in the study of the economic process. Economics had to examine carefully the development of individual peoples and of mankind as a whole. It had to produce an economic history of culture. Economic conditions were constantly changing and developing. Lastly, the historical school stressed the unity of social life. It focused on the interconnection of individual social processes and the organic, as against the mechanistic view of society. The economic whole is opposed to the factor of production, as part.

In effect, this historical school, despite the fact that it was deeply ingrained within the German national psyche, was eclipsed by Adam Smith, on the one hand, and by Karl Marx (1818–83), on the other. While one was the forerunner of capitalism in the 'west', the other, with his collaborator Engels, foreshadowed Communism in the 'east'. Moreover, because of the dogmatic character of Marxism most of us have lost sight of its developmental, 'wholist' underpinnings. These we want to focus upon here.

Marxism

The first developmental or evolutionary feature of Marx's thinking, which he drew from Hegel, was its dialectical nature. If capitalism was subject to change, what was its motive force? According to Hegel's philosophy of history, it had to be some contradiction inherent in the system. Such a contradiction of capitalism, Marx argued, was fundamental. For there was a clash between the increasingly social, cooperative nature of production—made necessary by the new productive powers which people possessed—and the individual ownership of the means of production.

Marx's principle of society is the social relationship as a whole, entered into for the purpose of social production. Moreover, this particular relationship is appropriate to a given development of productive power. It enables society to make the fullest use of these productive powers and increase them. But this very increase brings them into conflict with the social relationship which they had created. Marx and Engels, in effect, compared and contrasted two philosophical tendencies. The one they termed 'metaphysical', with fixed categories, the other 'dialectical' (Aristotle and especially Hegel) with fluid categories. For them all logic develops only from these progressing contradictions.

All successive historical systems are only transitory stages in the endless course of development of human society from the lower to the higher (Lowith, 1965, page 148). Each stage is necessary, and therefore justified for the time and conditions to which it owes its origins. But in the face of new, higher conditions which gradually develop it loses its vitality and justification. It must give way to a higher stage, which will also in its turn decay and perish.

Marx then, as far as Engels was concerned, discovered the law of development of human history. Such a law states simply that people must first eat, drink, have shelter and clothing, before they can pursue politics, sciences, art and religion. This law was developed by the well-known Armenian-American management theorist, Abraham Maslow, into his so-called hierarchy of needs (Maslow, 1964).

In the final analysis Marx and Engels were wrong, and Yeltsin today is paying the price. The demise of Communism in Europe today is living proof of their misplaced diagnosis and subsequently misconceived prognosis. For one thing, they failed to live up to their own dialectical perspective, by proposing that the State, together with the class system, would ultimately wither away with the advent of true socialism. For another, they replaced one kind of dogmatism, Hegel's idealism, with another, their own materialism. For that reason, there was a vehement reaction both towards totalitarian Marxism and also Hitler's fascism after the Second World War. Both were manifestations of the 'dark' side of wholism.

The German social market philosophy and policy that emerged after the war, as an amalgam of realism and idealism, served to combine economic classicism and romanticism. Its creators were the so-called German Ordo-Liberals.

In effect, the resultant 'culture clash' between Germanic idealism and Anglo-Saxon realism, as was the case for Japan in 1945, produced an economic blend that was much more effective than its constituent parts.

The social market

The intellectual framework for the German social market economy was provided by what is commonly known as the 'Freiburg Group', the leading figure of which was Walter Eucken. They are also known as neo-liberals or Ordo-Liberals. A second group, of whom the best known is Wilhelm Röpke, were closely associated. The Ordo-Liberals delineated the features of orderly markets and compared economic systems. Röpke and his followers embedded these principles, which are basically concerned with efficiency, into more metaphysical and ethical values. A social market economy is therefore represented as a sophisticated relationship between economic, legal, social and ethical systems. The *weltanschauung* of the social market may be said to encompass three broad objectives: the maintenance of political and economic *order*; the provision of some measure of *welfare*; and the preservation of *freedom and autonomy*.

For Eucken, the way in which everyday economic life proceeds depends on the nature of the country. This involves the race, culture and beliefs of its inhabitants, on the political institutions and structure of the State, in fact on the entire historical environment. Finally, Eucken maintains, the economic systems in the so-called 'capitalist' countries are so various and changing that the preconditions for the construction of a single theory to explain everyday life under capitalism do not exist. France's Michel Albert, as we have indicated, would be very much in agreement. Just as a great variety of words of different composition and length can be formed out of two dozen letters, an almost unlimited variety of actual economic systems can be made from a limited number of pure forms. It is the task of economics to investigate these as thoroughly as possible by extracting their significant characteristics.

If Eucken was the leading Ordo-Liberal economist, Röpke was its most respected social philosopher. Röpke saw the political and economic consolidation of Europe after the Second World War as needing to preserve what was of the essence of Europe. This was unity in diversity, freedom in solidarity, respect for human personality and for distinctions and particularities. We should be apprehensive about the idea of a European industrialism, he said, which drowns in sheer quantity everything that is qualitiative, diverse, varied, immeasurable and individual:

> The market's existence is justifiable and possible only because it is a part of a greater whole, which concerns not economics but philosophy, history and theology. Social rationalism misleads us into imagining that the market economy is no more than an 'economic technique' that is applicable to any kind of society and in any kind of spiritual and social climate.
>
> (Röpke, 1960, page 93)

Economics, for Röpke, is no natural science. The market economy is a constantly renewed texture of more or less short-lived contractual relations. It can, therefore, have no permanence unless the confidence that any contract presupposes rests on a broad and solid ethical base in all market parties (page 251). These social and economic theories, as we shall see from the economic historians Chandler and Shonfield, are borne out in German if not also in Dutch and Scandinavian practice.

Cooperative capitalism

Alfred Chandler, the American business and economic historian, recently published his comprehensive analysis of what he called German 'cooperative capitalism', between 1850 and 1950. He compared this with what he called 'managerial capitalism' in America, and 'personal capitalism' in the UK. Chandler's conclusions were very relevant to our findings here: 'The choice between competition and cooperation reflected more the nature of the product and the existing market than the predilection of either company for one type or another of interfirm relationship' (Chandler, 1990, page 472). The greatest difference, however, came in interfirm and intrafirm relationships. In the USA the new, large integrated managerial firms competed aggressively for market share and profits, in Germany many of them preferred to cooperate. Whereas in the USA the passage of the Sherman Antitrust Act in 1890 and its enforcement by the nation's courts reflected a shared belief in the value of competition, in Germany the strong support given to cartels and other interfirm agreements by the nation's courts reflected a shared belief in the benefits of industrial cooperation.

These beliefs were also evident in the larger role played by trade associations in Germany than in the USA. Moreover, German manufacturers paid much closer attention to the needs of their workforce. Thus the cooperation that developed between and within industrial firms can be considered, according to Chandler, as part of a larger system. The most striking legal difference lay in Germany's ability to enforce cartels and other agreements between competitors in courts of law. This meant that German industrials had much less incentive to merge into industry-wide holding companies. Instead, agreements as to price, output, and marketing territories were enforced through looser and more temporary federations. Such conventions, syndicates and communities of interest were based on legal devices rarely used in Britain or the USA. Moreover, by the turn of the century German universities and institutes were ahead of their American counterparts in providing industrial enterprise with technical and scientific knowledge and with skilled technicians and managers.

MODERN CAPITALISM

Germany cooperativism and French dirigisme
Friedrich List (1789–1846), German 'historicist' and inventor of 'national economics' in the 1840s, was scathing about classical English economics, which did not, he maintained, look beyond the principles governing a short-term profitable bargain. The establishment of powers of production, he said, were left to chance, to nature. The real issue of economic policy, of how to build up a nation's productive power, is therefore evaded. This is, of course, exactly in line with the traditional French as well as German view. In fact, what the great public and semi-public institutions are to the French economy the large banks are to Germany.

Intimate association and long-termism
There is a tradition, according to Shonfield, dating back to the early years of German industrial development whereby bankers have an intimate knowledge of all the phases of business. The ability to make a technical judgement is still the pride of German bankers. Moreover, one of the purposes served by the plural membership of the Supervisory Board—the *Aufsichtsrat*—is to provide a channel for the diffusion of advanced business practice. This brings to the attention of management new ideas and techniques that have been developed by other companies with which the banker is concerned.

In the 1960s the Deutsche Bank had one of its directors on the senior staff of the *Aufsichtsrat* of nearly every one of the dozen important German steel companies. During the period of the steel surplus in 1962, two of the largest steel companies, Thyssen and Mannesman, were dissuaded from going ahead with separate and expensive strip mills for the production of wide steel sheets. Instead it was agreed that one of them, Thyssen, would set up a single large plant, and be given an 8 per cent contract for wire rolling by the other. Once started on this type of venture, its momentum carried the steel companies forward into new experiments in collaboration. Moreover, these types of arrangements are not to be mistaken for an old style of cartel arrangement.

Banks as grand strategists of the nation

The large German banks have always seen it as their business to take an overall view of the long-term trend in any industry in which they were concerned and then to press individual firms to conform to certain broad lines of development: 'They see themselves essentially as grand strategists of the nation's industry, whereas the British banks, by contrast, were content to act as quartermaster general' (Chandler, 1990, page 472). The British system of specialized banking made the business of industrial investment the exclusive concern of the merchant bankers. Conversely, in Germany the all-purpose bank proved to be a remarkably powerful instrument for financing the rapid growth of a country which was a comparative latecomer to the Industrial Revolution.

The most prominent of the German banks is and has been for a long time, of course, the Deutsche Bank. Some observers believe that the influence of that institution over German business is unparalleled in any other Western country. The bank not only holds a 'blocking share minority' in Germany's leading industrial group, Daimler-Benz, it also owns 10 per cent of the leading German insurance company, Allianz, another 10 per cent of the largest reinsurance company in the world, Münchner Rückversicherung, 25 per cent of the retail chain Karstadt, and roughly a third of Philipp Holzmann, one of the largest internationally active German construction firms. These are only the better known of the stakes Deutsche Bank holds in German firms.

The influence of the bank is compounded by the tradition that German companies invite prominent bankers to become members of their Supervisory Board. The officers of the Deutsche Bank are particularly sought after as board members; as a result, they hold roughly 400 seats on Supervisory Boards. (The number per person has been limited in Germany to ten to prevent abuse.) Last but not least, one also has to mention the proxy rights that the German banks, like their counterparts in other countries, exercise in German shareholder meetings.

The power of the Deutsche Bank, and the two main competitors Dresdner Bank and Commerzbank which are smaller but still very substantial and influential in their own right, is, of course, frequently contested. When the Germans weigh the pros and cons, however, the majority still come to the conclusion that, for them, it is beneficial to have such a universal banking system. The biggest handicap is the power concentration in a few hands. Alfred Herrhausen, a former 'speaker' of the Deutsche Bank, roughly the equivalent of a CEO, once responded to a question about the power of German banks:

> I have never been one to deny that [Deutsche Bank] has power. The question is not whether we have power, but rather how we handle it and whether we use it responsibly or not.
>
> (Glouchevitch, 1992, page 77)

Therefore the belief is widespread that the bank has used its influence responsibly. There is also no immediate expectation that it should destroy this reputation of being prudent. Still, some observers even within Germany feel uncomfortable about this accumulated influence. However, this concentration of power in the hands of banks is by no means purely a German issue; in Italy, for instance, the State-controlled banks and financial institutions still account for two-thirds of activity in the banking system (Graham, 1991).

The prevailing system has offered Germany a number of substantial advantages. The most important ones are stability and a long-term orientation. Both are intertwined. German banks are deeply interested in a long-term relationship with companies; where a bank is a major shareholder, hostile takeovers are extremely rare. Management can devote its attention to the running of the business rather than worrying about an effective defence of it: 'Management does not live under the constant threat of restructuring forced on the firm from outside,' (Albert, 1992, page 129).

Reciprocal lines of influence

It would be wrong, however, to cast the German banks in the role of ringmasters. The lines of influence are reciprocal. What tends to emerge from this process is a consensus of big business about the affairs of an industry. Finally, the banks have an almost para-statal position. State subsidies, for example, are all distributed by the banks.

It would be wrong to assume that it is the banks alone that are responsible for the characteristic flavour of collective purpose in German industry.

They are the most noticeable expression of a much more general phenomenon.

Industrial collaboration in pursuit of long-range objectives is fostered by powerful trade associations in certain industries. And these spokesmen for the collective view have a direct *entrée* to the government machine. German *Verbände* (trade associations) have traditionally seen themselves as guardians of the interests of the nation's industries. The German penchant is for the orchestrated and purposeful, not the blind hand-to-hand encounter.

The two-tier board, or corporate governance system, is composed of a *Vorständ*, or management board, and a supervisory board. The latter is formed on the basis of the main outside interests on whose cooperation the company is dependent. These include customers for its products, suppliers of its materials, providers of finance and, of course, its employees, *Mitbestimmung*. The result is that one company will be represented on the *Aufsichtsrat* of another as supplier, and receive the representative of the second company as a valued customer.

Industries are thus somewhat cemented. Especially in the field of capital goods, what matters most to the potential buyer is that a new machine or piece of equipment should be the most advanced technical design. The opportunities for 'producer dominance' are much greater in such a market. The emphasis therein on guaranteed minimum standards, backed by substantive research effort and a national programme of supervised training, may provide a nation with a new competitive edge in the world of export markets.

Economic Dialectics
Moreover, whereas capital as 'finance' is most readily identified with London and New York, the Germans—like the Japanese—have recently been far more successful than their British and American counterparts in deploying capital to develop their economies. The ready association of 'capitalism' with free enterprise is therefore a significant misnomer. In fact, while the pragmatically oriented Anglo-Saxons have a natural affinity towards markets, it is the wholistically oriented Germans and Japanese who because of their developmental outlook have a natural insight into the meaning and influence of finance. More obviously, perhaps, the rational French are attuned to technology and, as we shall see, the humanistic Italians have an affinity with people. With regard to individual people, as the Danish existentialist Kirkegaard pointed out in the nineteenth century, Germany has experienced difficulty in transform-ing its collectively based wholism into individually oriented self-develop-

ment. In fact, the Ordo-Liberals, when they absorbed elements of Anglo-Saxon private enterprise and of entrepreneurial self-help, were unfortunately a generation too early to imbibe aspects of individualized learning and managerial self-development. This Germanic resistance to 'self-centred' management development of the British and American kind continues to this day, in parallel with the Anglo-Saxon resistance to collectively associated industrial development. We now turn—with a view to transcending the real East/West divide—to 'wholist' management concepts in general and to Bernard Lievegoed in particular.

Summary

WHOLISTIC PHILOSOPHY

Idealism
- For Kant, experience is no aggregate of sense impressions but a system—empirical rules of nature are particular instances of *a priori* rules of understanding.
- Goethe cannot stop with such a nature—the idea of metamorphosis becomes his guide, thinking not in systematic relations but in intuitive forms.
- Idealists are Hegelians, because—in contrast to the Latins—they instictively ascribe to evolution a deeper meaning and higher value than they ascribe to what is.
- Need and work, raised to the level of universality, constituted—for Hegel and Goethe—an immense system of solidarity and mutual dependence.

Romanticism
- The German economist Adam Müller stressed altruism and religion in opposition to what he regarded as Adam Smith's egoism and materialism.
- The State, Müller thought, must be regarded as an organism; the individuals who were the cells could not be thought of outside the totality of the State.
- The factors of production are nature, people and the past, including all capital—physical and spiritual—which has been built up in the course of time.
- All these collaborate in production, the object being both the multiplication of utility and the intensification of the economic and social union of the national household.

Historicism
- A developmental feature of Marx's thinking, which he drew from Hegel, was its dialectical nature.
- Marx's basic contradiction of capitalism lay between the increasingly social, cooperative nature of production and the individual ownership of the means of production.
- The relationship entered for the purpose of production is appropriate to a given development of productive power.
- It enables society to make the fullest use of these productive powers; but this very process brings them into conflict with the social relationship they have created.

WHOLIST ECONOMICS

Ordo-Liberalism
- The market's existence is justifiable and possible only because it is a part of a greater whole which concerns not economics but philosophy, history and theology.
- Economics, for the German Ordo-Liberals, is no natural science—it is a moral science and as such has to do with people as spiritual and moral beings.
- At the same time, economics does occupy a special position, insofar as its subject, the market economy, objectivizes subjective matters.

The social market
- The lines of influence in the social market are reciprocal. What tends to emerge is a consensus by big business about the affairs of an industry.
- State subsidies, for example, are all distributed by the banks—they are the most noticeable expression of a much more general phenomenon, a sense of collective purpose.
- Industrial collaboration in pursuit of long-range objectives is fostered by powerful trade associations in certain industries.
- Industries are thus cemented.

Business association
- Trade associations have traditionally seen themselves as guardians of the interests of the nation's industries.
- These spokesmen for the collective view have a direct *entrée* to the government machine, preferring the organized and the deliberate to the blind encounter.
- The membership of the Supervisory Board includes customers for the company's products, suppliers of its materials, providers of finance and employees.

- One company will be represented on the board of another as a supplier, and receive the representative of the second company as a valued customer.

12

Differentiation and integration: wholism in European management

The 'wholistic' approach to management thought, as it has evolved over the past half-century, has developed along a particular trajectory which we identify here as differentiated–integrated. In fact this theme was taken up at Harvard in the later 1960s by Paul Lawrence and Jay Lorsche (1968), in their seminal book *Organization and Environment*. The overwhelming concern, with them as with their European counterparts, has been with the creation of both differentiated and also integrated order within an ever-larger organizational and interorganizational field.

Such an order, spanning a continuum from Kant to Goethe, lends itself systematically to both reason and intuition. We start, systematically, with functions of organization, before moving on to systems theories of management. Thereafter we focus on Max Weber, emerging from the Kantian tradition, and then Bernard Lievegoed, who draws upon a Goethian stream of influence. Lievegoed, in particular, adopts a developmental approach to differentiation and integration that the Americans, Lawrence and Lorsche, never quite attained (Fig. 12.1).

Models of differentiation and integration

INSTITUTIONAL FRAMEWORKS

Federal political organization
The differentiation and integration, both in space and time, generic to 'wholism' is reflected both geographically and historically in Germany. The recent integration or unification of the two previously separated national entities represents a recurrence of a historical trend.

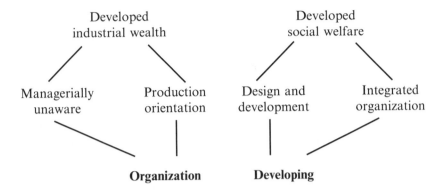

Fig. 12.1 The wholist branches

The differentiated *Länder* (states) which make up the old German federal republic have real political and economic independence. There is a visible north–south divide, which John Mole (1990) characterizes as hard–soft, and an east–west contrast between the solid Saxons and the cosmopolitan Rhinelanders. The French business leader, Michel Albert (1990), suggests that it is the Rhinelander, or what he terms 'Rhenish', capitalism that stands in stark contrast to the Anglo-Saxon model, and is also distinctively different from that of his country.

In fact if France is the best European example of rationally based, cultural centralism, West Germany represented the opposite pole. To start with, West Germany was a federal republic. Federalism is not only a political reality. Most of the *Länder* capitals—Berlin, Hamburg, Hanover, Düsseldorf, Frankfurt, Stuttgart and Munich—are regional centres in every respect, and industry is similarly dispersed.

Germany is best thought of geographically as a patchwork with differentiated enclaves and cities, reflecting the tribalism and ec-centricities of old dukedoms and principalities. The country has several business capitals—Frankfurt for banking and finance; Hamburg for trade; Munich for sunrise industries; and Düsseldorf–Dortmund–Essen for heavy industry. There is no dominating metropolis. At the same time, interestingly enough, Germany has not only—along with France—championed Western European integration but has also played a leading role in integrating economically with Eastern Europe.

Collaborative economic organization
Apart from State monopolies in most public services the government has major shareholdings in hundreds of German companies. The attitude to government participation in industry is based not on ideology but on a

sense of partnership with the business community. It extends to a local level where local authorities, schools, banks and businesses combine to establish policies of mutual benefit. Collaboration, in effect, between banks, government and business is seen to outweigh any conflicts of interest.

German organizations, like their Japanese counterparts, are best suited to a manufacturing environment where major decisions have a long life span. Germans are uneasy with uncertainty, ambiguity and unquantifiable risk. Technical competence rather than force of personality is relied upon. The concept of a team is a group of individuals each with given expertise, with a specific objective and a recognized place within the organization. This attitude derives from a strong sense that everything should be part of a purposeful, developmental pattern. It is not uncommon for employees to rise through the ranks. Training, predominantly technological, continues throughout an employee's career. Management education, as a separate discipline, is not viewed with enthusiasm. Companies prefer to instil their own methods. The spread of earnings between the highest and the lowest paid, unlike in the UK, is the lowest in the EC.

Harmonic education, training and development

Not only are there effectively no public schools in West Germany, there is also neither an Oxbridge nor an Ivy League university. There are really two considerations here. First, there are no universities in Germany which enjoy a particular social cachet. In other words, none are especially favoured by the upper class, after the manner of Oxford and Cambridge in England. Second, there are no universities which have a high reputation across the board. In Germany it is particular faculties which achieve repute. Hence there is no Oxbridge or grande école pattern background to success, arising from either the overall repute of particular universities or their social standing.

The German term *Wissenschaft* covers all formal knowledge, inclusive of the arts, natural or social sciences. The Germans employ a second term, *Kunst*, to refer to art. This term refers not in the British sense to the humanities but to the end products of art represented in paintings, statues and symphonies. Third, Germans use the word *Technik* with respect to manufacturing and the knowledge and skills relevant to it. The word *Technik* has no equivalent in English. Technique merely refers to a way of doing something, not necessarily related to manufacturing. Technology overstates the science–engineering link and does not pertain to skills. While journalists in Germany refer generally to technology, managers and engineers refer specifically to *Technik*. It is also, interestingly enough, a force for integration. The German company is *Technik* in organizational form (Lawrence, 1980, page 98). The skilled worker, the foreman, the superintendent, the technical director are all participants in *Technik*. It transcends hierarchy. It may also transcend particular functions, spanning most particularly research and development, design, production and production control, maintenance and quality control.

The book-keeping is done by clerks and the higher-level functions of financial control are in the hands of graduates of business economics. Moreover, there is to the outsider something rather purposeful about the German system. This sense of purpose comes over in two ways. First, there is the abundance of vocational and especially technical qualifications from the apprenticeship to the Ing. Grad., all of which testifies to the standing of German industry. Second, the mode of study is less geared to going to university for the sake of it and more towards getting a degree to demonstrate a general aptitude.

There is, in fact, no general concept of the professions in Germany. The word for profession, insofar as there is one, *Beruf*, is also the basic word for job or occupation. In that context a sales engineer is as good as a solicitor, a design engineer as good as a vicar. The German society, therefore, like its Japanese counterpart, is one in which much interest attaches to making things and this interest is largely diffused. It is a society which has a concept, *Technik*, to encompass the knowledge and skill relevant to making things and making them work. While *Technik* supplies Germans with a cultural umbrella, qualificational homogeneity enhances integration. Finally, as the British management analyst Peter Lawrence intimates, *Technik* is sufficiently pervasive to have some integrating effect over technical and commercial functions.

So much for the socio-political, cultural and educational backdrop to wholistically oriented management and organization. As we can see, it is substantively different from both the pragmatically and rationally based orientation, where personalized actions and depersonalized thought processes are respectively valued. For it is the interpersonal and interorganizational consensus that is all-important here. We now move on to wholistically based, developmental management concepts.

DEVELOPMENTAL MANAGEMENT CONCEPTS

As in the previous cases of experiential and rational management, there is a progressive evolution from simpler, outer-directed concepts to more complex, inner-directed ones. In the context of 'wholistic' management thought the progression is from differentiated systematic to integrated systemic perspectives.

Systems theory in organization and management

ORGANIZATIONS AS DIFFERENTIATED SYSTEMS

The basic functions of organizations, as revealed by the mainstream Germanic organizational theorist Erwin Grochla (1978), are systematically laid out, as in a manual for a well-oiled machine. Systems which are differentiated on the basis of division of labour and responsibilities, Grochla says, especially machine systems or socio-technical systems, need a set of rules which coordinate human activities and the functions of machines. Such rules need to be devised and implemented in a way which ensures that, regardless of the objective function, it is optimally attained. The system of rules, Grochla says, constitutes organization.

In reality, each system or set of rules reveals a pattern or an individual structure, the organization structure. The basic function of organization is therefore the systematic and permanent regulation of processes to fulful tasks. These in turn are carried out by people and machines according to the principle of the division of labour. In this sense organization or organization structure is an aid, a support system, an instrument. This instrumental notion of organization, duly systematic in its rule-bound approach, widely pervades the German management literature. This contrasts with the institutional concept of organization found in most pragmatically based approaches to the subject, which define the entire socio-technical system, including its interpersonal dynamics, as a human organization.

FROM SYSTEMATIC TO SYSTEMIC CONCEPTS

Systems thinking

The evolution and development of systems theory, according to Helmut Lehmann (1974), owes much to what is often described as 'holistic', 'holism', or 'systems' thinking. This approach can be traced back to the very beginning of Western civilisation, thereby being linked to Plato and Aristotle. In more recent times sytems thinking has taken on new forms, for example, in biology (neo-vitalism) and in psychology (*gestalt*).

Modern systems thinking can be traced back to the 1920s. In that decade a number of scientists in the English- and German-speaking worlds—Wiener, Bertalanffy, Kohler, Lotka—provided the foundations of systems theory in its two modern forms. The Anglo-Saxon approach has close links with cybernetics and with control engineering. The other more Germanic one, the so-called general systems theory, came about through the extension of holistic thinking to the social sciences.

In the context of business the subject matter of systems theory embraces material, goal-oriented or teleological systems designed by people, whose elements are linked to each other by a complex set of material and informational relationships. According to Ulrich (1978) management theory in Germany, initially influenced strongly by the empirically based Anglo-American approach, has subsequently acquired a stronger theoretical base in systems theory. However, systems theory has not led to any fundamental reformulation of the original approach to business administration in a systemic light. Rather, management, organization and strategy have been reformulated. Management, for Ulrich, is a process of shaping. It involves designing a model of an institution on the basis of characteristics that are sought.

It is also a process of development, involving the evolution of social institutions. While leadership theory, with its individual and empirical orientation, has generally followed behaviourist approaches, 'wholist' managemenent theory stands first and foremost under the influence of systems-oriented ones. For companies act in a complex and dynamic environment which makes their adaptation to changing conditions a precondition for survival. Opportunities and risks present in the external environment need to be harmonized with corporate strengths and weaknesses. These are embodied in the resources of the company and its systemic combinations. To cope with complexity involves reducing the load of external factors by measures involving the differentiation of systems, which is necessary because of people's limited ability to process complexity. The functioning of the management system, then, is the goal-oriented harmonization of the company, according to its functions in the envirionment. In economic-rational terms this process comprises phases of decision making, implementation and control. Socio-emotional harmonization dovetails individual workers' needs with the possibilities within the system, covering individual motivation and group coherence. The opportunities and risks in the environment provide management with a challenge to face potential possibilities and dangers by formulating a business policy specific to a particular system. The object of corporate strategy is to bring about a change in the company's present state which will gear it to future needs, at the same time heeding restrictions that are linked to the past. Many interdependent elements link strategy with structure and this makes simultaneous coordination essential; structure does not follow strategy in linear fashion.

MANAGEMENT BY EVOLUTION

Planned evolution

The German strategic thinker Werner Kirsch (1984), like Ulrich, has played a major part in bringing systemic ideas into management, most specifically in his case into business strategy. Classically systematic business thinking was solely concerned, he maintains, with operating profit and liquidity ratios. His systemic approach to business is different. With his broader interest in the dynamics of the development of companies and their environment, Kirsch investigates how to create and maintain the best prerequisites for future profit potential. In his approach, each individual step links into existing 'facts' and, in its turn, determines subsequent ones. The steering of this process takes place via a conceptual overview which in its turn is subject to evolutionary modification as a result of increased experience. Strategic management is therefore the direction setting and coordination of the long-term evolution of the company and its task environment via a conceptual overview of the company's policy. The planned evolutionary learning process for Kirsch is based on the concept of the evolving company as self-organizing.

Kirsch's developmental ideas on strategy can be likened to policy planning, as articulated in the design for evolution by the Swiss-German Erich Jantsch (1974). Both Kirsch and Jantsch introduce a frame of reference which facilitates policy integration, specifically linking up identity, image and socio-economic components. A reconstruction of the structural reality, constitution, policy and culture of the company provides for them both the institution's historically reshaped identity. This is often mirrored subconsciously in the changing value systems of employees. The redetermination of identity, by means of the reconstruction of that 'deep structure', takes as its point of departure the values, norms, rules and general behaviour which mark the decisions in the company.

Strategic management can only be built up through a lengthy step-by-step process, which itself has to be carried out as a multilayered learning process in pursuit of the idea of planned evolution. Such a strategic overview can be developed relatively autonomously from the perspective of a single field. If one is to achieve an internally consistent overview there has to be coordination (Board management). Coordination extends out of the organization, internally, into other organizations, externally. The web of interdependencies to which Kirsch alludes leads into cooperative strategy.

Inter-firm cooperation

Cooperation, according to Peter Schwartz (1979), is a purposefully created, goal-oriented, formal system of action with the aim of assigning specific tasks to otherwise independent actors. Partners in a cooperative agreement may be:

- Competitors in the supply and demand for similar goods and services—*horizontal cooperation*;

- Trading partners in a market situation—*vertical cooperation*;
- Suppliers of different products to the same customers—*heterogeneous cooperation*.

There are three discrete levels of cooperation within and between businesses:

- *Individual*—perceptions, attitudes and motives are particularly relevant;
- *Group*—formality and informality govern interactions;
- *Inter-group*—horizontal relations between departments and vertical ones between hierarchical levels. Codetermination roles apply here.
- *Inter-firm*—account must be taken of institutional characteristics and specific conditions of its system of operations.

We now turn more to Max Weber (1864–1920), whom many would see as the founding-father of 'wholist' organization theory.

Weber's developmental sociology

PROGRESSIVE RATIONALIZATION

The idea of the progressive rationalization of life, as the main directional trend of Western civilization, is the unifying theme of Weber's sociology. Just as Tocqueville saw the spread of equality as a master social process, Weber saw rationalization as similarly far-reaching. By 'rationalization' Weber meant the process by which explicit, abstract, intellectually calculable rules and procedures are increasingly substituted for sentiment, tradition and rule of thumb in all spheres of activity. Rationalization leads to the displacement of religion by science as the major source of intellectual authority. It involves the substitution of the trained expert for the cultivated man of letters, the ousting of the skilled handworker by machine technology. Similarly, it entails the replacement of traditional judicial wisdom by abstract, systematic codes. Rationality demystifies and instrumentalizes life (Wrong, 1970). For Marx the capitalist exploits the workers' productive capacities by subjecting them to the process of commodity production for the market. Weber forms an interesting contrast to Marx. For Weber, the techniques and social structures created by human rationality become actually stunting and constricting of the rational capacities of the people they dominate.

EVOLVING RATIONALITY AND INDIVIDUALITY

Weber proceeded from a conception of cultural evolution. In the centre of it stands the ever-recurring struggle of the creative individual with the forces of rationalization. Although Weber feared that in this combat the individual would finally be overcome, he did not simply take refuge in the cult of irrationality, but acclaimed rationality as pre-ordained (Wrong, 1970, page 34).

The spread of hierarchical, bureaucratic forms of social organization, then, stands in the same relation to social life as science, technology, secularism and legal formalism stand to their respective spheres of culture. In Weber's typology, therefore, the historical process may be described as a descent from a predominantly charismatic form, through traditional, to bureaucratic forms of life and dominance. These, in turn, were interrupted again and again, and directed into new courses by further eruptions of charisma. Historical development was a shifting battle between discipline and individual charisma.

For it was precisely within the rational environment that the individual was presented with the challenge of asserting his or her individuality. The principles of individuality and of rationality were in Weber's mind dialectical quantities. They belonged together. The conflict between the two principles was in his view the great theme of world history and, by implication, we might add, of management and organization. Bernard Lievegoed, a student of Goethe rather than Weber, was similarly concerned with this process of dialectical development, within organizations. Moreover, Lievegoed, unlike Weber, foresaw authentic integration between individuality and rationality through his developing organization.

Lievegoed's developmental management

Bernard Lievegoed, a prominent European management thinker, has turned Weber's general, historical analysis into specific organizational form. He establishes the context for his work on 'developing organizations' with his biologically based 'laws of development'.

LAWS OF DEVELOPMENT

Development for Lievegoed (1990) entails growth that continues within a certain structure until a limit is reached. Beyond this limit the existing structure or model can no longer impose order on the larger mass. The consequence is either disintegration or a step up to a higher level of order. We have here echoes of Marx and Hegel, if not also of Max Weber.

Lievegoed discerns the following developmental laws:

- Development is principally discontinuous.
- Within each stage a system appears that has a structure characteristic of that stage.

- The new stage has a dominant subsystem; this does not lead to a process of addition but to a shifting of all the relationships within the system.
- In a following stage the structure differs from the previous one in that it has a higher degree of complexity and differentiation.
- Development is not reversible—youth does not return.

Having revealed his developmental laws, Lievegoed sets out his approach to 'systems thinking'. In becoming familiar with the laws of development, Lievegoed argues, it is necessary to free ourselves from the actual situation of one's organization and to learn to think in terms of systems.

Lievegoed's mentor, Rudolph Steiner, the Austrian philosopher who in his turn was heavily influenced by Goethe, alluded to a threefold social system. Within it the economic subsystem was merely one part:

> If we contemplate life itself we shall find that the social life of man is threefold. If he is to contribute his share to the well being of the social order he must first of all possess individual capacity, talent or ability. In the second place he must be able to live at peace with his fellow men. Thirdly, he must be able to find his own proper place from which he can further the interests of the community by his work, his activity and his achievement. Through their mutual cooperation, moreover, the unity of the social organism can come about.
>
> (Steiner, 1947)

The enchancement of individual capacity is undertaken within the cultural field. The pursuit of peaceful relations with one's fellows arises within the political sphere. Work and achievement takes place within the economic realm. While the first, for Steiner, is an expression of liberty, and the second of equality, the third is a manifestation of fraternity. Human cooperation in economic life must be based on fraternity which is inherent in associations. As we shall see, in Lievegoed's 'wholistic' model of business and organizational development, fraternal association comes into its own once an enterprise realizes its full potential. The developing organization starts with pioneering.

THE DEVELOPING ORGANIZATION

The pioneering phase

In its pure form, for Lievegoed, the pioneer enterprise is run by the founder. It comes into being as a result of an entrepreneurial act of an individual person. Such a person has a realistic imagination, thereby a pragmatic orientation.

The business is an extension of the individual's ego, and the often autocratic style of leadership is based on the prestige he or she holds in the eyes of employees. The workforce functions as one big family. Problems are resolved by improvisation rather than planning. The pioneer is not only close to his or her workpeople but also to customers. Objectives are tangible and success or failure can be witnessed by all.

The close-knit character of the pioneering enterprise is both a strength and a potential weakness. If there is market growth so that personal contacts with customers are no longer possible, if extensive changes take place in the social structure so that a patriarchal style is no longer acceptable, the pioneering stage has reached its limits.

The differentiated phase

The main principles of the 'differentiated' phase, according to Lievegoed, are mechanization, standardization, specialization and coordination. Overarching rationality rules the day.

Through *mechanisation* technical resources are used wherever possible, in place of increasingly costly, unpredictable and relatively inefficient human resources. Rationally based techniques of production, distribution and sales, as well as finance and administration, displace empirically based instinct and feeling. *Standardization* involves interchangeability and uniformity of people and things. Standard parts and quality controls, standard job descriptions and performance appraisals, standard communications and control procedures become par for the differentiated course. Three particular kinds of *specialization*, according to Lievegoed, appear at this rationally based stage of business and organizational development. Functional specialization leads to similar activities being grouped under a departmental head. Hierarchical specialization establishes managerial authority, contained in and by vertical layers, constituting a veritable bureaucracy. Finally, Fayol's specialized management processes come to the fore. Ultimately, whereas competition is of pioneering essence, *coordination* is of particular importance at the differentiated stage. Fayol's principles of unity of command prevail to avoid contradictory instructions. Manageable spans of control are required according to the number of subordinates of whom a superior is able to retain detailed knowledge. Reliable communications are needed to ensure that staff remain appropriately informed. Systematic training is required to transmit necessary knowledge and skills throughout the company—all are involved.

The phase of differentiation, in effect, is as antithetical—and complementary—to the pioneering one as deductively based French rationalism is to inductively based English pragmatism. It is an essential phase that an organization needs to undergo, that is, from westernness' to 'northernness', as part of its development. Clearly differentiated functions have to be formed but, at a particular developmental threshold, can serve to deform in three ways.

First, formalization and bureaucratization can reduce the flexibility of the organization. To that extent, it increasingly fails to respond to market and social changes. Small functional kingdoms arise and communication breaks down. Second, problems of communication arise not only horizontally but also vertically. At the top less is known about what is happening at the base of the hierarchy and vice versa. Third, as differentiation overreaches itself, there is a steady fall in motivation to work and to buy. As the scale and impersonality of the organization increases, so does the individual's perceived impotence *vis-à-vis* the system grow relentlessly.

The integrated phase

For Lievegoed the third phase of integation represents the culmination of an organization's development. In that respect he perceives an evolutionary progression towards wholism, or systemic unity, albeit interspersed with crises of regression.

If we start with the entrepreneurial, individual initiative of the pioneer as our thesis, he says, the differentiated, rational management is in a certain sense the antithesis. The third step will have to be the synthesis of the positive elements of the first and second phases through a new integrating one, that is, the social subsystem.

Lievegoed's third phase is based on the premise that every individual can and wants to develop. Real fulfilment at work can be attained only if the individual need for ongoing development is satisfied. To accommodate this, a new form of integrated organization is required.

In Lievegoed's clover-leaf organization the Board no longer sits on the apex of the pyramid. It is now situated at the centre of the organization, at the crossing point of all the channels of information and communication. In effect, the clover-leaf model enables us to adopt a systemic view of the organization and its environment (Fig. 12.2). Pan-European *board management*, in this integrated setting, is somewhat different from its more parochially or nationally based counterpart:

- It shifts from an autocratic position at the top of a typically family based enterprise to the centre of a *socio-economic network*, where all the channels of communication underlying *process management* meet.
- It reorientates itself, interdependently, from the systematic formulation of competitively based strategies and structures towards the

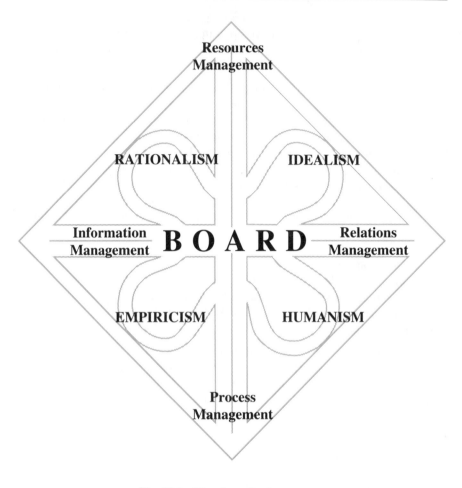

Fig. 12.2   The clover leaf as a system

cooperative development of a *systemic association* of producer/consumer, client/banker, employer/employee, in the context of *relations management*.

- It transforms an oppressively hierarchical structure into a *requisite bureaucracy*, with rationally based structures and functions which enable *resource management* to be undertaken appropriately, that is, fairly and efficiently.

- It turns from an embodiment of free enterprise into the focal point of a learning organization, in which the *information management* that it facilitates becomes the bridge between individual and organizational development.

The heart of darkness

LEFT OUT IN THE COLD

Interestingly enough, in our travels around the European businessphere it is in Germany, the most successful of our economies, that we come truly unstuck. Now there is an irony! The pragmatic Anglo-Saxon's influence on management goes without saying. The rationality of Fayol and Jaques has exerted some considerable influence on formal organization, and even humanism is now seeing the light of day, through the emergence, as we shall see, of flexible specialization. Wholism-in-management, however, has been left out in the cold, together with the strategic business perspective representing its own home ground. In other words, and on the one hand, what lives inside Germany's psyche is powerful enough to take it in 'real' life to the top of the European business tree. Yet, on the other, deep within those philosophical foundations of which Germany is so proud the 'whole' path to economic success lies buried. As a result, instead of perceiving the truth of the 'German miracle', as has been the case for Japan, the outside world is misled by surface features. Such clichés as 'they've lost the war, but they've won the peace', or 'what do you expect from that well-oiled machine?' seem not to do justice to the economic miracle of our 'wholistically' oriented neighbours. In fact, even somewhat more discerning assessments, like 'uninterrupted consensus' or 'meticulous engineering' constitute, at best, half-truths. Why, then, have we been willing to uncover the Japanese miracle thousands of miles away by probing so deeply into their Oriental ground while we have been unwilling to probe deeply into our own European soil?

TRANSFORMING DIALECTICAL MATERIALISM

There are two major reasons for this mutual self-deception, and very good ones at that! In the first place we European managers, unlike our Japanese counterparts, have shied away from those matters of the 'spirit', with which Germany is so richly endowed. On the one hand, we have shunted such descendants of Goethe like Rudolph Steiner off to 'the new age' where 'they can't hurt'. Their 'wholistic' economic and commercial strategies have therefore been lying dormant, rather than becoming manifest. On the other hand, outcast Bernard Lievegoed, and his global spread of management consultants—NPI—have been duly uprooted from their original, Germanic grounds.

In the second place, quite understandably, the combined traumas of Marxism and Nazism have tainted the formative influences of Germanic idealism. For, on the one hand, the emergent 'totality' in Leibniz and Hegel can alternatively degenerate into totalitarianism. On the other, their potentially life-giving force could represent, at one and the same time, that 'death-bearing force' of State socialism. The key to Europe's economic reformation in effect, and also spiritual renewal, lies in the transformation of dialectical materialism into developmental wholism.

Such an authentic version would embrace hierarchy and network, freedom and order, within a developmental whole. It would form the heart of a transformational approach to strategy formation in Europe. It would also help 'wholism' to exorcize itself from its own, totalitarian past. What, then, are the specific attributes of the wholistically oriented 'developmental' manager?

Summary

WHOLISTIC SOCIO-ECONOMIC FRAMEWORKS

Partnership economics
- Governments has shareholdings in hundreds of private companies.
- This is based not on ideology but on a sense of partnership with the business community.
- This extends to a local level, where local authorities, schools, banks and businesses combine to establish policies of mutual benefit.
- Hostile takeovers are virtually unknown.

Long-term industry
- Cooperative enterprise is suited to a manufacturing environment where major decisions have a long lifespan.
- Technical competence rather than force of personality is relied upon.
- This attitude arises from a sense that everything should be part of a purposeful, developmental pattern.
- The spread of earnings between the highest and the lowest paid is low.

Integral education
- There are no public schools, Oxbridge universities or grandes écoles.
- *Technik* is a force for integration—transcending hierarchy and business functions—encompassing the knowledge and skill required to make things works.
- While technical qualifications and apprenticeships proliferate there is no concept of professionalism—exclusive of or from job or occupation.
- There is a strong tendency for individuals to rise through the ranks, reinforced by the apprenticeship system.

WHOLISTIC MANAGEMENT CONCEPTS

Systemic management

- Wholistic management theory, initially influenced strongly by the competitive model, has subsequently acquired a stronger theoretical base in systems theory.
- Management is seen to involve a process of shaping, that is, designing a model of an institution on the basis of characteristics that are sought.
- Opportunities and risks present in the external environment need to be harmonized with corporate strengths and weaknesses.
- These are embodied in the resources of the company and its systemic combinations.

Developing organization

- For Lievegoed, growth continues within a certain structure until a limit is reached.
- Beyond this limit the existing structure can no longer impose order on the larger mass—the consequence is either disintegration or a step up to a higher order.
- In a following stage the structure differs from the previous one in that it has a higher degree of complexity and differentiation.
- A first, economically based pioneering stage is followed by a technologically differentiated one, culminating in a socially integrated stage of development.

13

The developmental manager

Beyond Management
Whereas pragmatically oriented societies feel particularly at home with personalized leadership and rationally based ones thrive on depersonalized management, the 'wholistic' one is neither here nor there. In fact, as Peter Lawrence (1980) has pointed out, the vocabulary employed by German managers is not particularly managerial. That is, it does not reflect the language of the business school or the concept of management as a systematic entity that can be analysed in general terms. The same goes, indeed, for the Japanese (see Fig. 13.1).

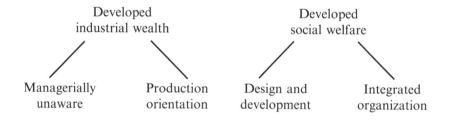

Fig. 13.1   The fruits of developmental management

Workmanship
What does distinguish the German manager's vocabulary is the abundance of words denoting positive attitudes to work and achievement. *Arbeitswille*, the will to work, *Arbeitsfreudigkeit*, delight in work, and *Arbeitseinsatz*, getting down to work, are very common expressions. *Einsatzbereitschaft*, the willingness to engage in purposeful action, and *Durchsetzungsvermögen*, the ability to get things done, are common. Without doubt, there is similar terminology in Japan.

VALUING CONCRETE EXPERIENCE

Germans have a conception of themselves as doing particular jobs in manufacturing companies, rather than of themselves as managers. They tend to think in practical rather than in abstract terms. Ideas about motivation, communication or human relations are secondary to what gets made and sold, in that they all tend to imply society's, or at least management's, effort at amelioration rather than sincere appreciation. What seemingly happens in industry in America or Britain can only be redeemed by a strong dose of 'human relations'. Omissions of these in Germany, and in Japan, tend to suggest, somehow or other, that industry is more domesticated, less alienating than in America where these concepts and shibboleths arose (Lawrence, 1980). Their apprenticeship system, moreover, tends to bear this out.

Apprenticeship

The German apprenticeship system is deeply rooted in German history; it can be traced to the fourteenth century. A crucial test came when the Industrial Revolution arrived. The use of machines supposedly reduced human labour to perfunctory, rote tasks. As a consequence, in most European countries the training of skilled labour was phased out, but not in Germany. There is no simple explanation why German industrialists took on the job-training role when many of their counterparts did not, though it is interesting to note that an aristocrat like the German Imperial Chancellor Otto von Bismarck introduced far-reaching, pioneering social legislation as early as the 1880s. The impact of the apprenticeship system on the German economy, though, can hardly be overstated. It generates the rather self-confident, versatile *Facharbeiter* (skilled craftsman) who in many ways represents the real backbone of German industry.

The system uses a dual approach: the apprentices generally work three days a week on the job and spend the other two in a vocational school. During the first phase, the trainees earn only about DM 200 a week, which makes the system palatable to the German companies who have to finance it. Currently more than half a million companies in Germany offer apprenticeships in some 450 professions.

The typical duration of that type of training is three years. Due to its success in blue-collar professions, the scheme has also been extended to the commercial side of business.

A key feature of the system is that it is locally administered but nationally coordinated. A person who has gone through an apprenticeship in, say, North Rhine-Westphalia can easily join a firm in Baden-Württemberg, as his or her new employer has a good understanding of the formation of the job applicant as soon as the latter presents a *Gesellenbrief* (certificate). In this way a pool of skilled labour is generated by the system. The lengths and intensity of it as well as the combination of hands-on and conceptual approaches ensure that a graduate of the system has a 'gut feel' for the business (Smyser, 1992, page 74).

The system is undeniably very expensive. According to some estimates, employers spend about DM 50 billion a year on this type of training. The firms, though, recognize that it is a necessity. As an apprentice in his or her third year of training is already quite productive, at a still relatively low wage, the firms are usually willing to accept more apprentices than they plan to employ afterwards. In the late 1970s and early 1980s when the 'baby boomers' reached the age when an apprenticeship is typically started, private enterprise was eager to accommodate them.

The number of placements available for vocational training was increased from roughly 500 000 to 720 000 in a relatively short time. The same happened after German unification, when thousands of East German youngsters had to be absorbed after the firms who traditionally would have taken them as apprentices had collapsed.

Against this backdrop it becomes clear that one of the greatest benefits of the apprenticeship system is a social one. The unemployment among the population under 24 years, as a percentage of total unemployment, is relatively low in Germany (14.45 per cent). The three other economies in the 'quartet' registered higher figures (in 1990): France 30.03 per cent, the UK 31.49 per cent and Italy 49.69 per cent (Wachter, 1992, pages 21–37). The positive attitude of German managers towards the creation of such a pool of qualified labour has several additional benefits.

A second benefit is a high labour productivity. Although the skills of the labour force are only one aspect of productivity ratio, it is important enough to mention the labour productivity in this context. In 1990 the added value per employer per hour amounted in Germany to US$34.44, in comparison with France (US$29.77), Italy (US$28.68) and the UK (US$20.92). We now turn from apprenticeship in particular to developmental 'management' in general.

Does the path to economic success lie beyond management? Is there a good reason why the Germans and the Japanese have substantially ignored the business schools? What are the key managerial attributes of the 'wholistic' or developmental 'manager', and why might they be so successful?

Work not management

Managerially unselfconscious

Germans, according to Lawrence, simply do not have a strong concept of management. The status of industry is high, the organization of production, selling goods and running firms are activities which are taken seriously and well rewarded. But the Germans, and in many respects the Japanese, are much less prone than the Americans, or British, to think in terms of 'management'. It is just not an entity that can be extrapolated, analysed and talked about in general terms.

There is no particular mystique of authority in developmentally oriented companies, no fetish about having it, being fit for it, or in positions of it. There is more emphasis on the rational and less on the hierarchical element. Ask a German manager what are the requirements for such and such a post and you will be bombarded by *fachspezifisch* statements. *Fachkompetenz* means job proficiency, *Fachwissen* means specialist knowledge, and *Fachkenntnisse* means knowhow in one's specialism. Developmental managers, then, think about the functionally specific rather than the managerially general. That is, they, like the Japanese, are managerially unselfconscious (Lawrence, 1980). The relatively slight engagement of 'wholistically' oriented nations like Germany and Japan in the management movement means that they are less likely to expect that their problems will be solved by exposure to 'management science'. If one rationally abstracts management work, analyses it, treats it as a discrete entity and assigns to it its own laws and dynamics, then all this implies some depreciation of what it is that is being managed. What it is that is managed matters in the 'whole' scheme of things, because what is emphasized is the product, its quality and knowledge and experience of it.

Collegiate style

What might be termed a German management style has the following characteristics (Smyser, 1992):

- Collegiate more than hierarchical or individualistic
- Oriented to achieving consensus, not issuing orders
- Conscious of the employees and respectful of expertise
- Closely attentive to the company's product, to quality, precision and service
- Loyal to one company and to its long-term prospects
- Long-term orientation to innovation by evolution
- Less apt than American or Asian managers to react quickly to developments

- Committed to foreign market position
- Involved in communal affairs
- Committed to quality of work, not quantity

The glory of West German production, moreover, has been through the *Mittelstand*, that is, the medium-sized firms, who employ 80 per cent of German workers.

Gemeinschaft

There is, in Germany, a long tradition of patriarchic responsibility for the social welfare of the workforce. At the same time, bureaucratic principles have always played a significant role in the organization of social and personnel affairs. However, and at the same time, 'scientific management' has always been a subject of debate in German management.

Eugen Schmalenbach, the founder of German business economics, was very sceptical about the introduction of 'mechanistic' planning and organization procedures that would, in his view, undermine responsibility in the organization and hamper the 'feeling' for economic principles. From the mid-1920s there was an influential debate among engineering professors on *Arbeitsfreude*—the enjoyment of work—as an essential precondition of efficient production. With its strong emphasis on *Gemeinschaft* (communalism) as opposed to *Gesellschaft* (contractual relations), and with its promise of reconciliation of labour and capital it had strong ideological undertones.

PRODUCTION AND DESIGN

Unfortunately, because of the comparative lack of focus on individual managerial behaviour within the Germanic culture, we have less material to draw on than in the pragmatic and rational cases. Moreover, as has already been indicated, 'wholism' leads, on the one hand, to a greater value being placed on a product for which one can feel rather than on productivity about which one think. On the other hand, there is more focus on design and development than on finance.

Production orientation

The relative strength of the line as opposed to staff and the rejection of arm's-length management and the down-to-earth approach to management problems all contribute to a positive evaluation of the production function. Germans are immune to American-style analyses of management, as an abstracted entity, and are susceptible to the pervasive influence of *Technik*. The 'whole' idea is that the firm is not a 'money-making machine' but a place where products get designed, made and eventually sold with profits ensuing (Lawrence, 1980, page 93).

In Germany and Japan this whole approach tends to restrict the allure of accountants and financial controllers and to dignify the makers and those associated with them. Profit is never the direct object of the verb 'to make'. Companies do not make money; only the mint does that. They make goods and services. A visitor to a German company will always be told about the product range.

People doing quite ordinary jobs are concerned that they should be done well. There is a tendency for the worker not just to do the job but to internalize its purpose. Postmen worry if the letters they are to deliver have unclear or incomplete addresses. Bus drivers worry if they fall behind schedule. Repairmen worry if they cannot effect a repair quickly. Finally, the foreman is a key figure in production. This person often addressed, therefore, by the boss as *Meister*. The foreman's behaviour, however, is not noticeably authoritarian. The basic demeanour is one of quiet confidence. Blue-collar jobs in production in Germany involve more work components, more skill, more versatility and more autonomy than the equivalent jobs in Britain or France.

Organizational integration
According to Lawrence, the organizational hierarchy is also shorter in the German firms than in the French. In most of the firms the proportion of non-manual workers is also lower in Germany (less task specialization and a smaller administrative component). In the German firms there is little compartmentalization between unskilled workers, skilled workers and technicians and non-manual workers. Conversely, in French companies each of these groups is regarded as being discrete and as having separate promotion ladders. Similarly, Lawrence found that the German firms exhibited less compartmentalization between office staff, junior and senior management than the French and British. Moreover, they had a higher proportion of senior managers who had begun work as junior employees or manual workers. The German companies had fewer supervisory personnel external to the main body of production workers, and these supervisory grades were less clearly defined than in French companies.

Both German and Japanese management, then, are self-contained, not easily influenced from without, non-doctrinaire, and characterized by the ability to make collaborative top management work. German management is relatively uninterested in modern techniques of planning and control—except production control—and in mathematical aids to decision making. They are not particularly prone to formulating and formalizing company goals. Rather, they are inclined to intuit the development of their companies, based on their historically based appreciation of their individual circumstances.

In the final analysis, moreover, they are more likely to argue forward from products rather than backward from profits. If one asks German managers what, as representatives of the company, they are proud of, they tend not to give answers in terms of profits, turnover or market share. The performance indicators more often alluded to are orders and exports. German and Japanese managers tell you proudly, too, that you cannot tell the difference between the personnel manager and the lathe operator. Everyone arrives with a briefcase:

> Meetings have a strong dash of egalitarianism. One gets clerks and chargehands alongside managers. There is a lot of speaking your mind and answering back, the use of titles not being widespread.
>
> (Lawrence, 1980, page 107)

Design and development

Lawrence cites such statements from managers as 'Ich bin mit Leib und Seele Ingenieur' (I'm body and soul an engineer) from a technical director of a company, and 'Er ist Vollblutingenieur' (He's a full-blooded engineer) from a personnel manager about one of his employees. A Greek purchasing agent commented 'we always buy German; we know the Germans live with the idea of making things from childhood on'. A distinctive feature, therefore, of both German and Japanese industry is the standing of design/or development. These are often regarded as prima donna functions, and the reason for this is interesting. Part of it is the idea that people in it are creative, or have inventive talent. This is perhaps a variation on the British theme of the academic *élan* of research-oriented 'boffinism'. The second and more particularly developmental consideration in this connection is the view that design and development are the areas where the company can really distinguish itself.

Germany, then, would be expected to play a prominent role within Europe in the field of research and development. This is in fact the case. In Table 13.1 we illustrate the *research and development orientation* in the four countries compared and contrasted in this book, as revealed by the *World Competitiveness Report*.

The lower part of the table gives the different categories (and ways to measure) R&D expenses. Germany stands out in all cases, followed by France, the UK and Italy. Christopher Lorenz (1992) of the *Financial Times* argues that the Germans, and even more the Japanese, excel in undertaking a steady flow of incremental product and process improvements, as opposed to less frequent and much riskier great leaps forward which 'is one of the reasons for those countries' industrial success in the past 20 years against the more breakthrough-oriented US and UK'. Lorenz urges the UK to take advantage of the devaluation of the pound in

1992 to boost the relatively short-run development (i.e. the 'D') as distinct from riskier long-term research (the 'R' in R&D).

Table 13.1   Comparative R&D

R&D orientation	France	Germany	Italy	UK
Time to innovate	46.4	48.7	50.9	47.0
Time to market	50.4	52.1	50.9	46.2
Total expenditure on R&D (1990, in US$ million)	28.613	42.062	14.744	18.874
Total expenditure of R&D (1990, percentage of GDP)	2.4	2.83	1.35	2.26
Business expenditure of R&D (1990, US$ million)	17.612	30.916	8.414	12.439

Source: Garelli (1992).

Developmental managers, more oriented towards the collective product than towards personal prowess, are less overtly concerned with ambition and status than their Anglo-Saxon counterparts. They take seriously preparation for a company career but have little folklore on 'how to get to the top'.

In the final analysis, 'wholistic' thinking about work in industry, covering who should do what and how, is remarkably free from separatist typecasting. The sort of antitheses which are often felt to exist between theory and practice, thought and action, specialist knowledge and generalist judgement, commercial and technical aptitude, even line and staff, do not seem to bother the Germans or the Japanese. They do not seem to show much zeal, according to Lawrence, for putting people into boxes. They do not seem to fear that clever people will be 'bad at action'.

The evolutionary *cul de sac*

WHY NO *ma*?!

In conclusion, and unlike the cases of the pragmatically and rationally oriented managers, it is difficult to draw up a coherent connection between the cultural roots and managerial fruits of 'wholism'. Whereas the linkage between the collective consciousness of Germanic and Japanese societies, and the organizational integration that ensues, is relatively clearcut, the connection between the 'spirit of becoming' and the production orientation is less so.

Interestingly enough, in the Japanese case, the linkages between underlying cultural predispositions and surface managerial manifestations have been much more actively pursued than in the German one. Here is one illustration from Richard Pascale's oft-quoted book *The Art of Japanese Management* (1982):

> The Japanese treat the parenthetical *ma* as we would a punctuation mark. However, '*ma*' directs the reader to stop and conjure up all thoughts as images of spring. Having done so, he is ready to proceed, bringing all his mental pictures of spring into juxtaposition with the poem's next words, 'as dawn'. Symbolically, '*ma*' tells the reader to pause, wait and experience before proceeding (page 93).

For some strange reason we have taken much less time and trouble to explore our central and eastern Europe heritage, insofar as it has influenced our own European managerial thought and practice, than we have done for the Far East.

Undoubtedly Germany and Japan—as Michel Albert (1991) has high-lighted—have much in common in business, sharing a developmental *weltanschauung*. But they are also significantly different. After all, Germany is not quite an Oriental civilization!

IMPASSE

Philosophical impasse
As indicated in Chapter 12, the philosophical impact of Germanic 'idealism' on business and management has been somewhat curtailed in the past. This is, at least in part, because of the combined, traumatic effects of Nazism and Marxism on Europe. The negative drift of 'wholism', whether as reflected in the romantic economists, in the philosopher Hegel, or in the composer Wagner, towards absolutism has led us to tread wearily along this otherwise positively developmental front. This weariness, while understandable, has served to distort business and management theory towards the experiential and rational. The only substantive developmental ideas available to us, besides our own work (Lessem, 1990), and, of course, that of Bernard Lievegoed and the NPI (1990), are those writings based on the Japanese.

Yet they remain far more remote from our European heritage than the Rhinelanders. Meanwhile, German management thinkers such as Kirsch and Ulrich overlay their developmental concepts with markedly rational overtones. The division, therefore, between depth philosophy and surface application, particularly at the level of the individual manager, remains very strong.

Psychological impasse

Unfortunately, moreover, further reinforcing the philosophical impasse is a psychological one. As we have already mentioned, the 'whole' manager, while intuitively centred, also occupies a psychological periphery. On the thoughtful periphery lie the rules and regulations, the sytems and procedures, the workflow bureaucracy that characterize Germanic management. Unlike the rational case, however, such codification is secondary, rather than primary. On the feeling periphery lies the practical involvement with product that is so much a part of the German *Technik*, and industry focus. Again, it is important to emphasize that this feeling orientation is secondary rather than primary. It is the intuitive appreciation of the 'developmental', as opposed to the rational or pragmatic, and of the 'whole', as opposed to the part, which is of the real essence.

Yet because the intuitive centre lies below the immediate surface it is the other psychological orientations which appear to gain the upper hand. The same applies, incidentally, to Japanese management. If the Americans, particularly, had not taken the time and trouble to probe below the Oriental managerial surface we would never have gained the distinctive perspective on the Japanese that we have now. So it now behoves us, in the interests of European management as a whole, to move forward where others have feared to tread. Moreover, there is the fourth, and final, humanistic brand of management.

Summary

DEVELOPMENTAL MANAGERIAL ATTITUDES

Work not management

- Developmentalists are not definitively 'managerial' in their attitudes and outlook.
- Their 'managerial' vocabulary is dominated by words denoting positive attitudes to work.
- These include the will to work, the love of work and getting down to work.
- Above all, a willingness to engage in purposeful action dominates the management lexicon.

Concrete not abstract

- Developmental 'managers' have a concept of themselves as doing particular jobs in manufacturing companies rather than of themselves as managers.

- They tend to think about work in practical rather than abstract terms.
- Ideas about motivation, communication or human relations are secondary to what is made and sold.
- Industry is more domesticated and less alienating than in the competitive and coordinated business environments.

DEVELOPMENTAL MANAGERIAL BEHAVIOUR

Quality product
- Developmental 'managers' focus on the functionally specific rather than the managerially general.
- They rely on specific job proficiency rather than abstract management science.
- Such abstract science serves to depreciate what it is that is being managed.
- What is emphasized is the product, its quality, and the knowledge and experience that the 'manager' has of it.

Production orientation
- The developmental 'manager' is concerned with the design, production and sale of products rather than with making money.
- Companies do not make money—they make goods and services, leaving the mint to make the money!
- There is a tendency for the worker, therefore, not just to do the job but to internalize its purpose.
- Blue-collar jobs involve, as a result, more skill, more versatility and more autonomy in cooperative than in competitive or coordinated management.

Intuitive integration
- There is less compartmentalization between junior and senior management than in the other management domains.
- Top management operates in collaborative mode, with the chief executive as *primus inter pares* and every worker coming to work with a briefcase!
- The development of the business is contemplated historically, and intuited reflectively, rather than assessed analytically.
- Arguing forward from products rather than backwards from profits.

Design for development
- Design and development, for cooperative management, are the prima donna functions, in contrast to marketing or finance.
- The former are the areas in which management and worker can see themselves most making their mark.

- Distinctions between management and worker, theory and practice, line and staff, specialist and generalist, are much less clearcut than in the competitive case.
- In the final analysis, personal achievement at work is of much greater importance than getting to the top.

Part V

Humanism—Convivial

14

The net and the quest: Humanism in European business

> The Body Shop produces products that cleanse, polish and protect the skin and hair. How we produce them and how we market them is the most interesting thing about us. We are innovative, we are passionate, and we care. We are innovative in our formulations; we are passionate about environmental issues; we care about retailing. The image, goals and values of our company are as important as our product.
>
> Anita Roddick, founder, The Body Shop

The humanist space

Anita Roddick, an Italian by descent, has captured the public imagination not only in Britain, where her corporate headquarters are based, but also around the world as a business humanist. Whereas the wholist is rooted in what Jung termed a collective self (Jacobi, 1962), that is, a storehouse of latent memory traces from our ancestral past, humanism is much more immediately communal in its orientation:

> The sense of equality which permeates all collective life is different from the French idea of equality. Latin equality, being a living sense, is unconsciously assumed whereas Gallic equality, being an idea, is aired and asserted.
>
> (de Madariaga, 1968, page 37)

In de Madariaga's terms Anita Roddick is much closer to Spain than to France and England. 'Managing people', therefore, as reflected in pragmatic leadership, in rationally based human resource management or in the totality of organization development, is anathema to the man or woman of the people.

Such a perspective, in fact, is much more southern than western or central European. Socialized management and organization displaces the personalized–pragmatic, depersonalized–rational, and transpersonalized–wholistic equivalent. In fact the absence of such a 'human' approach has led to adversarial industrial relations not only in Zambia or Zimbabwe but also in Britian and France, as well as in the United States of America.

Humanism in time

The problem with the humanistic approach to business and management around the world is that it has remained stuck in what might be termed its primal groove (Lessem, 1989). De Madariaga gives an illustration of this approach to human affairs in Spain, which could be replicated in San Salvador or in Saudi Arabia, in Sri Lanka or southern Italy:

> Spain's humanism provides the root of that 'personalism' which is so often observed. The importance of personal contacts is well known wherever people of the Spanish race are concerned. Whether the question in debate is a trivial affair or the most important business, a relation of man to man is indispensable if results are to be obtained.
>
> (de Madariaga, 1922, page 47)

There are only two notable European examples in which such primally oriented personalism has been upgraded into a more intricate form of business and managerial humanism. These are the cases of central Italy, in general, and of the Mondragon cooperatives in northern Spain, in particular. In the Italian case the kinship bonds of the extended family have been transformed into the communication linkages of an extended socio-economic network (see Fig. 14.1).

While it was the Renaissance Italians in fourteenth-century Florence who originated business as we know it today, those same people now seem to be developing a genuinely new form of business entity for the twenty-first century. While the down-to-earth subject of communal enterprise has been the feeling-centred, extended family, the more elevated object of humanistic concern has been the socially inclusive human family.

The business patriarch or matriarch, managing by *ad hoc* improvisation, has been reviewed as an 'impannatore' like Adriano Benetton, managing by purposefully flexible specialization. Similarly, the humanistically oriented business institution, having been established as a localized communal enterprise, is now beginning to emerge as a regionalized socio-economic network. Let us now review the cultural roots from which springs such a humanistic enterprise.

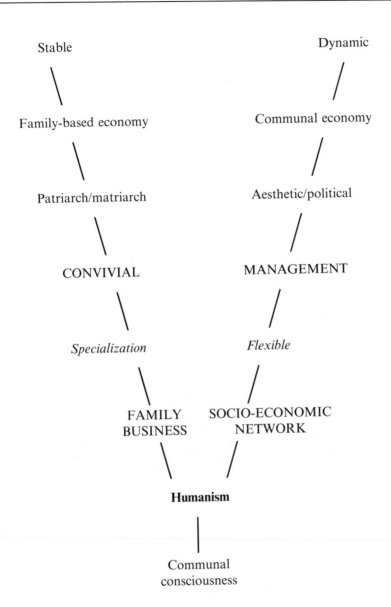

Fig. 14.1   The humanist tree

Images of community—the roots of humanism

FEELING LIFE

Two European nations, according to English social historian Faulkner Jones, i.e. Spain and Italy, have as their special task the recapitulation of a social consciousness in a way suitable for our era. Dante, Goya and Michelangelo have made it possible for us to realize to what sublime heights the feeling-life of people can rise. The shadow side of that feeling life has revealed itself in the dark passions behind the Spanish Inquisition. Disunion, bloodshed, and treachery disfigure the annals of the Italian city-states, even at their greatest. The same can be said for the Mafia today.

In fact, because of the innate egalitarian instinct within such communal societies, it is necessary, in de Madariaga's terms, to 'superimpose cohesion' on a grand scale through the State, the Church or the Army. As a result, small-scale activity tends to be more human in such communally oriented societies than the large-scale organization.

SMALL IS BEAUTIFUL

In a remarkably closely observed study of communal activity in southern Europe, the English political economist Ralph Glasser (1977) portrayed, life in a typical village in southern Italy:

> San Giorgio insists that we see man in society in organic terms always, and that we demand to know, before anything else, what kind of emotional and spiritual life must underpin his workaday existence. It indicates compellingly that a certain type and size of small, self-generating township—or growth unit—is the right social model to strive for. Such a unit can be fully known to itself, and therefore helps the individual to maintain the reciprocal relationships of obligation and response required to support the community's emotional network.

Therein the individual can feel he or she is integral and within it can make manageable emotional relationships.

THE IMAGE OF THE NET

The image of the net, for Glasser, is a useful piece of shorthand:

> The culture is the net. Each individual is a filament within it. So every person is constantly checking his position (identity) within the net by referring to that of everyone else. He does this by observing all of them in every action and statement, in their mutual interactions, and in his own interactions with them. This is one reason, for example, why everyone in a network community needs constant and complete information about everyone else. Exact, mutual knowledge is vital to the process of perception and reperception, and to the

monitoring of how the net is responding to whatever forces are bearing on it (page 166)

The requirement of complete knowledge means that the community must not be too large. That is why each Body Shop franchise, for example, like each part of the Benetton whole, is kept to a small size. If everyone must know everyone else sufficiently to be secure in pursuing whatever relationships are required by economic or personal affairs, two circumstances are necessary. People must first not live too far from anyone likely to be relevant to their lives. Second, they must meet often in order to be aware of any changes in behaviour or in the influences affecting their life. How does this communal activity fit in with the humanistic idea as it has evolved through the European ages?

The communal idea—the main stem of humanism

HUMANISTIC PHILOSOPHY
Pragmatists and rationalists have between them in Jungian terms continually straddled the divide between sensation and thought. Meanwhile, wholists have positioned themselves between reason and intuition, and humanists—like Anita Roddick—have occupied the ground connecting feeling with intuition. The last's primary mode of expression in that regard has been artistic rather than philosophical.

However, there is a distinctive brand of humanistic philosophy, as we shall soon see, that can be traced back to Giambattista Vico in the seventeenth century and extended by Benedetto Croce into modern times. Derivative economic philosophies, though hard to come by, can be gleaned from the work of Alberti in the fifteenth century and Galiani in the eighteenth. Finally, the contemporary management thinkers who have drawn upon the emergent, humanistic heritage are the two MIT-based professors of economic history, Piore and Sabel, and the Spanish originator of the Mondragon cooperatives, Father Arizmendi. Humanism originated, though, in the Renaissance.

Renaissance humanism
Renaissance humanism was, first and foremost, a revolt against the other worldliness of medieval Christianity, a turning away from preoccupation with personal immortality to making the best of life in this world. For the Renaissance the ideal human being was no longer the ascetic monk but a new type—the universal man, the many-sided personality, delighting in every kind of earthly achievement. The philosophy of humanism,

according to Corliss Lamont, an American historian of philosophy constitutes a profound and passionate affirmation of the joys and beauties of existence upon this earth. It heartily welcomes all life-enhancing and healthy pleasures, from the simple gratifications of food and drink, sunshine and sport to the more complex appreciation of art and literature, friendship and social communion:

> Humanism believes in the beauty of love and the love of beauty. All the manysided possibilities for good in human living the Humanist would weave into a sustained pattern of happiness.
>
> (Lamont, 1965, page 227)

According to the tenets of humanism, therefore, a society in which most individuals are devoted to a communal wellbeing will attain greater happiness and make more progress than one in which private self-interest and advancement are the prime motivation. First, a society of socially conscious individuals will be able to achieve and maintain those higher material and cultural levels that provide the broadest foundations for happiness and progress. Second, we are gregarious creatures. Because we are social beings we experience our deepest and most enduring joys in association with others. Third, loyalty to a worthwhile social aim can bring stability and harmony into our lives, giving us a central purpose around which we are able to integrate our personalities. In such a way the sociable Humanist strives to the best of his or her ability to further the good of family, local community—city, town or village—State and nation. The altruistic person, moreover, is continually looking beyond his or her native land to the world at large and thinking about the wellbeing of the peoples of the world.

We now turn from humanism in general to one of its earliest and best-known philosophical exponents, Giambattista Vico (1668–1744).

Vico's new science
Vico was for humanism in the eighteenth century the equivalent of Bacon for empiricism, Descartes for rationalism and Hegel for idealism. In comparing ancient and modern methods of study Vico argued that the moderns have instituted great improvements in the physical sciences. However, they had unduly depreciated those studies whose matter depends on the human will. Those involve vicissitude and probability, and include languages, poetry, eloquence, history, jurisprudence and politics (Fisch and Bergin, 1944, page 38).

Modern history, Vico maintained, rested on the discovery of man as a peculiarly historical being, subject to a development transcending the life of any individual, nation or race. He argued that it is by virtue of this discovery that modern history has been the complement and polar opposite of modern physics in the making of the modern mind. Wherever the impact of this discovery is felt, the interest in history departs from personal feats and exploits, wars, treaties, alliances and dynastic successions. Instead it focuses on customs, laws, institutions, forms of economic and social organization, languages, arts, religions, sciences and climates of opinion (Berginand and Fisch, 1948, page xxii).

Vico continually maintained that as the poets had first 'sensed' in the way of vulgar wisdom so the philosophers later understood in the way of esoteric wisdom. Therefore the former may be said to have been the 'sense' and the latter the 'intellect' of the human race. The human mind does not understand anything of which it has had no previous experience. Similarly, and by implication, the business manager needs to have a 'feel' for a situation prior to being able to grasp it, aesthetically or conceptually. In other words, we must trace the beginnings of poetic wisdom (or, by analogy, market insight) to a crude metaphysics or basic business hunch. This brings us to Benedetto Croce (1866–1952) in our own century.

Croce's aesthetics

Croce took as his point of departure Vico's 'bold and revolutionary innovation' that 'poetry represents the imaginative form of knowledge' logically prior to intellect and free from reflection and reasoning. By analogy, the new business enterprise has a 'primal' form, logically antecedent to the rationally managed organization that succeeds it. Thereafter Croce was to arrive at the all-important conclusion that there are not just one but two relatively autonomous forms of knowledge.

For Croce man is both a knower and a doer. As human knowledge manifests itself in two distinct forms so does human conduct. On the theoretical plane man not only lives by reasoning, he lives also by intuiting, that is, by producing images and enjoying them for their own sakes. This being the case, knowledge may either have as its object particulars (images), which are the products of intuition (art), or universals (concepts), which are the product of reasoning (logic). Correspondingly, on the practical plane man lives not only by moral promptings but also by economic incentives. Hence human conduct may have as its objective either the satisfaction of needs, which are particular and in reach (economics) or the satisfaction of those that are universal (ethics).

It is interesting at this point to compare and contrast the humanists Vico and Croce with the empirically minded Bacon and Revans. We can see, with Croce as for Vico, that the so-called doer, or the 'sensed' world, is closer to intuition and to feeling than it is to pragmatically based sensation or action. The humanists retain that very close affinity with art and artifact—both plastic and political—which re-emerges in economic settings. In fact, as we have already intimated, for Vico and Croce art is not only the starting point for human enterprise it is also the ultimate physical reality (Bergin and Fisch, 1948, page 217). In that respect they seemingly place themselves at an opposite pole from the 'sense'-based pragmatists.

If it is asked why art cannot be a physical fact, Croce emphasizes that it is necessary to state, first that physical facts lack reality. On the other hand, art, to which so many devote their whole lives and which fills everyone with heavenly joy, is supremely real. The proof itself, he affirms, is being acknowledged by the physicists themselves, when they conceive physical phenomena as manifestations of principles which go beyond experience. Physical facts make themselves known not as something truly real but as a construction of our intellect for the purposes of science (page 25). Similarly, we might argue, a balance sheet or a profit and loss account is not a fact. Rather, each is a logical construction for the purposes of nominal financial reporting, which is subject, in turn, to 'real', creative accounting! How, then, has such aesthetically based humanistic philosophy been reflected in economic thought?

Economic plasticity

THEORY

The humanistic economists
Leon Battista Alberti, the fifteenth-century Italian humanist, has been introduced to us already in Chapter 3.

How often have we had Italian managers on our programmes who have an irrepressible desire to convert thoughts into visual images?! It teaches us how to take the world apart, discover the relations between its parts, and then put it together again in an ideally completed form. So too in politics:

> The world is not goods to be consumed or a field to be dominated. It is a field for the creation of an ideal form in human affairs.
>
> (Coates, 1965, page 21)

The artist for Alberti removes himself from his subject in order to see better the ideal harmony and order reflected in the relation between the parts. So does the industrial designer or the 'impannatore'.

Ferdinando Galiani, the eighteenth-century Italian abbot in diplomatic employment in Paris, similarly condemned dogmatic rationalism. As we have seen, he called for flexible policies in line with historical and geographical conditions rather than for adherence to immutable principles of allegedly universal applicability.

Galiani's doubts about the power of reason to deduce eternal truths reflect the influence of Vico, who opposed the anti-historical rationalism characteristic of French Cartesianism. In his approach to history, as we have just seen, Vico stressed the evolution of social institutions. Galiani's historical sense makes him see value not as an inherent quality of goods but as one that will vary with our changing appreciation of them. He recognizes the effect of social forces and stresses the role of fashion as a determinant of our desires and thus our values. In so doing he anticipates the economic developments in central Italy that we are witnessing today.

Societal flexibility

THE AMERICAN MODEL IN CONTEXT

Since the beginning of this century, Giorgio Inzerelli at Holland's Erasmus University points out that industrial organization in the Western world has been transformed by ideas and principles developed in the United States:

> The American model of industrial organisation based on large scale mass production is driven by the systematic application of Adam Smith's principles of division of labour, specialisation and standardisation, which were refined by Taylor early in this century.
>
> (Inzerelli, 1990, page 7)

Interestingly enough, in terms of the European model we have developed here, mass production represents an amalgam of pragmatism and rationalism, with perhaps even more emphasis on the latter than the former.

In fact, network-based humanism is wholly antithetical to hierarchically based rationalism. Inzerelli argues, in the spirit of both Vico and Galiani, that such a mechanistic view of organizations tends to give little consideration to the socio-cultural elements:

> This scientific approach implied that management principles had, ideally, universal validity, and could be abstracted from the specific context of managerial activity. As such it was in line with the classic view that economic activities could be understood in isolation from the social context in which they are embedded (page 7).

THE ITALIAN 'SUCCESS STORY'

Considered not long ago as a developing country, Italy is now the fifth largest economy of the world, after the USA, Japan, Germany and

France. Italy has historically been burdened by an inefficient government administration and by the relatively undeveloped southern regions. Yet the ability of the Italians to improve the efficiency of their economy is shown by the high rate of productivity growth they have achieved in recent years. Between 1979 and 1987 the real GDP per employee has grown by 4 per cent per annum compared to 2.9 per cent for Japan, 1.49 per cent for Germany and 0.66 per cent for the USA.

The country in fact is geographically and economically divided into at least three parts. The south is still relatively underdeveloped. The north has a concentration of large firms conforming to the American model. Finally, the central north-east (CNE) area has been recently industrialized by a proliferation of small firms. This third area of the country has grown the most rapidly in recent years. Moreover, this particular economic region serves to contradict the basic tenet of classical economics that industrial growth necessitates the disappearance of the 'traditional' sector in favour of the 'modern' one. The CNE area comprises seven administrative regions that account for over 40 per cent of the Italian GDP, compared with 35 per cent and 24 per cent for the north-west and south. The CNE economic model, in fact, can also be found in the Jutland province of Denmark (textiles and clothing), the Småland province of Sweden (machine tools), Germany's Baden-Württemberg (textiles, machine tools, car components), France's Rhône Alps region (plastic injection) and around Madrid (electronic components).

Political sensibility

PLASTIC AND POLITICAL ART

It is interesting to see that the first major European challenge to the conventional economic wisdom, as Inzerelli points out, is emerging from that region of Italy whence modern capitalism came, some six centuries ago. Interestingly enough, moreover, there is a common cultural thread connecting Vico's poetic wisdom with the primal, Italian family business. Similarly, his rationally articulated intellect can be associated with Italy's modern-day flexible specialization. Finally, the combination of 'plastic and political art' that Alberti identified in the fifteenth century is a part and parcel of the well-known Italian talent for improvisation today.

SOCIALLY WELL-ATTUNED—INDIVIDUALLY ILL-ATTUNED

Absent sense and sensibility

Like wholism, moreover, Italian or Spanish humanism is a long way removed from the immediate sense and sensibility—to use the English novelist Jane Austen's phraseology—of the individual, pragmatically oriented manager. While productive enterprise in central Italy, or in the Mondragon region of Spain, is well integrated with its social context, it is not clearly differentiated at the level of the individual. In that respect it is far removed from its experientially and rationally minded European neighbours.

In Italy, as in Spain or Portugal, feelings flow into one another, thereafter to be synthesized by aesthetically based intuitions. However, they are not conceptually differentiated in duly generalizable form. While thought and action form the pragmatic way, feeling and intuition constitute the humanistic way. Inevitably, European management needs both. The humanistic model, in effect, provides an example of an economic system whose strength derives, to a large extent, not from its differentiation but from its integration with the social structure. To the extent that this is true then the survival of the system will depend as much on economic factors as on the ability of economic, social and political actors to maintain a high level of mutual integration. This leads us on to the concept of 'humanism' in European management.

Summary

HUMANISTIC PHILOSOPHY

Vico's Humanism
- Giambattista Vico involved himself with studies on the human will, covering languages, poetry, history, politics.
- For this fifteenth-century Italian, philosophical wisdom can only come into its own by recovering its particular poetic, or creative origins.
- Moreover, there is such an original and individual birth for each new institution, and for each nation.
- The nations of which Vico speaks constitute a world in itself, which he calls 'il mondo delle nazioni'.

Croce's aesthetics
- For the contemporary humanist Croce, there is, first a simple or intuitive form of knowledge, and second, a complex or conceptual form, each enjoying its own theoretical value.
- The first phase of mankind's journey corresponds to its aesthetic form, the second to its logical, the third to its economic, the fourth to its ethical.
- Each form is conceived dialectically, that is as four stages of development mutually involving each other.

- The proper study of philosophy, finally, involves the story of mankind—for the world of human history is the stage where the eternal 'drama' of mankind is enacted.

Plastic and political art

- Fourteenth-century Italian political economist, Leon Alberti, believed that humanity achieves its highest expression in two arts, plastic and political.
- In the plastic art man discovers order and harmony in nature, while in the political one he translates that order and harmony into social terms.
- Fifteenth-century abbot Galiani called for flexible policies in line with historical and geographical conditions, rather than adherence to immutable principles.
- Galiani's historical sense made him see value not as an inherent quality of goods but as one that will vary with man's changing appreciation of them.

SOCIO-ECONOMIC POLICY

Complex web

- Middle Italy provides an example of an economic system whose strength derives from its integration with the social structure.
- To that extent the survival of the system ultimately depends on the ability of economic, social and political actors to maintain a high level of mutual integration.
- Each mid-Italian industrial district is composed of a core of more-or-less equal small enterprises bound in a complex web of competition and cooperation.
- Structure shades into infrastructure, competition into cooperation and economy into society.

Fluid process

- The very fluidity of the resources that makes the system flexible, paradoxically also makes it necessary to create institutions that facilitate cooperation.
- Trade associations, unions, guilds, purchasing cooperatives, cooperative marketing all prevail, but no single institution formally links the productive units.
- Federated enterprises hold one another's stocks and have interlocking boards of directors; sometimes the firms share financial and marketing facilities.
- 'Solar' firms frequently treat external suppliers as collaborators, and often cooperate with community institutions in research, education and welfare.

15

Flexible specialization

The humanistic management model will be the last of the four that we shall be identifying. As such, it is important to make some general points now with reference to European management. In the first place it is necessary to stress that any one generic approach—be it pragmatically or rationally, wholistically or humanistically based—is by no means exclusive to a particular part of Europe. It is, however, most strongly rooted there.

For example, in the case of 'flexible specialization', which we shall shortly be reviewing, this particular model of managing is to be found throughout the Continent. However, it is especially well attuned to central Italy. At the same time, it would make sense for each part of Europe to diversify its management and organizational portfolio and to purposefully develop exogenous structures and functions as well as indigenous ones.

Moreover, any one European region is naturally predisposed to focus on the individual insofar as it is pragmatically oriented. Similarly, it is predisposed towards the organization to the extent that it is rationally based, the collective from a wholistic perspective, and the community as humanist. To the extent that it focuses in one direction it will be liable to pay correspondingly less attention to others. As a result, where the focus is weak the extent of differentiation and integration of that particular factor of ultimate production will be crude rather than sophisticated.

For example, an individual in Lisbon will be less clearly differentiated than in London, and a community in Paris less so than in Padua. To fully realize itself, from its particular cultural and philosophical perspective, each of the four parts of the European whole has to interact with each other, that is, individual–organizational–collective–communal. An authentic, Europeanwide division of labour would therefore need to be carefully orchestrated in order to balance the best of all worlds rather than obtain an imbalance of the worst. The same applies to any corporation.

For example, IBM in its heyday combined pragmatic individualism—respect for the individual—with organizational rationality through its motto 'Think'. Moreover, a sense for the collective—interdependence with the society without—was combined with communally shared values within. Conversely, in an underdeveloped country, individual enterprise may be thwarted by an inward-looking bureaucracy, while the collective authority (urban government) is distanced from the communal one (rural village) (Fig. 15.1).

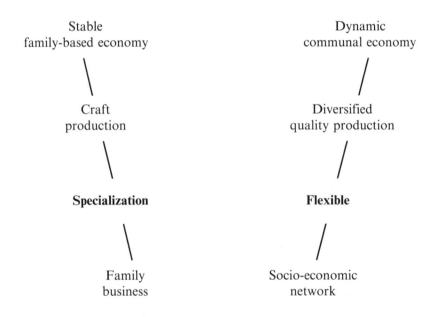

Fig. 15.1   The humanist branches

Models of communal management and organization

FAMILIASM VERSUS INDIVIDUALISM

The family business, in fact, lies at the heart of a humanistic approach to business, albeit at the primal end of its socio-economic development. In the words of Leon Danco, an Italian American who founded the Center for Family Business in Ohio: 'Family businesses are unique because they are composed of a flow through time of people with conflicting needs, concerns, abilities and rights, who also share one of the strongest bonds human beings can have, a family relationship' (Danco, 1980, page 8). For

Danco a family business is so much more than an economic enterprise. It is a stew of family relationships, based on both love and resentment.

Blood ties, moreover, are not the only qualifications for this family. Business 'relatives' are the long-term employees who become like brothers to the founder because they grew up in the business together. The exanding family requires the same care and interest the founder expended on developing his or her own children for the future:

> It is by nature explosive, because of its ever expanding complexity. Each time a new person is added, a new and unpredictable pole of influence is brought into the family.
>
> (Danco, 1980, page 127)

Italy is therefore a matrix of interests and loyalties. Horizontally divided into regions, it is vertically divided by factionalism. All aspects of Italian life, according to John Mole (1990), are divided by rival interest groups, including political parties, private and public sector, employers and unions, Church and State. There are 20 regions which have considerable autonomy in health, education and police. Moreover,

> affiliation to at least one interest group is essential. Belonging to a political party or to the church, to the Mafia or to a Masonic lodge, to a trade association or to a trade union is not merely a sociable association of like minded people, but an economic necessity. Affiliation, and the rights and obligations that go with it, replaces what passes for a wider social awareness in countries (like France or Germany) whose political and social institutions are more universally accepted. There are national policies in abundance but they do not percolate to the level of ordinary life.
>
> (Mole, 1991, page 49)

Hence the instability of Italian politics.

For most Italians, according to business journalist Dalbert Hallenstein (1991), if not also for the Spanish, the family, in effect, is the substitute for the State:

> Loyalty is centred almost exclusively on the family and its members. The family is the only institution which can be trusted and relied upon. Some loyalty may be devoted to one's native town or village, or even to the region where one was born, but an Italian's true allegiance is to the family—and to nothing or nobody else (page 26).

Indeed, Hallenstein adds, one of the reasons the Italians are the greatest savers in the world, even more so than the Japanese, is that any family may share four or five incomes, plus various pensions. Not surprisingly, therefore, in Italy the family has become the largest bank. Often houses and even entire factories are constructed using family (virtually interest-free) loans, without any recourse to the banking system with its long delays and high interest rates.

The Italian's capacity for work, moreover, according to Hallenstein is limitless provided it is for his family, and that his or her employer is not some amorphous corporation, like a bank or the State. There is no concept of public service, and members of the public are defined by the State employees as fools (*fessi*) if they believe that they are entitled to such a service. Italy's bureaucracy, in Hallenstein's words, is second only to India's in its diabolical complexity. Government is popularly viewed as a group of separate cliques working for themselves. The payment of taxes, for example, is seen not as a duty to the community but as an exaction to be evaded. If there is to be cooperation, in Italy or in Spain, it is likely to be close to home. As a result, both countries, at least in particular regions, have a strong cooperative tradition.

Personal and cooperative enterprise

While cooperative enterprise is widespread in Italy, as, for example, compared with Britain or the Nordic countries, it is in the Spanish Basque country that the renowned Mondragon cooperatives have emerged. Therein today some 55 000 people are employed in a wide range of industrial enterprises. The Mondragon cooperative experiment was initiated by a Basque priest, Father Arizmendi. He first set out in 1941 to be an adviser to young people. The Basque nation, to which he was committed, had a strongly nationalistic streak to it and had vigorously opposed General Franco during the Spanish Civil War. Arizmendi's first priority, as he saw it in the 1940s, was to establish a technical school for young people. He immediately enlisted the community's support, as he continued to do for all of his subsequent activities. In fact he soon realized that technical education without industries in which to subsequently apply it would leave the youths frustrated. So he encouraged five of the graduates of the initial technical school to set up the first of the Mondragon cooperatives.

A small part of the start-up capital needed to buy a bankrupt business came from the savings of the five founders. The remainder was raised from the Mondragon community and particularly through friends and contacts in drinking clubs—*chiquitos*—which are a strong feature of Basque life. These clubs are quite small and encourage lasting relationships of high trust and solidarity among members. Thereafter as the five initial founders set up their operation to manufacture heating stoves in the mid-1950s the Catholic Father was purposefully occupied in setting up a cooperative bank:

One of the most powerful arguments that Arizmendi had used in urging that the bank be set up was that the isolation of the individual cooperatives involved the most formidable risks to which their members should not be exposed. Another had been that the potential for cooperative enterprise would never be adequately developed if the task of encouraging and midwifing new initiatives was left to the individual enterprises themselves.

(Oakshott, 1978, page 171)

In the subsequent 15-year period, between 1961 and 1976, more than 60 cooperative enterprises were created at Mondragon, bound by the following seven structural and functional elements, which combined personal and cooperative enterprise:

- Each worker-member must purchase a significant stake whose value would alter with the enterprise's fortunes.
- Ultimate control rests with the general assembly.
- A significant proportion of the cooperative's capital remains collectively owned and indivisible.
- Wage and salary differentials are set to take account of both market factors and the needs for solidarity.
- The isolated cooperatives have continuous access to professional advice, to capital for expansion, and to skilled manpower.
- Through their support for educational and social projects, the cooperatives enjoy continued communal back-up.
- While the independence of the individual cooperatives is guarded, they are essentially integrated into a group.

As we can see, the Mondragon cooperatives are a true amalgam of small-scale, combined personal and communal enterprises.

In fact the backbone of the Italian economy, as is the case in Spain, is formed by thousands of small family and cooperative businesses. Therefore industry and commerce as a whole is dominated by the family firm, in just a few cases rising to the powerful heights of the huge Agnelli, and De Benedetti 'condottieri'-run concerns. Similarly, the retail trade, agriculture and construction industries are dominated by cooperatives, themselves grouped into consortia.

Business owners retain their indentity within the small group partly out of a psychological need for familial independence and partly out of commercial self-interest. It is invariably profitable to keep out of the hands of the tax authorities, the bankers and the trade unions. While banks are highly regulated and are not allowed to participate in the ownership of commercial companies, unions are highly politicized and the relationship between management and unions is normally confrontational. There are two labour markets: the official one which, according to Mole, is biased in favour of the employee, and the unofficial one accounting for some 25 per cent of employment, which is duly unregulated.

The extensive public involvement in industry is primarily through the intermediary State holding companies—IRI, ENI and EFIM—each of which is highly diversified. Real control is, in fact, in the hands of the political parties and not the State bureaucracy. IRI, the largest of the three, is a Christian Democrat stronghold. Government spending, as a proportion of the GDP, is the highest in the European Community. Yet only one in five employees are public servants, as opposed to one in three in Germany and the UK. Public enterprise, in Italy as in Spain, is not noted for its rationally based organization!

L'arte di arrangiarsi

In the final analysis, even though Italian life may appear to be chaotic and disorganized, there are very strict rules under the surface.

> Perhaps the most remarkable of Italy's informal institutions is what is defined as the *l'arte di arrangiarsi*, or the art of making do. This seemingly simple ability has been developed by the Italians over the centuries into a fine art. It explains their ability to cope as a nation in the face of conditions—the crime-ridden south, an appalling transport and postal system, and the highest level of national indebtedness in western Europe—which would have crushed any other community.
>
> (Hallenstein, 1991, page 124)

It also explains how Italian industry, despite its apparent lack of planning, is one of the most inventive in the world. Virtually nothing of importance is done according to the book. The Italians invented accountancy and, as Mole tells us, 'have remained creative with their accountancy ever since!' They have also, and perhaps more significantly, played a leading role in developing a new form of business and social institution, which is heralding what has been termed a second industrial divide!

Craft based production

THE SECOND INDUSTRIAL DIVIDE

In 1984 Piore and Sabel, two professors of economic history at MIT in Boston, Massachusetts, wrote their seminal work *The Second Industrial Divide*. Their claim, like that of Inzerelli at Erasmus (see Chapter 12), is that the deterioration in economic performance in America is due to the fact that its industrial development is founded on mass production. They argue, therefore, that the technologies and operating procedures of most modern corporations, together with the forms of labour market control defended by many labour movements, must change. Similarly, the instruments of macroeconomic control developed by bureaucrats, administrators and economists in the welfare states and the rules of the international monetary and trading systems established immediately after the Second World War must be radically altered: 'All must be modified, perhaps even discarded, if the chronic economic diseases of our time are to be cured' (Piore and Sabel, 1984, page 4).

In their view the first industrial divide came in the nineteenth century. At that time the emergence of mass production technologies, initially in Britain and then in the United States, limited the growth of less rigid manufacturing technologies, which existed primarily in various regions of Western Europe. These less rigid manufacturing technologies were craft systems. In the most advanced ones skilled workers used sophisticated general-purpose machinery to produce a wide and constantly changing assortment of goods for large but constantly shifting markets.

Best of both worlds

Yet mass production has, Piore and Sabel maintain, always necessitated its mirror image, craft production. During the high noon of mass production, craft production was used by firms operating in markets too narrow and fluctuating to recoup the specialized use of resources of mass production. Craft production supplied luxury goods and experimental products. It provided the specialized equipment used in mass production and the standardized goods for which the demand was too unstable to make the use of dedicated equipment profitable. Craft production thus appeared either as a residual category, taking up the markets rejected by mass production, or as a limit on the pace of the introduction of mass production. Yet, in the 1990s, such 'reborne' craft production heralds the 'second industrial divide'.

Integrated producers today have tailored their setups to exploit possible combinations of craft and mass production. Computerized process control equipment, for example, allows firms to regulate the carbon content of steel more precisely and to add a sequence of different alloys without interrupting the flow of production. New factories are being designed to manufacture a diversity of products, using a wide range of starting materials. The institutional environment required to support them, as history shows, is very different from the one required to support mass production.

Familiasm and municipalism

Three support systems, in fact, according to Piore and Sabel, can be distinguished for encouraging permanent innovation through the reshuffling of resources. These were *municipalism, welfare capitalism* or paternalism and an entrepreneurial use of kin relations that Piore and Sabel call *familiasm*. Any given industry might move from one system to the other as it adopted new technologies and entered new markets. Municipalism, first, involved guaranteeing the mobility of resources by protecting the firms against paralysing shocks from the market and by providing access to skills and knowledge that the firms lacked. Second, welfare capitalism involved the industrialists in creating an extraordinary network of social institutions. There were schools for mechanized weaving and spinning, an Ecole Supérieure de Commerce in France, a savings society, and a society for maternity care. Familiasm, finally, the *système motte* (named after Alfred Motte of Roubaix, France) was to pair each family member who had come of age with an experienced technician from one of the family's firms. These two were provided with start-up capital, after which they established together a company that specialized in one of the phases of production that was still needed. Contemporary versions of each of these support systems are most likely to be found in central Italy, and to a lesser extent in southern Germany. Central Italy's textile industry is a particularly suitable case in point.

The case of central Italy

The most mature of the mature industries is textiles. Between 1966 and 1976 employment in the Western European textile industry was declining by about 25 per cent in France and West Germany and by more than 35 per cent in Britain. But employment in Pratese textiles remained steady and exports boomed. Prato's success rested on two factors: a long-term shift from standardized to fashionable products and a corresponding reorganization of production. This involved a move from large integrated mills to technologically sophisticated shops, specializing in various phases of production. With constant experimentation on the finishing of cloth the Pratese achieved a variety of textures and finishes that gave products 'born poor' the appearance of luxury.

While these small shops were springing up they needed to be formed into a network. To combine them into a flexible production system became, from the late 1950s, the function of the *impannatore*, a descendant of the early modern *Verleger* (putter-out). The *impannatore* became a designer, responsible for shaping and responding to fashion, as well as for organizing production, also urging firms to experiment with materials and processes:

> More significantly, the local banks, the trade unions, and artists and industrialists' associations collaborated in a vast project. They began to devise computer based technologies to increase the flexibility of the links among the firms, as well as the efficiency of each production unit. The expectation was that technology could be suited to the region's vocation as a collective specialist rather than adapting regional structures to the technology used in advanced mass production firms.
>
> (Piore and Sabel, 1984, page 135)

Four coincident factors were crucial in the Italian case. These included the Italian extended family, the view of artisan work as a distinct type of economic activity, and the existence of merchant traditions connecting the Italian provinces to world markets. Finally, municipal and regional governments were often allied to the labour movement, to help create the infrastructure that the firms required but could not themselves provide.

The story of Prato textiles can be retold, in Italy, for many industries. There is the mini steel mill of Brescia; the ceramic building materials industry of Sassuolo; the high-fashion silk industry of Como; the farm-machine industry of Reggio-Emilia; and the special machinery and motorcycle industry of Bologna. That is why central Italy has today taken the lead in Europe in reversing the trend towards mass production.

Community and flexibility

In introducing us to the concept of flexible specialization Piore and Sabel have cited past examples of regional conglomeration in Italy, Germany, France and Spain. Each of the industrial districts therein was composed of a core of more or less equally small enterprises bound in a complex web of competition and cooperation. Trade associations, trade unions, guilds, purchasing cooperatives, cooperative marketing all prevailed. But no single institution formally linked the productive units. The cohesion of the industry rested on a sense of community; ethnic, political or religious.

Flexible specialization therefore works by violating one of the key assumptions of classical political economy: that the economy is separate from society. Markets and hierarchies are the two categories that dominate contemporary theory and practical reflection in the organization of industry. Both presuppose the firm to be an independent entity. In market models, the firm is linked by exchange relations to other units. In hierarchy models, it is so autonomous as almost to constitute an industry in itself. By contrast, in flexible specialization it is hard to tell where society ends and economic organization begins. Among the ironies of the resurgence of craft production is that its deployment of modern technology depends on its reinvigoration of affiliations that are associated with the pre-industrial past.

Flexible specialization requires a fusion of competition and cooperation that cannot occur in the market model, where economy is distinct from society and firms are independent competitive units. In contrast, within a system of flexible specialization, firms depend on one another for the sharing of skills, technical knowledge, information on opportunities and information on standards: 'Structure shades into infrastructure, competition into cooperation and economy into society' (Piore and Sabel, 1984, page 216) Interestingly enough, according to Piore and Sabel, large firms in mature industries, like IBM, are trying to transform themselves from self-contained corporate communities into organizational centres of industrial districts. They are doing so by moving towards Just-in-Time production systems, which blur the distinction between internal and external suppliers while encouraging the spatial concentration of production.

Today, in parts of Europe as in Japan, federated enterprises hold one another's stocks and have interlocking boards of directors. Frequently, the managers of a going enterprise in the federation are despatched to serve in a new one. Sometimes the firms share financial and marketing facilities. But the group is not as integrated as the mass production corporations, and member firms are not hierarchically arranged.

Despite their large size, the modern 'solar' and workshop firms frequently treat external suppliers as collaborators. Subcontractors retain considerable autonomy; and unlike the mass producer, the solar firm depends on subcontractors for advice in solving design and production problems. These firms are large and central enough to their respective industries to supply internally many of the services that in a regional conglomeration would be supplied by the community. But firms in this category often cooperate with community institutions (for example, in research, education and welfare).

PRODUCTIVE KNOWLEDGE

In mass production the central problem is stabilizing and extending the market. Once this is done the corporation as a self-contained unit has the interest and capacity to advance the division of labour through the simplification of tasks. This requires the creation of special-purpose machines, thereby lowering production costs and setting the stage for further growth. In a system of flexible specialization, in contrast, the problem of organizing innovation merely begins with the creation of a market. Because its product only appeals to a limited number of customers there is no presumption that cuts in production costs will substantially increase the market. In fact, the very fluidity of the resources that makes the system flexible paradoxically also makes it necessary to create institutions that facilitate cooperation. Three such examples predominate.

Mass production's entire division of labour routinizes and therefore, for Piore and Sabel, trivializes work to a degree that often degrades the people who perform it. In contrast, flexible specialization is predicated on cooperation. Moreover, the frequent changes in the production process put a premium on craft skills. Thus the production worker's intellectual participation in the work process is enhanced and his or her role revitalized. Moreover, craft production depends on solidarity and communitarianism. Production workers must be so broadly skilled that they can shift rapidly from one job to another; even more important, they must be able to collaborate with designers to solve the problems that inevitably arise in execution. Such craft workers are bred, not born. Moreover, the formation of their identity as persons is bound up first, with their admittance into a group of workers and second, with their mastery of productive knowledge.

Towards European integration

THE HUMANISTIC TRAJECTORY
The journey from patriarchal family business, based upon primal family bonds, to flexible specialization, underpinned by Piore and Sabel's complex relationships, is a long one. It is indeed a long stretch from Danco's family patriarch—whose human concerns are confined within his own extended family—via central Italy, to Mondragon's Father Arizmendi—whose humanistic concerns reached out to the whole of the Spanish Basque country.

However, each shares common ground. In all three cases there is an identifiable and localized community—in the first case an extended family, in the second a Prato type district, and in the third the Mondragon region of northern Spain. In each situation, moreover, competition and cooperation are locally juxtaposed. Interestingly enough, of course, as the humanistic orientation deepens and broadens, so both the geographical and psychological scopes of the managerial undertaking are extended. In geographical terms, quite evidently, there is a development from a single family, like Danco's, to an entire community, like

Mondragon's. In psychological terms, Danco's fundamentally patriarchal, Zeus-like enterprise is transformed by Piore and Sabel into a matriarchal, communally based organization.

THE UNCOMPLETED EUROPEAN JOURNEY

At the same time, we have come a long way on this European journey, from the self-interested universe of Adam Smith to the socially centred world of Father Arizmendi. Yet, paradoxically enough, while Smith was the armchair philosopher, Arizmendi was a man of business affairs!

In the final analysis, though, Arizmendi kept himself apart from the specific running of the individual firms. For he had not worked out a way of integrating himself-as-manager with the human society around him. In other words, he had failed to undergo the complete learning cycle.

ALMOST COMPLETING THE EUROPEAN JOURNEY

For the complete journey, European management has its inner and outer dimensions. Inwardly, the individual manager has to journey through him- or herself, that is, through sensing, thinking, intuiting and feeling. That inner journey will be reinforced by a strong exposure to those four cultural and philosophical world views—pragmatic, rational, wholistic and humanistic—in which those psychological types are strongly and respectively rooted. Moreover, unless such an exposure in each case includes elements of active experimentation, abstract conceptualization, reflective observation and practical experience, the learning will be incomplete.

In addition, and from a managerial perspective, the completeness of the outer journey will be predetermined not only by the nature of the exposure but also by the scope. In other words, in a pragmatic context it will be of most benefit to be exposed to an individual enterprise. In a rational one it will be most fruitful to position oneself at the interface between a public and private organization. In a wholistic context the structure and dynamics of all participants in an industrial constellation would be of the essence. Finally, in a humanistic setting one would want to learn from an entire socio-economic network. We now need to turn, before concluding our journey, to the specific managerial attributes of the 'convivial' manager.

Summary

CONVIVIAL INSTITUTIONAL FRAMEWORKS

Family affiliation
- The extended family lies at the heart of the convivial economy and society.

- The convivial community, by extension, is a matrix of interests and loyalties, horizontally divided into regions and vertically into factions.
- Affiliation to at least one faction or interest group—be it a political party, a trade union, the Masonic lodge or the Mafia—is essential.
- Such affiliation, and the rights and obligations that go with it, replaces what passes for wider social awareness in other kinds of societies.

Craft production
- While mass production has dominated in individualistically competitive and rationally coordinated societies, craft production has held its own in convivial ones.
- In craft production the worker embeds his or her knowledge in ever more varied products.
- Alongside this convivial form of production, familiasm, municipalism and welfare capitalism come into their own, serving to protect firms against paralysing shocks, providing access to skills, and creating a network of supportive social and educational institutions.

Convivial banking
- In a convivial society the family is the substitute for the state, as the only institution that can be trusted and relied upon.
- The family in Italy has become the largest bank, with each one combining together four or five incomes and providing interest-free loans.
- Government is viewed as a group of separate cliques each working for its own members, not for the common good.
- The payment of taxes is viewed as an exaction to be evaded rather than as a duty of the community.

CONVIVIAL MANAGEMENT CONCEPTS

Flexible specialization without
- Flexible specialization works by violating one of the key assumptions of classical political economy—that the economy is separate from society.
- In market models, the firm is linked by exchange relations to other units; in hierarchy models, the firm is so autonomous as almost to constitute an industry.
- In contrast, flexible specialization depends on its reinvigoration of affiliations that are associated with the pre-industrial past.
- It is therefore hard to tell where society ends and where economic organization begins.

Flexible specialization within

- Whereas mass production's entire division of labour reduces work to a mere routine, often degrading the people who perform it, flexible specialization is predicated on cooperation.
- The frequent changes in the production process put a premium on craft skills, enhancing the production worker's intellectual participation in the work process.
- Production workers must be so broadly skilled that they can shift rapidly from one job to another, collaborating with designers to solve problems that arise in execution.
- Such craft workers are bred, not born, through their admittance into a group of workers, on the one hand, and their mastery of productive knowledge, on the other.

16

Artist and politician: the convivial European manager

The experiential manager seeks in thought a practical result. The rational manager seeks in action an intellectual outcome. The developmental manager intuitively pursues an idea. The convivial manager seeks in action and thought a result in terms of passion, that is, direct experience of and through people and things. Such a passionate quality, which smacks of good company, good friendship, good food and good wine, was converted by the European cleric and radical social philosopher, Ivan Illich (1972) into his 'tools for conviviality' in the 1960s. Such 'convivial' technology, as opposed to mass production is, in Illich's terms, intrinsically social, as is convivial management in our own context here. At his or her best, then, the convivial manager is a social artist as well as a cultivated politician (Fig. 16.1).

For such 'convivial' managers, moreover, their point of reference will be neither the individual nor the organization but, in fact, the extended family, or community. Such a family will be represented by either a patriarch or a matriarch, an 'impresario' or an 'impannatore'. Its managers will be politically cultivated and socially artistic.

Personal and familial

POLITICALLY CULTIVATED

Therefore while rational management behaviour is subject to intellectually based principles, in convivial management the moving forces are not principles but personalities and communities. The Italian or the Spaniard is held by the vicissitudes of continual battles for power. Political allegiance is more personal and familial than objective and institutional. Standards of ethics principally apply to personal and social relationships, the inverse of more rationally based cultures where civic responsibility outweighs personal morality:

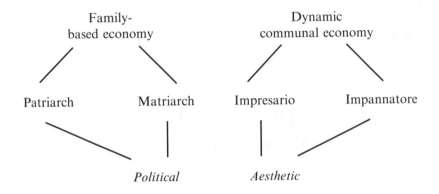

Fig. 16.1 The fruits of managerial humanism

> Whereas, then, at first sight the political structures of western European countries are the same as democracies organized under a parliamentary system, in reality they are as different as the national characters would lead us to expect. In England political institutions are the outcome of a pragmatic evolution. In France they resulted from a constitution carefully planned beforehand. In Italy politics is in a plastic state.
>
> (de Madariaga, 1922, page 74)

The key word in describing the Italian managerial approach, for Mole (1991), is flexibility. The disorganization apparent to someone from a more rational background is therefore often illusory. Flexibility, for the convivial manager, means concentrating on what is essential to get a job done without getting bogged down in principle. There is a strong, temperamental aversion to planning among such managers. They thrive on ambiguity and risk, duly exploiting a market niche without waiting for an in-depth analysis. This view of Mole's runs counter to Hofstede's (1991) 'Latin' perspective.

'DIETROLOGIA'—THE STAGE FOR MEETING

In a convivial setting communication channels are invariably complicated. Informal contacts are vital in every aspect of convivial life, and information is one of them:

> There is never a shortage of opinion but facts are usually in short supply. They are secretively guarded and traded on a transactional basis. The word 'dietrologia' sums up the belief that behind every event there are powerful personalities or organizations manipulating everything. Things get done without apparent reason.
>
> (Mole, 1991, page 60)

In formal meetings, moreover, decisions taken and agreed may not ever be implemented. It may never be clear, in fact, why a meeting has been called in the first place. Sometimes it feels they are merely social gatherings to reinforce a sense of togetherness. You may get the impression, according to Mole, that nothing is happening or a dozen things at once:

> A meeting is often a stage for exhibiting eloquence and is consequently a free-for-all of opinions, comments and ideas. Everyone is entitled to make an opinion, is listened to and apparently agreed with. The weight of the idea resides not in the idea itself but in the importance and influence of the speaker. The purpose of meetings, moreover, is to evaluate the mood of others, to sense supporters and test the water, not to make decisions.
>
> (Mole, 1991, page 59)

Formal presentations, moreover, are seldom called upon.

Opinions must not be imposed but must be agreed to. While people will not publicly go out on a limb to fight for a minority view, they will not submit to a majority decision. They will abandon the group or undermine its work from the inside. The guiding principle is not to offend the 'dignità' of a dissident but give him or her time to change their opinion and save face. If there are signs of entrenched positions the skilled chairperson will often adjourn the meeting. When it is reconvened, after some subtle lobbying, the objections will have disappeared.

SOCIAL ARTISTRY

Talent for improvisation

In contrast to the pragmatists, most particularly, the humanists have an aesthetic attitude. In de Madariaga's opinion, this attitude is 'natural, spontaneous, innate and general'. Hence the exceptional wealth of popular art and industrial design, in different degrees, according to local climate, occupation and economic conditions.

Convivial managers, therefore, are receptive to fresh ideas, new solutions, inventiveness and imagination. They have a talent for improvising solutions, and will cooperate with others as long as they get a chance to demonstrate their own skills. We have seen, de Madariaga tells us, the pragmatist taking from the object of which he or she thinks all that is useful at the moment. The rationalist looks at the object systematically with initiative and premeditation. The humanist, in his or her turn, thinks by contemplation:

He waits in an apparent passivity for the object to reveal itself to him. He lets the stream of life pass through him until chance will suddenly imbue it with new light. In intuition the object contemplated reveals itself all at once in its essence, with all its connections and all the connections which attach it to the rest of life.

(de Madariaga, 1922, page 49)

'Bella figura'

For the convivial manager being a cultivated artist is not a social grace but a social necessity: 'The most mundane conversations amongst managers are peppered with references to sources ranging from Aristotle to Umberto Eco, Adam Smith to John Kenneth Galbraith' (Mole, 1991, page 62). Making a good impression matters deeply. The excellence of taste and design are an expression of the Italian desire to make a 'bella figura'. This is not superficial. It extends to the kind of conversation you make, the kind of person you are. While role playing comes naturally to most Italians they are equally adept at sensing if there is a solid base of competence behind the facade. The high quality of engineering and design does not come from mere networking skills. The status of technical people, alongside artists, is consistently high. Italians, moreover, generally feel they can do a job better than their bosses and do not readily take instructions unless they feel a personal commitment to what they have to do. But once such commitment is obtained, de Madariaga indicates, the energy, flair and creativity applied to execution will be extraordinary:

It is precisely when he is most egotistical that the humanist is most universal. He seeks universality without meaning to do so. For his egotism functions precisely in letting the life stream pass through him, in all its spontaneity and integrity.

(de Madariaga, 1922, page 54)

From patriarchy to patrimonial; from matriarchy to cooperative

In more conventional terms Italian or 'Latin' managers, as differentiated from the more rational Belgian and French, could be labelled as either patriarchal or matriarchal. Whereas the former are characterized by the private enterprise and the latter by the cooperative, the State bureaucracy has no convivial basis for its operations. Hence, as de Madariaga emphasizes, its manifest distance from the people:

The individual philosophy of the man of passion implies a nature rebellious to the chain of collective life. Such collective life is seen by the humanist as the connecting of individual lives to a system of gears. In such a gear only a small sector of each wheel is actually connected at every moment, and playing an active role, while the man of passion is at every moment present with his whole self wherever he is.

(1992, page 47)

Such a convivial manager lives and works in an intensely social world. Whether the question at issue is a trivial affair or the most important business, a person-to-person relationship is indispensable, de Madariaga maintains, if results are to be achieved.

THE PATRIARCHAL MANAGER

For Leon Danco, to whom we were introduced in the previous chapter, the founder-patriarch chooses his business associates out of the limited group of people he knows. He puts a relative into sales because it sounded a good idea after a few glasses of wine together. He picks his partners from among the extended family because he needs people to keep the books straight or to contribute cash. He gathers his employees through desperation or fantasy, a distant cousin here, a sister-in-law there, the only way he can cajole anyone to join a struggling, marginal business. Add to this recruitment roulette, Danco maintains, the fact that most founders have not the slightest idea what kinds of skills they are going to need in the people they bring to the company, and you end up with a very explosive personnel policy.

While 'papa' ploughs through the early years of the business stamping out one brushfire after another, 'mama' has to watch from the sidelines as he drains the bank account, mortgages the house and borrows on the insurance. The business founder, therefore, needs much more than his spouse's understanding, and possibly her active participation: 'The help he really needs is someone to talk to, someone with whom he can share his worries; someone who can appreciate his victories and understand the nature of his coming battles' (Danco, 1976, page 33).

What may hurt most is that 'mama' is unable to help her husband other than to act as a sounding board for his great ideas, an audience for his victories and a repository for his complaints. His dreams, his frustrations, his defeats, his fears he keeps to himself because he does not want to burden her.

The kids grow up with 'mama' and what picture they get of 'papa' comes mostly from her:

> The image he gives them is one of an absentee relative who drops into their lives on his way to or from elsewhere. When he is around, he makes them feel inadequate. I often wonder how many of the sports cars on the road are actual guilt offerings from dads to their neglected kids.

(Danco, 1976, page 37)

Meanwhile, the founder's dream is to be someone, to be able to point to something he built, and to be remembered with love by those who follow. Therein lies a paradox. The founder in fact has two personalities. From his employees, as from his family, he demands compliance, flexibility, pliability. As the same time, he will do anything in the world to placate a customer.

The lines of authority on the chart of the average family business, according to Danco, tend to take two basic forms. The first is what he terms the *spider* form, where the boss sits in the middle of a series of radiating lines. The trademark of the spider organization is that none of the lines of authority touch or cross each other. There are no meetings. Everyone, other than the boss, hangs immobile and solitary in the web, awaiting his or her summons in a state of suspended animation.

The second common form is what Danco calls the *rake*. At the top is the boss. Way down at the bottom are the helpers, usually all spread out at the same level: 'In between, somewhere in the system, you can bet there's the little old lady with the moustache who's hiding the books' (Danco, 1976, page 91). The business owner, surrounded by people in various relationships, must contend not only with his or her managers, suppliers, competitors and customers but also with the family. Family business is a process involving complex relationships among many people.

According to John Mole (1991), moreover, this kind of personalized, convivial structure repeats itself within the higher echelons of the large-scale organization in Italy or in Spain:

> In the large companies a conventional hierarchy in the sense of clear reporting lines is only to be found at the lower levels of the organization. At the middle to upper levels the true hierarchies are built on personal alliances (page 55)

that is, between people in the organization who trust each other and rely on each other to get things done. Formal appraisal, therefore, is very difficult for either side to manage, as is any direct criticism, unless it is in the context of a direct, personalized relationship.

The transfer of economic control in a convivial setting, from personalized ownership to rational management, commercially and psychologically as well as economically or politically, has not yet occurred. In fact, perhaps, it should never occur in anything more than a partial sense.

The very large private firms in Italy and Spain, therefore, as a continuation of the patriarchal line, remain under the domination of a few, well-organized financial groups. They can usually be pinpointed to specific individuals, while the State enterprise is subject to the control of political groups. In both cases, just as in the family-run firm, managers—with duly subdued rationality—are often excluded from long-term decisions, which are therefore made on an emotional and intuitive basis.

The matriarchal manager is less visible an influence than his or her patriarchal counterpart in Europe. Perhaps this is because the relatively fertile humanistic grounds in Italy and Spain are more masculine in character than the less fertile (in this convivial respect) but more feminine, Nordic ones. Nevertheless, cooperative enterprise in southern Europe is of a matriarchal character and is relatively widespread.

The Italian cooperative movement is the biggest, by far, in Western Europe, and the most diverse (Holmstrom, 1989, page 21). Like the socio-economic network that has given birth to flexible specialization, so also the cooperatives help one another, formally through consortia and informally through the mediation of the regional cooperative movement. Coopcam of Bologna, a typical cooperative was founded in 1945 by workers who loaded, unloaded and cleaned trains. The founding-president, who was still in office in 1979, canvassed local authorities and found there was a market for installing and servicing street lights. Coopcam made little or no distinction between management roles and elective or 'political' ones. The president performed both. Indeed, in the early days the cooperatives were suspicious of any form of specialized management, since the only sort they knew was the hierarchical management of conventional firms. The point of the cooperative was to avoid this. By the 1950s, however, the cooperatives were too large to be managed in this *ad hoc* way. The work became more complex, especially in the new manufacturing firms and in the building industry.

By a series of new initiatives and mergers with smaller cooperatives, Coopcam took on various other manufacturing and services activities:

> The relation between the member and the enterprise was no longer the idyllic, romantic one that existed in the traditional, small co-op. It is now mediated and filtered through various institutions: the members section, the workplace assembly, the departmental assembly. What unifies the people is common ownership of the enterprise and the formal equality of the members; what divides them is the difference in level of professional skill, culture and real power.
>
> (De Santis, 1980, page 36)

Although this communal approach to business is more clearly associated with cooperative than with private enterprise it has its more generic roots set deep within humanistic grounds.

Humanistic grounds for cooperation

Humanistically oriented business relationships, as we have already indicated, are based on mutual dependence. This sense of mutual obligation is most easily satisfied with members of the extended family. A purely salary-based contractual relationship, characteristic of pragmatically based cultures, is not enough:

> Once a relationship has been established, based on a common purpose where everyone will visibly profit, there will be total cooperation and commitment. If the relationship has not been created colleagues will be highly competitive to the point of undermining each other.
>
> (Mole, 1991, page 59)

Humanism, as a philosophical force, and conviviality, as a managerial one, thereby exercises a 'plastic and political' influence. For Derossi, then, the concept of

> the corporation as a public institution is more advanced in Italy than in most developed countries, and the public and social control over corporate decisions is stronger. Political and social control over the firm in Italy does not appear to be so much the result of industrialisation as of processes taking place in the entire society and within economic institutions.
>
> (Derossi, 1984, page 182)

The humanist trajectory

OVERALL BREAKDOWN

The 'humanist' trajectory, through which a communal consciousness expresses itself in convivial, managerial form, is the least actualized of the four European domains that we have investigated. In effect, this trajectory is distinctively southern as opposed to western, northern or eastern in character. It reflects the passionate, communal people of not only Italy, Spain, and Portugal but also of much of Africa and Latin America. Unfortunately, the antipathy that such peoples feel towards rationalized structures has given rise to oppressively personalized forms of economic and political authority. Familial conviviality, close to home, has been supplanted by corrupt bureaucracy, at large.

BREAKTHROUGH IN CENTRAL ITALY

The one evident breakthrough has been in central Italy. There a fertile combination of patriarchal personality and matriarchal community has given rise to flexible specialization. Flourishing, family-based private companies co-exist with proliferating cooperative enterprises, most particularly in Emilia-Romagna. Individuality and community are juxtaposed in many different commercial and social contexts.

Seemingly, central Italy, like the Mondragon region of Spain, is well positioned between the rationality of the north and the humanism of the south. In the same way it is poised midway between patriarchal and matriarchal forms of behaviour. As such, conviviality comes into its own as an appropriately rational as well as emotionally binding approach to management.

The notion of family is truly extended, in the case of a Benetton in Italy or an Arizmendi in Spain, to richness of the product line, to the diversified marketplace and to the intricacy of organization. Cultivated political behaviour and social artistry is used to good rather than to ill effect, as form is aligned with function.

ABSENT CONVIVIALITY

Because conviviality, in the guise of the 'political and plastic artistry' to which Alberti originally referred, has never been conceptualized as a business or organizational form, students of management have been bereft of its influence. While experientially based managers, as we have seen, have Reg Revans to draw on, the rationally oriented have Elliot Jaques and the developmentally inclined have Bernard Lievegoed, the humanists draw a blank.

Whereas today we have the so-called 'humanistic psychology' of the Armenian American, Abraham Maslow (1964) and of the Italian, Roberto Assagioli (1974), to draw upon, both of their sets of concepts are 'over-psychological' and 'under-plastic/political'! In fact the people side of management has been most heavily influenced, until now, by the experientially based Anglo-Saxons and the developmentally oriented Japanese, with a small dose of rationality to add to the mix. Is it not now the time for us to turn towards the south, for a newly-to-be-discovered convivial manager, who would play his or her part in correcting the current North–South European, and global, imbalance? We now turn, by way of conclusion, from national to corporate, industrial and professionally based cultures.

Summary

CONVIVIAL MANAGERIAL ATTITUDES

Familial respect
- Managers are expected to make decisions paternalistically or maternalistically, in both cases with a protective outlook, conveyed as alternately domineering or nurturing.

- A close interest, in the form of either supervision or counselling, is welcomed by employees.
- Employees avoid outright disagreement with the boss, whereby the sense of mutual obligation and response would be torn asunder.
- People only trust others 'in the family'.

Security valued
- Direct conflict and competition is to be avoided within the family while being encouraged without.
- While creativity is valued insofar as it enhances family values, deviance from the familial norms is threatening.
- There is a concern with security, at both an economic and an emotional level;
- The convivial manager searches for absolute quality rather than quality that is relative to customer requirements.

CONVIVIAL MANAGERIAL BEHAVIOUR

Patriarchal and matriarchal
- A person-to-person relationship is indispensable to doing business.
- Co-workers are selected from the extended family or the adjacent faction/interest group.
- Conventional hierarchy is to be found only at lower levels or organization—above are patriarchs or matriarchs sitting in the middle of a series of radiating lines.
- Large private firms remain under the domination of a few, well-organized financial groups, controlled by individuals, while public enterprise is subject to political control.

Matriarchal and patriarchal
- Convivial enterprise is cooperatively based, personally and communally, whereas so-called 'cooperative' management involves transpersonal and systemic collaboration.
- Such matriarchal conviviality—of the personal and communal variety—supplants hierarchy, as well as any distinction between managerial and elective roles.
- What thereby unifies people is not individual power and authority but common ownership of the enterprise, and felt—as well as legalized—equality.
- Once such a relationship of familial equality is established there is likely to be total commitment.

Politically cultivated

- Political allegiance is more personal and familial than objective and institutional—standards of ethics principally apply to individual and social relationships.
- Convivial strategy formulation, in this political context, involves plasticity and flexibility, there being strong temperamental objection to formalized planning.
- Behind every move is a powerful personality or communal connection—the weight of an idea resides not in the idea itself but in the importance and influence of the speaker.
- Opinions must not be imposed but agreed to, the guiding principle being not to offend the 'dignità' of a dissident.

Social artistry

- An aesthetic attitude comes naturally, spontaneously, innately and generally to the convivial personality, whether in Italy or Spain, southern France or Portugal.
- Convivial managers are generally receptive to fresh ideas, new solutions, inventiveness and imagination.
- A meeting is a stage for exhibiting eloquence, and a free-for-all, to express opinions and ideas, and role playing comes naturally.
- Being a cultivated managerial artist, then, is not a social grace but a necessity—excellence of taste and design is an expression of the desire to make a 'bella figura'.

Part VI

Conclusion

17

A generic typology of cultures

The major focus of this book has been upon national or ethnically based as opposed to 'corporate', 'industry' or even 'professional' culture. Yet, as every practitioner knows, the influence of a particular company, be it Philips or Olivetti; a particular industry, be it chemicals or fast foods; or a particular profession, be it engineering or catering, will be a major influence over the way things are done. As a result, for example, if an accountant is working for Fiat within the automobile industry in northern Italy he or she will be lodged in four respectively professional, corporate, sectoral and national cultures.

Fortunately there is a way of cross-correlating them all. Specifically, and in turn, as indicated below, 'westernness', 'northernness', 'easternness' and 'southernness' can be applied to professional, corporate and sectoral cultures (see Appendices 1 and 2 at the end of Chapter 18 and Table 17.1), whereas:

- The west's *business* transactions create a *commercial* culture
- The north's *managerial* order forms a *bureaucratic* culture
- The east's *system* of work produces an *industrial* culture
- The south's *service* relations animate a *familial* culture

Table 17.1 The four worlds

	Sphere	*Form*	*Substance*
1	Western	Individual transaction	Commercial
2	Northern	Organizational order	Bureaucratic
3	Eastern	Technical system	Industrial
4	Southern	Social	Familial

Table 17.2   Comparative cultures

Commercial	Administrative	Industrial	Familial
Bias for action	Productive work	Work ethic	Working together
Enthusiasm for results	Enthusiasm for objectives	Enthusiasm for *Technik*	Enthusiasm for people
Action planning	Cognitive orientation	Work discipline	Group mind
Entrepreneurial flair	Strategic planning	Quality circles	Shared values
Commercial improvisation	Organizational coordination	Technical association	Social affiliation
Salesmanship	Management control	Production process	Personnel
Short-term outlook	Long-term forecasting	Long-term outlook	Management as an art form

COMPARATIVE BEHAVIOUR

The comparative behaviour of enterprises in these respectively businesslike, managerial, work-oriented and communal cultures is illustrated—in summary terms—in Table 17.2.

We can now visit each of these worlds, in turn, paying particular attention to the prevailing images, ideas, frameworks and attributes. Having thereby oriented ourselves towards each world, we can then pay attention to the national, sectoral, corporate and professional cultures that prevail within them. Finally, it is important to stress that our focus here is on cultural attributes that are not only richly engrained but have also become distinctively incorporated into a specific field. Such purposeful incorporation, for example, has not yet taken place in the developing countries, where an explicitly articulated Bangladeshi or Zimbabwean business or economic way has not so far become manifest.

World 1: Commercial—Westernness

PRAGMATIC   TRADING
COMPETITIVE   ENTREPRENEURIAL

Commercial 'world 1', which we call typically 'western', is pragmatic in national outlook, trading in sectoral orientation, competitive in corporate culture and entrepreneurial in professional approach. The underlying western image, moreover, is that of an island race.

ORIENTATION

Image
The archetype of 'world 1' at a national level is the pragmatic island race, both insular and warlike, self-seeking and self-reliant. A sectoral

archetype would be a commercially based trading company, living on its wits, thereby trading off opportunities. A corporate archetype would be the competitive Hanson Trust, that Anglo-American industrial conglomerate, wheeling and dealing forever and a day. An individual archetype, finally, is Ross Perot who, having made his millions from his own entrepreneurship, fought (but without success) his lone battle against all odds to become President of the United States.

The overall image of 'westernness' is of a field of play. The traditional image of a *battlefield*, which still prevails today, is one in which you shoot or get shot, you conquer or are conquered, you gain or lose territory, you outmanoeuvre the enemy or lose your own ground. The contemporary sporting image, usually that of a competitive baseball or football *game*, contains its proverbial *winner or loser*, its first base and its home run, its own goals and its long shots. In both military and sporting analogies, moreover, there is the image of the *hero*, that is, an individual standing out against the odds. In the EC context, for example, the image of a level playing field has predominated in the Anglo-Saxon mind, within which individual countries can battle it out for victory.

Idea
The general philosophy underlying the competitive field of play is that of empiricism and, together with it, *pragmatism* and *utilitarianism*. The general idea is that what counts is what works, what is worth while is what is useful. Furthermore, *seeing is believing*, and action speaks much louder than words. *Common sense* transcends analytical prowess or 'self-indulgent' feeling. Intuition is only valid if it can be converted from something remote and esoteric into an *everyday hunch*.

The differentiated *factors of* economic *production* are deemed to be land, labour and capital, and the integrating one is enterprise. The factors are considered to be *freely tradable*, at the right price, and are required to be eminently mobile. At the same time, the freedom to *hire and fire*, to acquire and dispose of physical, financial and human assets is sacrosanct. Furthermore, *each* sector of the economy—commercial, industrial and governmental—makes its own *separate* way. As a result, the upholders of labour and capital are pitted politically against one another, both within and without the enterprise.

Framework
The 'macro' frame of reference is that of the market. Such a marketplace is dominated by the *exchange* of goods or services, knowledge or favours. Everything, or every person, has its price and life and work is an ongoing *transaction* between one person and another, governed by implicit or explicit *contract*. In such a world, be it based in Wall Street or in the City

of London, the *deal* is what matters, sometimes even more than the actual matter at hand.

The 'micro' frame of reference is the enterprise. Such an enterprise stands alone, pitting itself against its environment, and only the *fittest* shall *survive*. It is in that sense that Britain, or Lloyd's, remains a nation or a corporation of *individual shopkeepers* or solo names. *Lines of influence* radiate out from the entrepreneurial centre, and these supplant any functionally or structurally ordered hierarchies of command. This is typical, for example, of a youthfully aggressive salesforce. Each individual or enterprise paddles their own canoe. *Every* man is an island!

Attributes

'Western' behaviour is typically *business* oriented, and entrepreneurial. A bias for *action* is accompanied by enthusiasm for *results*. Action *planning* is coupled with *entrepreneurial* flair. A capacity for commercial *improvisation* goes together with *sales*manship. Finally, such business oriented managers possess a characteristically *short-term* outlook.

The *individual 'world 1' need to achieve* has been identified as a driving force for such business executives, who therefore stand out from the crowd, strive to be number one, and exert their will and influence on others. Such a drive has been attributed to *personal insecurity*, to the *Protestant ethic*, and to the *desire to be free* from the constraints of the political, social or economic establishment.

CATEGORIZATION

Pragmatic spheres

The world of business generally, more so than those of politics and economics, art and science, lends itself to pragmatism. The art of the possible, often associated with political life, is even more characteristic of commercial activity around the world. That having been said, the Anglo-Saxon world—inclusive of Australasia, Britain, North America—is the most culturally inclined to be empirical. At the same time, the Dutch and the Scandinavians have strong pragmatic tendencies while also being influenced by other cultural spheres.

Within business, the phase which particularly lends itself to pragmatically based opportunism is the early, entrepreneurial one, when one's senses need to be the most sharply honed. It is at this point that a 'nation of shopkeepers' flourishes. Within the Anglo-Saxon world the English, in fact, are the most markedly pragmatic. In the United States the prevailing economic empiricism has been mixed with strong doses of organizational rationality and inspirational management. Finally, through the influence of the American business schools, their management literature, and their multinational companies, the pragmatic orientation has been spread across the world.

Trade sectors

Trade, as differentiated from industry, is intrinsic to 'world 1'. The primal market, in fact, is to be found in unfashionable parts of Paris, in the streets of Tangiers, as well as in the City of London. Commercial activity, on a large scale though, stands alongside pragmatic enterprise as a 'western' phenomenon. The trading houses of Hamburg, the *sogo shosha* of Japan, the London Stock Exchange and the market women of Nigeria are variations on the same pragmatically based commercial theme.

Within the company the commercial activities of purchasing and sales—of goods and services, of commodities and properties, of stocks and shares—are inner manifestations of 'westernness'. Pragmatically based opportunism also lends itself to exploration-based industries, in the oil and gas fields, and to agro-business enterprises, extending from developed into developing countries. Finally, within an industry, the advent of counter trade and the need to hedge against fluctuations in exchange rates enhances the role played by commercial activities.

Competitive companies

In their corporate cultures some companies are more single-mindedly competitive than others. Coke and Pepsi in America, the Hanson Trust in Britain and business empires established by such commercial impresarios as Agnelli and De Benedetti in Italy, are prominent cases in point. Such 'macho' or 'work hard–play hard' cultures are renowned for their acquisitiveness and for their commercial (as opposed to social or technical) orientations.

Such competitive companies, finally, are inclined to build up a strong sense of competitiveness within their organizations, as well as without. Harold Geneen at ITT in the 1970s, for example, was renowned for playing off one division against another.

Entrepreneurial professions

Some professions or occupations are innately more entrepreneurial than others. Typically, the unqualified trader, on the one hand, and the gifted amateur, on the other, swell the entrepreneurial ranks. Between these two is the professional salesperson or financier, both of whom may or may not have acquired an accredited training. Self-made people within both their own enterprises and established organizations retain their individualism. The classical scholar becomes an insurance broker, the chartered accountant becomes a commodity broker and the chartered surveyor becomes a property dealer. Inevitably, such individuals are more likely to come into their idiosyncratic own in countries, notably Anglo-Saxon ones, where such individual initiative is encouraged. At the same time, throughout the world intrinsically commercial sectors and highly competitive companies encourage such businesslike behaviour. Things are different in world 2, up north!

World 2: Bureaucratic—Northernness

RATIONAL   ADMINISTRATIVE
COORDINATED ANALYTICAL

Bureaucratic 'world 2', which we term typically 'northern', is rational in its overall cultural outlook, administrative in its sectoral orientation, tightly coordinated in its organizational approach and analytically inclined in its professional attitude. Its guiding image, moreover, is that of 'measure'.

ORIENTATION

Image
The archetype of 'world 2' at a national level is the rational person who must measure, deliberate and calculate, being methodical and analytical. A sectoral archetype would be a mass producer or mass marketer, ranging from an assembly line-based production unit to a supermarketing organization. A corporate archetype would be Alcatel. An individual archetype today might be Jacques Delors, symbol of 'Brussels bureaucracy'.

The overall image of 'northernness' is of a bureaucratic machine. The traditional image of a small *cog in a* large *wheel* still prevails today. Organizational *mechanisms*, reflected in rules and procedures, are accompanied by managerial *instruments* for monitoring and controlling what goes on. Specialization of functions, *standardization* of process and regulation of performance all have a mechanical ring to them.

Idea
The general philosophy underlying the bureaucratic machine is that of rationalism and, together with it, *logical positivism* and *structural-functionalism*. The general idea is that what counts is what can be counted, that is measured or validated in one's mind's eye. Truth lies in

what can be *deduced from first principles* and not in what can be induced from direct experience and observation. *Methodical analysis* therefore surpasses common sense as a prelude to action and *thought precedes action* as a basis for individual and organizational activity.

Physically based land, for the original French Physiocrats, rather than individually *constituted* labour formed the basis for material *wealth*. Subsequently, for the rationalists, *technology and industry* formed the basis for productive enterprise. In France the invisible hand of Adam Smith's marketplace is replaced by the visible hand of 'le plan'. The *State* thereby exercises its formative and centralizing influence on the *integration* of the different sectors and regions of the economy.

Framework

The macro frame of reference is that of the 'l'état'. The centralized governmental administration, as the *economic brain*, directs business proceedings among the constituent industrial and commercial enterprises. While the market mechanism serves to activate the economic parts from without, the *central administrative brain controls* the overall economy from within. Each enterprise is therefore a part—individual and depersonalized functionary—within the whole—impersonal organizational structure. People and information, goods and services are *ordered* rather than exchanged.

The 'micro' frame of enterprise is the organization. Such an organization is rationally structured, with a view to efficient and effective functioning. It is divided between *commercial* and *financial* as well as *technical* and *managerial* functions, and is structured in accordance with a perceived need for *order* and *equity*. The lines of command are vertical, from head to foot, in a descending *hierarchy* or progressively increased dependence and dependability.

Attributes

'Northern' behaviour is typically *managerially* oriented and essentially analytical. *Productive* work is accompanied by an enthusiasm for pre-established *objectives*. A *cognitive* orientation is coupled with *strategic* planning. Organizational *coordination* is combined with formalized management *control*. Finally, *long-term forecasting* adds subtlety to an otherwise regimented approach to planning the future.

The drive for *formalization* is a recognized attribute of such administrators. They want to create order out of chaos and to exert depersonalized control over an unduly personalized world. Such a depersonalized drive has been attributed by the German sociologist Max Weber to the need for *progressive rationalization* within organizations.

CATEGORIZATION

Rational spheres

As business enterprises grow in size and scope so the need arises for ever greater rationality in their systems and structures. In fact, most developing countries have been held back in their economic development not for lack of entrepreneurial spirit but because of their relative failure to grow appropriate rationally based functions and structures. Such scientifically based rationality has been predominant in the north, as opposed to the south, and is most strongly embodied in Gallic culture. At the same time, large-scale enterprises in America as well as in the northern parts of Europe are receptive to such rationality.

Within business, the function that lends itself to analytical rigour is that of control, related to both finance and data processing. Moreover, this rationally based approach to business administration has been enshrined within the MBA, which has become the flagship of every business school. The formalized business functions, originally articulated by French engineer Henri Fayol, have thus remained sacrosanct. Finally, whereas pragmatically based managerial practices are particular to business, rationally based functions apply to all organizations, public and private.

Administrative sectors

Mass production and retail activity, subject to large-scale routine management and organization, lend themselves to rationality. As such, traditional sectors of the chemicals industry in which the European 'north' is so strongly entrenched, civil engineering projects in transport and construction, as well as mass marketing activities in food retailing, and in media communications, fall into this so-called 'administrative' sector. Interestingly enough, automobile production, which used to be in this rational 'Fordist' category, no longer is so, as we shall see.

Within a particular organization such rationally based routine activity is a prime target for automation. It therefore lends itself to the branch of business termed 'informatique', for which the French are particularly noted. The increasing role played by information technology in business, moreover, enhances this rational base.

Coordinated companies

Well-coordinated companies are better known for their internal structure and functioning than for their external competitiveness. An American case in point is McDonalds, in fast foods, and a British one is Sainsbury's, the leading supermarketeer. In France Michelin, the tyre manufacturer, would be a case in point. Such scientifically managed companies are renowned for their tightly knit structures and systems rather than for their dynamic leadership.

In these companies, finally, functional differentiation is supplemented by tight integration at the top. Vertical distance between layers is water-tight, and strict formality is maintained.

Analytical professions

In France, mathematics is the basis for professional competence, supported by the Grande Ecole, in both engineering and administration. In Britain the equivalent analytically based professions would be accounting and economics, positioned closer to money than to things. In Germany the legal and engineering professions are similarly oriented, and in Italy it would be design, also associated with aesthetics.

In the 'northern' world, then, professionally and administratively based prowess stands one in better stead than commercially based competence. Moreover, prior schooling and higher education provides one with a lifelong base in that professional respect. They provide the basis for enduring meritocracy. Germany and Japan are different, again.

World 3: Industrial—Easternness

WHOLISTIC   INDUSTRIAL
COOPERATIVE   TECHNICAL

Industrial 'world 3', which we typify as 'eastern', is wholistic in its national outlook, industrial in its sectoral orientation, cooperative in its organiza-tional approach, and technically inclined in its professional attitude. The image which springs to mind here is a 'harmonic' one.

ORIENTATION

Image

The archetype of 'world 3' at a national level is that of a harmonic state, with somewhat autonomous but simultaneously interdependent regions. A sectoral archetype would be an industrially based company engaged in diversified quality production. A corporate archetype would be a Honda in Japan or a Mercedes-Benz in Germany, each manufacturing a complex family of product lines. Finally, an individual archetype is the well-known *Technik*, with which manager and worker, banker and manufacturer identify.

The overall image of 'easternness' is captured in the composition of a chamber orchestra. While there is a conductor present, he or she is one of the leading players. Moreover, it is of major importance that everyone is *in tune*, that *each plays their part in the whole*, and that there is *an overall harmony*. There is a place in a chamber orchestra for a solo player, but such places will change during the course of the music, so that players alternate in taking the key parts. What counts, in the final analysis, is the *quality of the playing*—technical and artistic. The individual is ultimately *subservient to the work*.

Idea

The general philosophy underlying the cooperative field of playing is that of idealism, wholism, or *gestalt* psychology. What counts therefore is what serves to *integrate the parts into a working whole*. A systemic world view of interrelatedness predominates over a rational view of dependence, or a pragmatic one of independence. Intuition, as a higher form of rationality, is based on *depth of reflection* rather than upon gut feel!

The integrated factors of production are deemed to be *people, nature and the past*. Capital, in its essence, is both spiritual and material, human and physical. *Productive relations*, as identified by Marx, are intimately associated with *social relations*. In that context market and society are inextricably interwoven, in the form of a so-called social market. Whereas in Germany this pervades the economy as a whole, in Japan it predominates within the extended business family. A national *consensus* over economic affairs is therefore a characteristic of 'world 3'.

Framework

The 'macro' frame of reference is that of a particular *Technik* with which people identify. Each field of technical, artistic and social endeavour has its *norms of conduct*. Every thing or every person has a *quality*, which is only realizable in association with others in a particular configuration or *gestalt*. The exchange of goods and services, essential as it might be in the conduct of everyday business, is considered subservient to the *work itself*.

The 'micro' frame of reference is the *'meta-enterprise'*, 'industrial cluster', what is termed in Japan the *kereitsu*, that is, a firm and its associates. Typically, a manufacturer, a bank, subcontractors and possibly distributors will be intimately interlinked. As a result, *interorganizational relations* become as important as those within a particular organization. The meta-firm becomes an *interdependent system*, as opposed to an independent enterprise or dependable organization, developing in close association with its physical, economic and social environment.

Attributes

'Eastern' behaviour is typically *work* oriented, and technically focused. A strong *work ethic* is accompanied by enthusiasm for the *task*. Mental *discipline* is coupled with social discipline through *quality circles*.

An inclination towards industrial *association* goes with a preoccupation with the *production process*. Finally, such technically oriented 'easterners', through their identification with their work-in-society, are able to project their activities into the *long term*.

There is a perceived need for interpersonal and interorganizational harmony, on the one hand, and for a *harmonization* of rules and regulations, on the other, both within the organization and without. Moreover, 'easterners' find it easier than 'westerners' to develop their perceived part of the technical, economic and social whole in a spirit of *partnership*, rather than seeing manager and worker, product and market, business and environment, in adversarial terms. However, the down side of interdependence, contrasted with independence, is that *their view of the totality can descend into totalitarianism*.

CATEGORIZATION

Wholistic spheres

The economic ascendancy of Germany and Japan in recent years, superficially associated with the 'fresh start' each made after the Second World War, is more realistically the result of their pre-eminent 'easternness'. When a wholistic approach to business is combined with elements of rationalism and pragmatism the sphere of economic influence grows in leaps and bounds. To some extent, the Dutch, the Swiss and the Scandinavians harbour elements of 'world 3'. Finally, in the world at large, explicit manifestations of 'easternness' are emerging in South Korea, Singapore and Taiwan.

Within business this integrated phase of development surpasses the previously pioneering and differentiated stages. Any truly large-scale enterprise, even a US-based multinational (culturally ill attuned to wholism), needs to assume such interdependent proportions if it is to grow and develop.

Industrial sectors

Industry, as differentiated from trade, is intrinsic to 'world 3'. Unlike 'world 2', moreover, technology lacks an intrinsic status of its own. Priority is given to technology that works. The electronics industry is a prime case in point, where the developmental Japanese are gradually surpassing the innovative Americans. Interestingly enough, over the course of the last twenty years the automobile industry has shifted from the 'west' and 'north' to the 'east', and thereby from mass to so-called 'lean' production:

> European automobile plants experienced in the 1950's what the Americans had experienced in the 1930's. The situation of stagnant mass production might have continued indefinitely if a new motor industry had not emerged in Japan. The truly lean plant transfers the maximum number of tasks to those workers actually adding value to the car on the line. In the end it is dynamic teamwork which emerges as the heart of the lean factory; workers respond only when there exists some reciprocity.
>
> (Womack *et al.*, 1990)

Cooperative companies

Joint ventures, strategic alliances and co-partnership agreements are swelling the ranks of so called 'meta-enterprises' that are generic to 'world 3'. Interestingly enough, this trend was anticipated by the great Anglo-Dutch combinations, Shell and Unilever that were created early in this century.

The Japanese, in the second half of this century, took over in the cooperative vein. For example, in the 1950s Toyota began to establish a new, 'lean' production approach to component supply. The first step was to organize suppliers into functional tiers. First-tier suppliers were responsible for working as an integral part of the product development team. Toyota encouraged its first-tier suppliers to talk among themselves about ways to improve the design process. Each first-tier supplier then formed a second tier of suppliers under itself. Because second-tier suppliers were all specialists in manufacturing processes it was easy to group them into suppliers' associations.

Toyota retained a portion of the equity in its first-tier suppliers, and the suppliers themselves acquired much of the balance in one another. In addition, Toyota often acted as banker for its supplier group. Finally, Toyota would lend them personnel to deal with workload surges, and it would transfer senior personnel not in line for senior positions within Toyota. Today such companies as Alcatel in France, Siemens in Germany, ICL in the UK, Mitsubishi in Japan, and IBM in America are engaged in a proliferation of cooperative ventures.

Technically oriented professions
Some professions or occupations are more steeped in a particular *Technik* than others. Typically, the craftsman, on the one hand, and the engineer—who is more interested in specific applications than in general concepts—on the other, are cases in point. Moreover, both of them, in this 'eastern' context, are inclined to work in a team rather than to show off their individual ingenuity, as in the 'west'. Finally, the logic of teamwork is integral to the task rather than in winning the 'world 1' game.

Interestingly enough, in the 'west', such astute managerial thinkers as Harvard's Robert Reich (1991), in heralding the new work of nations, and Shoshana Zuboff (1988), in pronouncing her 'age of the smart machine' are urging Americans to engage in a more collective form of enterprise. Seemingly, the new era of flexible specialization, as we will now see in Italy, calls more upon group *Technik* than individual ingenuity.

World 4: Familial—'Southernness'

HUMANISTIC   SERVICE
COMMUNAL   SOCIAL

Familial 'world 4', which we have typified as 'southern', has an indigenously 'humanist' approach to everyday life. Its sectoral orientation is towards service, its organizational approach is innately familial, and its professional attitude is inherently social. The prevailing image is that of 'mother-earth'.

ORIENTATION

Image
The archetype of 'world 3' at a regional or national level is that of the all-embracing mother-earth, on the one hand loving and bountiful, and on the other, full of intrigue and mystery. A sectoral archetype would be a service industry, such as travel and tourism, where hospitality is of the essence. A corporate archetype would be the communally based Mondragon group of cooperative companies in the Spanish Basque country, and an individual archetype might be the Benetton family, based in Italy.

The metaphor of 'southernness' is that of a communal dance. For within 'world 4' a personal *joie de vivre* is inextricably interlinked with a *social* interplay. Moreover, such an interplay has a *natural rhythm* to it. Like the ebb and flow of the tides, so work and life take on a communal rhythm, that 'western' or 'northern' business enterprises have tended to ignore. The dance is filled with *passion*, and each dancer has his or her distinct personality, but ultimately it is the rhythmical *movement* that takes over, in the dance, as gospel singing, as well as in the road gang or productivity festival.

Idea

The general philosophy underlying the communal enterprise is that of humanism. What counts *unites* people and things altogether. Things that are *enjoyable* are worth doing; nice people are worth working for. As such, *people and love* (as well as 'tribe' and hate) surpass profit and loss as the real 'P' and 'L' of business. *Communal values* transcend individual ones; knowledge shared is knowledge gained. The *art of living* is the greatest of all. What ultimately undermines humanism, however, is *nepotism*.

At the heart of the 'southern' economy is the *family*. The family business, in its turn, is *interlinked with the communal economy*. Where the 'northern' economy scores by marrying public and private interests at the national centre, the 'southern' economy succeeds when it merges society and economy together *at the local periphery*. The local municipality, the family business, and the regional education authorities become a *latter-day extended family*. Manager and worker function as parent and child, lodged in either a *patriarchal or a matriarchal* relationship.

Framework

The 'macro' frame of reference is that of the socio-economic network. Such a network is dominated by the *relationships* between family businesses, in and between themselves. *Mutual trust* underpins such relations, and *reciprocally based duties* and obligations mobilize trade and industry. As a result, contracts are more effective when they are personally and socially—as opposed to impersonally and legally—binding. *Social structure fades into infrastructure* as business intermeshes with community.

As such, affiliation to at least one interest group is essential. Belonging to a political party or to the Church, to the Mafia or to a Masonic lodge, to a trade association or to a trade union is not merely a sociable association of like-minded people but an economic necessity. *Affiliation*, and the rights and obligations that go with it, *replaces* what passes for a *wider social awareness* in countries like France or Germany whose political and social institutions are more universally accepted. There are national policies in abundance but they do not percolate to the level of ordinary life.

The 'micro' frame of reference is the mode of flexible specialization that has come to be associated with an upgrading of familiar, craft-based production. In such a craft-based set-up trade associations, trade unions, guilds, purchasing cooperatives, and cooperative marketing all prevail. But no single institution formally links the productive units. The *cohesion* of the industry rests on a sense *of community*, ethnic, political or religious.

> Among the ironies of the resurgence of craft production is that its deployment of modern technology depends on its reinvigoration of affiliations that are associated with the preindustrial past. Within a system of flexible specialisation, firms depend on one another for the *sharing of skills*, technical knowledge, information on opportunities and information on standards.
>
> Piore and Sabel (1984)

Attributes

'Southern' behaviour is typically *people* oriented and social. Working *together* is accompanied by an enthusiasm for *people*. A *group mind*, within, is coupled with *shared values* in manipulating the world, without. A capacity for *social affiliation*, as opposed to task or 'human resource' management, goes with a real empathy for those *groups* and institutions that are part of the 'world 4' network. Finally, *management as an art form* brings light to situations which, because of the often turbulent environment in which the 'southerner' works, may appear to a 'northerner' to be very dark.

The socially oriented *need for affiliation*, then, is dominant among 'southerners'. Hitherto, this attitude has led to less economic success than the achievement motivation in the 'west'. At the same time, among the *workforce*, as distinct from management, and often among *women*, as distinct from men, 'world 4' is the prime force that prevails. Generally, the 'easterner' has found it easier to come to terms with this than the 'westerner' or the 'northerner'. Moreover, 'world 4' can also be unpredictable.

For the temperament of the 'southerner' is inevitably more passionate than that of his or her cooler counterparts:

> No longer the supple and continuous curve adapted to all forms of nature, which we have observed in the man of action; nor the series of straight lines successively correcting each other by sudden turns, as in the intellectual; but a kind of *rest followed by a sudden explosion* of conquering will which, soon exhausted, falls back to the first indifference—a series of horizontal lines of action cut by abrupt peaks of over activity. The first struggles in order to do things; the second in order to possess them in knowledge; the third to *let off his surplus energy*.
>
> (de Madariaga, 1922)

CATEGORIZATION

Humanistic spheres

The developing world as a whole is predominantly 'humanistic' in orientation. To the extent that countries therein have often been run by inhuman dictators, it is because the latter have removed themselves from the common people. For Salvador de Madariaga, that astute Spanish observer of the European scene, the 'southerner', embodied in the Spaniard, no matter what his or her standing, is *of the people*.

Thus the Spanish or 'southern' attitude to equality does not follow a hierarchy of the English type, which implies a spontaneous recognition of inequalities. Nor does it provide the basis for the erection of a State hierarchy after the 'northern' pattern, since the sense of equality is subconscious, and it does not level the people to a flat plane of citizens. *'Southern' collective life*, therefore, counts on *superimposed cohesion*, through the Church or Army.

Service sectors

Service, as distinct from industry, is intrinsic to 'world 4'. Italian restaurants, Zimbabwean hotels, Indian hospitality, all come to mind when we contemplate 'southern' services. It is the personal services rather than the knowledge work that particularly exemplifies 'world 4'. Commercial and social services, on the other hand, are much more western and northern in nature.

Within the company, such 'southernness' is notably absent from the mainstream business functions. Human resource management characteristically lacks the warmth and enthusiasm that is more often associated with secretarial and craft-based activity. However, the sales force, particularly in cases where closeness to the customer replaces a hard-sell approach, will often embody such 'southern' flavour in their way of being.

Communal companies

Generally, companies tend to be more communal at the earlier phases of their existence, when they tend to retain that family feeling. Thereafter, many variations are to be found on the 'southern' theme. The central Italian region, as a whole, has developed a reputation for growing familial companies and Mondragon, in northern Spain, likewise.

Benetton is probably the best-known company which, while growing large, has maintained strong, comunally based values. In Japan, companies like Honda and Mitsubishi maintain the sense of *uchi*, or household, in the company. Though this is generally a phenomenon, in

Japan the typically 'southern' warmth—that dance of life—tends to be missing. Finally, in America, two companies stand out for their known communality around the world: Mary Kay Cosmetics and 3M. Both manage to combine 'western' enterprise with 'southern' community, the former in feminine and the latter in masculine guise. In fact, Tom Peters' (1982) pre-emphasis upon shared values is a reflection of such a communal orientation, albeit set in the context of an indomitable 'world 1' will to win.

Social professions

Those professions oriented towards the 'southern sun' are characteristically of a caring nature, such as nursing and primary school teaching, which fall outside of the business realm. Similarly, 'people-oriented' professions such as hotel and catering management may fall into this 'southern' category. The increasing emphasis being placed, however, on 'customer care' programmes is putting pressure on many professionals to become more effectively 'southern' in their approach.

Cultural spheres

So much for national, sectoral, corporate and professional cultures. In summary, as can be seen below, they—western, northern, eastern and southern—relate to each other in the way that we have now described (Table 17.3).

Table 17.3 Cultural spheres

Sphere	Sector	Corporation	Profession	Business sphere
Pragmatism	Trade	Competitive	Entrepreneurial	West
Rationalism	Administration	Coordinated	Analytical	North
Wholism	Industry	Cooperative	Technical	East
Humanism	Service	Familial	Social	South

Finally, how do these cultural spheres relate to the more conventional wisdom on the *functions* of business and the *styles* of managers? This question is addressed fully in Chapter 18.

18

Cultures and functions

Functions

Commercial—a good deal
'Westernness', strongly reflected in the Anglo-Saxon world, epitomizes the actively commercial functions of business. These are crudely embodied in buying and selling and more elaborately in purchasing and sales. The image of the wheeler-dealer, living off his or her wits, applies most particularly in this first case. The outcome sought is a good deal.

Financial—effective control
'Northernness', with its Gallic overtones, epitomizes the abstractly financial functions of business from an administrative and analytical perspective. Such activities are crudely embodied in 'doing the sums' and more elaborately in planning and resource allocation. The image of the boffin mathematician, buried in a computer, applies in this second case. The outcome sought is effective control.

Technical—quality product
'Easternness', best represented in Germany and Japan, epitomizes the inherently technical functions of business. These are crudely embodied in making things that work and more elaborately in development and engineering. The image of the master-craftworker applies in this third instance. The outcome sought is a quality product.

Social—good relations
'Southernness', best reflected—in economic terms—in central Italy, epitomizes the concretely social functions of business. These are crudely embodied in the family and more elaborately in community relations, both inside and outside the business. The dual image of the patriarch or

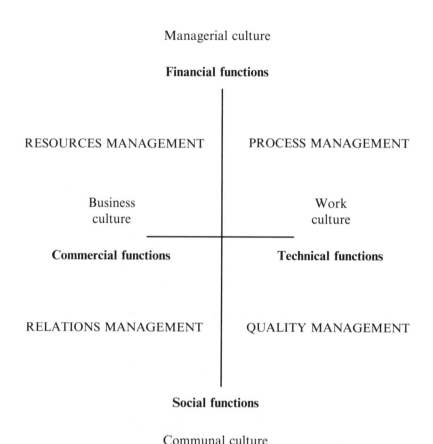

Fig. 18.1   Cultures and functions

matriarch is the appropriate one in this case. The outcome he or she seeks is one of good relations. We now turn from the traditionally based, generic functions, to the emergent combinations of functional forces (see Fig. 18.1).

DERIVATIVE FUNCTIONS

Relations management—south/west—promoting exchange
'Relations management' at its best, inclusive of *marketing*, combines the business orientation of the west with the communal ethos of the south. Coca-Cola, lodged in the American south-west, is a case in point. As such, it brings together sales and promotion with community and public relations. In effect, this happens less often than it might, because the

marketing function has been dominated by the north-western, as opposed to the south-western, quadrant. The recent emphasis on 'relationships marketing', however, has begun to redress this northern imbalance.

Resources management—north/west—exploiting resources

The well-developed 'resources management' function, inclusive of *management control*, combines the commercial acumen of the west with the administrative prowess of the north. The Hanson Trust in the north of England, to which we have already referred, is an obvious case in point. As such, this composite function often links together mergers and acquisitions, accounting and finance, data processing and management information systems, as well as—on some occasions—strategic management. The outcome it seeks is an effective allocation of resources, from both an entrepreneurial and an analytical perspective.

Process management—north/east—instilling Technik

'Process management' at its best, inclusive of *production*, combines the work ethic of the east with the administrative prowess of the north. German manufacturers, such as Siemens and Volkswagen, are typical cases in point. They bring together design and engineering *Technik*, on the one hand, with production planning and control, on the other. The more traditionally based operations management function, associated with the combined business/administration of the west/north, is a poor relation of such process management. As such, it is only partially heeded by the Germans and Japanese.

Quality management—south/east—producing harmony

Moving south-east, we come to 'quality management', inclusive of *personnel*, which serves to combine the work ethic of the east with the communal orientation of the south. Japanese manufacturers, such as Mitsubishi and Toyota, embody such a quality approach. They combine a desire for continuing self-improvement, on the one hand, with a propensity to work in harmonic quality circles, on the other. Without the corresponding self-discipline and group harmony required, so-called 'TQM' becomes antithetical to the south-eastern cause, that is, one of producing technical and social harmony. We now turn from impersonal functions to personal styles.

Cultures and styles

GENERIC STYLES

Entrepreneur—winning

The archetypical 'westerner'—be he Bill Gates at Microsoft or Lee Iacocca at Chrysler—is a business *entrepreneur*, recently elevated to the corporate equivalent, that is, the so-called 'intrapreneur' (Pinchot, 1985). Such an enterprising manager (Lessem, 1987) is a calculated risk taker, a proverbial opportunist, a habitual wheeler-dealer, a persistent achiever, a gamesperson who enjoys winning, a committed product champion and a powerful influence in the organization. As such, he or she is the antidote to the analytically based executive.

Executive—directing

The archetypical 'northerner'—be he Alfred Sloane at General Motors or Henri Fayol in France—is an *executive* manager, epitomized by a director-general or chief executive officer. Such an analytical manager methodically plans and controls, has a coherent sense of direction through which to coordinate the functioning of the business. He or she thereby communicates effectively with a view to serving the organization and society.

Adopter—facilitating

The archetypical 'easterner'—as an individual—is much less well known than his or her business and managerial counterparts in the west. However, the typical Japanese organization has become nothing short of legendary in its reputation. A case in point is Honda, albeit that the company is somewhat more westernized than, say, Toyota. Its managing director from 1973 to 1983, Kiyoshi Kawashima, implanted five principles in the company: 'follow your dreams; respect theory, new ideas and time; as well as love your work and make your workplace bright and positive; ensure a harmonious flow of work; and make research and dedicated effort a daily habit' (Mito, 1991). It is the last three of these five principles which are most typically 'eastern'. These have been associated with the operating style of an adopter (Lessem, 1989), that is, someone who, in submitting to the work, adopts the company faith and facilitates such adoption in others.

Animateur—sharing

The archetypical 'southerner', while well known outside business for their 'love of life', is less well known within. Typically, such an *animateur*—a word adopted from the French, where it is set in the context of community work—operates informally, making social connections. He or she establishes rituals and ceremonies to unite people, builds up a community to which people feel they belong, thereby also animating their social lives. Furthermore, he or she creates a cohesive culture in which values are shared. Whether in Italy or in Spain, Africa or Latin America, such a style of operating is yet to gain prominence on the global business and organizational stage (Fig. 18.2).

We now turn from the generic styles—of west and north, east and south—to the emergent combinations, or derivatives.

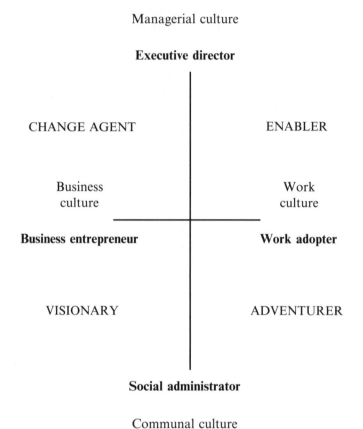

Managerial culture

Executive director

CHANGE AGENT   ENABLER

Business   Work
culture   culture

Business entrepreneur   **Work adopter**

VISIONARY   ADVENTURER

Social administrator

Communal culture

Fig. 18.2   Cultures and styles

DERIVATIVE STYLES

Visionary—south/west—transforming
Starting out in the south/west, the business *visionary* is the most originative, albeit the rarest, of managers. Combining western enterprise with southern inspiration he or she has the courage to dream, and with it the ability to envisage the future. Duly impassioned, and as an originator, he or she is able to impart fundamental values, thereby transforming people and things. The Californian Steve Jobs, who created Apple

Computers, like the Anglo-Italian Anita Roddick, who created The Body Shop, are recent examples of such charismatic individuals.

Agent of change—north/west—adapting
Set in the north/west, between the entrepreneur and the executive, is the contemporary *change agent*, who is typically a professional, whose learning exceeds the rate of change. Ever inclined to experiment, both socially and technically, he or she has the flexibility of mind to continually adapt to change. As a contemporary troubleshooter, John Harvey-Jones, the former chairman of ICI, is a typical agent of such change.

Enabler—north/east—enhancing
Towards the north/east, reaching towards Germany, is the sense for the *gestalt*, and for Jung's process of individuation, whereby the individual realizes his or her part in the whole. The *enabler* typically enhances an individual's or group's ability to play their fitting part in the whole, not only in the context of the work to be done in the organization but also through the individual's work as a vocation. In fact, German unification could be seen in that light if Chancellor Kohl were able to play a genuinely enabling role. As such, he would be acting as a link person, recognizing potential for development, and harnessing individuality-in-interdependence, being duly in touch with the forces inhibiting and enhancing economic and cultural evolution.

Adventurer—south/east—enacting
Finally, towards the virgin territories of the south/east, we have such contemporary business *adventurers* as, indeed, Richard Branson of Virgin Airlines. Drawing off the raw energy of the south, operating close to nature, they also bring the action bias of the west into play. As activators and energizers, they bring their natural rhythm of work and play into their individual and organizational lives, as director-general Jean Riboud will have done, by turning Schlumberger into a transnational company, while in close contact with the oilmen.

So much for the collective functions and individual styles that draw off the four worlds—commercial, administrative, industrial and familial. We now need to conclude the cultural argument.

Cultural integration
In conclusion, and as by now may have become apparent, a country, sector, company or professional manager that is able to become more 'worldly' in approach is bound to be more successful. No one world can succeed in isolation. A business that deals, an organization that manages,

people and things that work, and a community that binds are generic parts of a global whole. Germany and Japan are the obvious examples of countries that managed to combine their 'industrial' with enough of a 'commercial'—and, to some extent, 'administrative'—to renew themselves after the Second World War. In the airline industry, 'managerial' efficiency has had to be combined with 'communal' style customer care for success to be enduring. A company like McDonalds, while well entrenched in 'world 1', has had to combine this entrepreneurial orientation with rationally based 'world 2' systems in order to succeed on a global scale. Finally, a profession like banking, in recent years, has had to link up its 'managerial' efficiency, with some significant degree of both business and community-mindedness (Fig. 18.3).

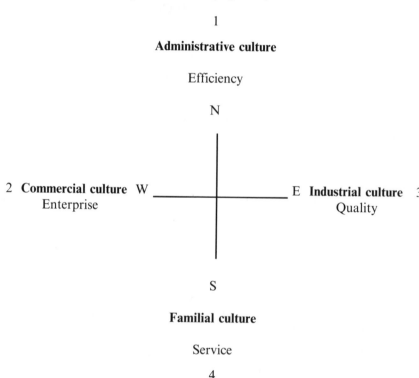

1

Administrative culture

Efficiency

N

2 **Commercial culture** W _____ E **Industrial culture** 3
   Enterprise   Quality

S

Familial culture

Service

4

Fig. 18.3   The four cultures

That having been said, many countries and companies around the world are failing because they are not being true to their primary selves. For a growing nation, sector, company or profession needs to build upon firm indigenous foundations. The path to successful cultural evolution lies in an ability to remain true to oneself while reaching out to others. The

Japanese, therefore, have gained a worldwide reputation for retaining an 'eastern' spirit while adopting 'western' techniques. It remains for us, as managers, to tap our alternately western, eastern and southern European techniques—individually or in combination—while retaining our globally 'northern' spirit. Such is the challenge of our time. Therein lies the basis for Europe as a learning community.

Appendix 1: Optimal cultural performance inventory

Think of a time when your country, industry, company or profession is or
might be performing at its best. Now rank each of the seven sets of
statements laid out below, from 1 (lowest) to 4 (highest), thereby
indicating what kind of high-performing activity applies to your particular
national, sectoral, corporate or professional culture. When you have
finished, add up all the 1s (world 1); 2's (world 2); 3's (world 3); and 4's
(world 4).

Physical performance

1. We have a strong bias for action

2. Our productivity is second to none

3. We physically come together frequently, across levels and
   functions, to make things work

4. We love doing things together

Social performance

1. We're incredibly enthusiastic

2. We operate in highly effective teams

3. The quality of our work is something we can afford to be very
   proud of

4. We're a family

Intellectual performance

1. We're very shrewd operators

2. Our planning and control procedures are clearly established
   for all to see

3. We have the opportunity to lift ourselves from the shopfloor to senior management

4. We learn from one another all the time

Economic performance

1. We have an absolute will to win

2. Our plans are methodically coordinated

3. Our strategy is directed at the development of our full technical potential

4. We have shared values that our whole community is working towards

Organizational performance

1. We are able to improvise on the spot

2. We are efficiently and effectively structured

3. The different parts of our working community are in harmony, one with the other

4. Our enterprise is like one big family

Environmental performance

1. We have a very good feel for what is happening in the outside world

2. Our powers of analysis are highly developed

3. We plan the development of our work, and technology, in intimate association with others

4. We develop opportunities by keeping closely in touch with the communities around us

☐

Creative performance

1. We have enough imagination to be able to see around corners

☐

2. We are able to manage innovation systematically

☐

3. We are able to continually renew our business and society

☐

4. We share a beautiful vision of our future

☐

Appendix 2: Minimal cultural performance inventory

Think of a time when your country, industry, company or profession is or might be performing at its worst. Now rank each of the seven sets of statements laid out below, from 1 (lowest) to 4 (highest), thereby indicating what kind of low-performing activity most applies to your particular national, sectoral, corporate or professional culture. When you have finished, add up all the 1's (world 1); 2's (world 2); 3's (world 3); and 4's (world 4).

Physical performance

1. We only work because we have to live ☐

2. We work mindlessly because they tell us to ☐

3. Work is a necessity, not something meaningful ☐

4. We work because our families have to eat ☐

Social performance

1. It's a case of 'us' managers against 'them' workers ☐

2. The workforce will kick the system at every turn ☐

3. They've become so interested in the quality of their lives, they're not producing quality work ☐

4. Community around here turns into 'communism' ☐

Intellectual performance

1. We try to cut corners ☐

2. Managers' plans are so perfect that they've become totally out of touch with reality ☐

3. We're so keen to perfect the job that we are out of touch with why we're doing it ☐

4. There's too much flair and too little compromise ☐

Economic performance

1. Short-term strategies take over completely ☐

2. It's a case of paralysis by analysis ☐

3. Protectionism is the name of the game ☐

4. Blood feuds take over the family enterprise ☐

Organizational performance

1. We're forever reorganizing ☐

2. Rules and regulations stifle performance ☐

3. We conform so rigidly to the system we can't take any initiatives ourselves ☐

4. The whole place is corrupt ☐

Environmental performance

1. It's a jungle in here and out there ☐

2. The bureaucratic machine rolls on regardless, in blissful ignorance of what's happening around it ☐

3. We operate as a closed cartel, only serving our own interests ☐

4. The owners have no interest in people outside 'the family'

☐

Creative performance

1. Imagination is a tool used to commercially manipulate rather than technically create

☐

2. Creativity degenerates into building castles in the air

☐

3. There's no place for creativity in our 'keep your heads down' environment

☐

4. Nepotism is rife in this scheming atmosphere

☐

19

Creating a European management system

The variety of Europe gives to each of its characters in its inner conversation enough definiteness and richness for the discussion to be lively. The unity of Europe, on the other hand, preserves enough common ground for the conversation to be stimulating and fertile. It is this perennial argument ever going on in the recesses of the European being which has determined its evolution.

Salvador de Madariaga, *Portrait of Europe*

Think global—act local

In this final chapter, having now related national to corporate cultures, it is time to draw together the threads of this book while relating them to our current, managerial concerns. The words on every international manager's lips are 'think global—act local'. Ostensibly, there lies the key to managing diversity. Yet such local variety is inevitably circumscribed. In other words, and on the one hand, local variations are likely to be so multifaceted that no sharply differentiated features emerge. In Spain, for example, 'personal connections' are liable to be all-important; but they are also likely to be so in Britain and France, albeit different kinds of connections. On the other hand, globalization leads to standardization, so that fundamental differences are bypassed. McDonald's in Moscow, for instance, is no different from its equivalent in Manchester. In fact 'think global—act local', in its blandness, is actually antithetical to European-ness. There is no underlying conversation, in de Madariaga's terms, to stretch the European mind.

Interestingly enough, if we conduct a properly European debate we find, participating within it, a global set of managers of a different kind. For

European 'globality', potentially if not yet actually, implies heterogeneity rather than homogeneity, individuality rather than uniformity.

The problem is that in management until now there has been no properly conducted European argument to tease out the essential character differences. Both the North–South debate between rich and poor and the East–West debate between Communism and capitalism have focused on political and economic rather than managerial and organizational differences. Neither has served to identify unity-in-variety, or variety-in-unity. What we have proposed instead is a philosophically based division of European labour, containing enough definiteness and richness of character for the discussion to be not only lively but also mutually enriching! In reality, of course, there will be significant overlapping. Northern Italy, for example, is both 'northern' and 'southern', in our terms, while the Netherlands is both 'western' and 'eastern'. While France may be predominantly 'northern' rational, it contains additional elements of all three 'nesses', not to mention the all-pervasive American influence.

COLLECTIVE UNITY—INDIVIDUAL DIVERSITY

To the extent that Europe embodies, in Jung's terms, all four psychological types—thinking and feeling, sensing and intuiting—and in our terms a complete set of philosophical systems—rationalism and humanism, pragmatism and wholism—so a rich argument between each is facilitated (Fig. 19.1). Such an argument, as we can see in Table 19.1, can be conducted on many different planes, across what de Madariaga terms, respectively, horizontal and vertical European axes.

The cast of European characters

While Hamlet and Don Quixote are horizontal characters, types of manhood whose tensions and relations move sideways towards other men, Faust and Don Juan are vertical characters whose chief tensions are in the realm of absolute values—life, death, destiny, God.

(de Madariaga, 1968)

For de Madariaga, while the Greeks made gods of the forces of nature, we Europeans have substituted these gods with human features that have been wrested out of ourselves. Pre-eminent among these are the four figures which Shakespeare, Goethe, Cervantes and Tirso de Molina have sculpted out of the Europeans of their days, and of the generations that came before them. 'Born definitively English, Spanish and German they are always European, indeed universal, with that specific branch of

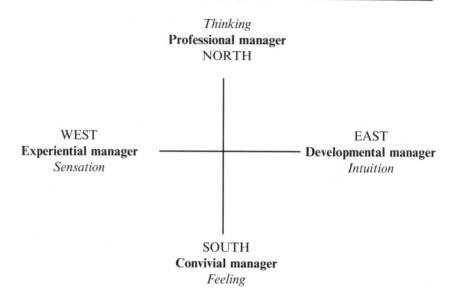

Fig. 19.1 European globality

universality that derives from its Socratic brain and from its Christian heart' (de Madariaga 1968). These culturally laden images, implicitly though not yet explicitly, underlie European managerial attributes. In fact to the extent that we are able to draw purposefully upon our cultural heritage, so the European manager, within the European organization,

Table 19.1 European management characters

Dimension	Characteristic			
	Western	*Northern*	*Eastern*	*Southern*
Corporate	Commercial	Administrative	Industrial	Familial
Managerial attributes				
Behaviour	Experiential	Professional	Developmental	Convivial
Attitude	Sensation	Thought	Intuition	Feeling
Institutional models				
Function	Salesmanship	Control	Production	Personnel
Structure	Transaction	Hierarchy	System	Network
Societal ideas				
Economics	Free market	*Dirigiste*	Social market	Communal
Philosophy	Pragmatic	Rational	Wholistic	Humanistic
Cultural images				
Art	Theatre	Architecture	Music	Dance
Culture	Anglo-Saxon	Gallic	Germanic	Latin

will be able to play his or her authentically economic part in the social whole. Between these cultural images and distinct managerial attributes lie particular conceptual models and generic European ideas.

INDIVIDUAL/GROUP—WEST/EAST

Hamlet and Don Quixote, according to de Madariaga, are symbols for the first of the most European of problems, that of the balance between the individual and the group.

The experiential 'western' manager

Shakespeare's Hamlet represents, on the one hand, the tortured soul of a man born free who lives in a community too strong and exacting for him. His soliloquies constitute inner adventures—sallies of the man of action driven to passion by social pressure, forcing him to explore his inner self. Driving Hamlet inwards, like inward spirals, Shakespeare anticipates Reg Revans's experientially oriented manager, who in the process of changing his outer world needs to change himself. Interestingly enough, moreover, the Shakespearean character and Revans's learner are both called upon to act. In each case, as for the empiricist or pragmatist, the intention is that knowledge bears fruit in works!

The Anglo-Saxon then, like Hamlet, is a man of action hemmed in by a society very much aware of itself, watchful of its standards and alive to its traditions. Adam Smith's market economy, in which the pursuit of multiple individual goods is thought to lead to the good of all, is a natural outcome of this world view. The transactionally oriented business world, in fact, to which Shakespeare belonged before he devoted himself to the theatre is eminently suited to a marketplace in which individuals wheel and deal. Salesmanship, therein, is of the business essence, and being on the stage, whether theatrically or commercially, applies in each case. In duly arousing our attention, interest, desire and action the gifted salesperson and the talented actor have a good deal in common. The individualistic 'westerner' is our first archetypical European character, who is represented in even more vivid terms, today, in the United States. He or she also prevails throughout Europe at the formative and entrepreneurial stage of a business's development. As the embodiment of enterprise, therefore, this pragmatic individual has carried the business day for some three centuries in Europe and America. Furthermore, even in the 1990s when the Anglo-Saxons seem to have lost their business way, the image of 'the independent man of action' seems to live on in the public imagination, whether in Prague or in *perestroika*, in Copenhagen or in Krakow. That is why John Harvey-Jones's books are all bestsellers.

The developmental 'eastern' manager

Individually based free enterprise in the 'west' has recently been somewhat eclipsed by the collectively based economies of the 'east'. Most distinctly embodied in Japan Inc. they are also, and in European terms, strongly reflected in Germany's social market. While, for de Madariaga, Hamlet was the personification of man born free, Cervantes' Don Quixote personified man born social. While the former had to live in a society too strong and exacting for him, the latter was obliged to live in a society too loose and rarefied for his liking. In European terms, therefore, Quixote represents the social whole that suffers by being torn apart.

Germany in fact, like Japan, tore both itself and the world apart when their fascist regimes obliterated the individual within the totality. Forced, after the Second World War, to imbibe doses of individualism from the west, these 'eastern' societies rebalanced themselves to good effect. 'Japanese spirit, western technique', a combination of intrinsic collectivism and extrinsic individualism, has proved to be better adapted to today's global economy than 'westernness' in isolation.

Since the Second World War the Germanic orientation towards wholism has led to a similarly systemic approach to productive activity. The close interconnectedness between worker and manager, as well as between banker and manufacturer—all with a view to enhanced product quality or *Technik*—is unparalleled in other parts of Europe.

The focus in Germany, then, and to some degree in Holland and Sweden is upon product and production rather than upon market and sales. At the same time, the developmental orientation leads towards a design process that takes the consumer into account, as part of the whole. The deeper Germanic intuition, although often hidden beneath the so-called 'well-oiled machine', is attuned to patterns of evolution in both product and market as in individual and organization. The implicit sense for harmony, as represented in the classical music of Bach or Mozart, is explicitly reflected in the consensus approach to management, where the captains of industry are 'first among equals' rather than 'up-front' individual leaders. Overall, a collective rather than individual approach to management and organization prevails.

The individual is only able to be free to the extent that he or she is able to find an appropriate part in the whole. This is borne out, for example, by the 'partnership' philosophy espoused by Bertelsmann's Reinhard Mohn. The collective spirit of 'Eastern' Europe, at least within the economic realm, has all too long been represented in the form of State socialism, set in the context of Communism. This has served to blur the outline of the second of our European characters. The more authentic version, as we have now seen, is that of the social market, established within the context of wholism. It is embodied in the developmental manager, who has more affinity with the social whole than with the individual part.

As such, he or she identifies more with the whole industrial process rather than with the part business function. Such a manager is therefore typically Japanese or German rather than British or Italian. We now turn from the horizontal individual/group axis, that is, west–east, to the vertical one, represented as north–south.

MIND/WILL—NORTH/SOUTH

The divisions between first and third worlds, like those between capitalism and Communism, were never embodied creatively in the hearts and minds of great Europeans. Rather, for de Madariaga, just as Hamlet and Don Quixote symbolize the first individual–social European field of force, Faust and Don Juan represent the second. Therefore, the field of creative tension between mind and will separates and also integrates purposeful intellect and intelligent impulse. Strictly speaking, will without mind is mere impulse and mind without will is mere dilettantism.

The professional 'northern' manager

Goethe's Faust stands for the spirit of inquiry. He represents that higher rationalism, that faith in 'the inner light of the human spirit which, from the days of Socrates has led Europe to the discovery of science of the planet and of the inner continents of man' (de Madariaga, 1968). For de Madariaga Faust is symbolic of the rules and principles that regulate life, so clearly apparent in Gallic culture. For more than any other country, France has developed a *dirigiste* economy, underpinned by sophisticated planning mechanisms that are drawn out of its rationalistic outlook on life and business. Moreover, unlike State socialism the Gallic approach to a planned economy is based on an innate appreciation for form, for clearcut structure and function. As a result, the French uphold professionalism in the field of administration like no other nation.

Valuing thought processes above action or passion, the managerial culture so ingrained in the French upholds formalized planning and control, direction and coordination. A hierarchy of functions is structurally ordered. There is a progressively increased ability to cope with complexity as one rises up the organizational tree. In that respect the intricate architecture of 'la Tour Eiffel' is an appropriate symbol.

In the final analysis the professional manager focuses, unlike his or her experiential or developmental counterparts, not on the individual or the group but on the institution. His or her perspective is therefore impersonal rather than personal or interpersonal. In that respect, objective, scientific, rational 'northernness' shines through, as was the case for the industrial engineer Henri Fayol who wrote the first book on 'industrial and general administration'. Fayol, who first articulated the functions of management and organization, in the 1920s, embodies the third of our 'northern' European characters, the professional administrator, rational to the core. Personified in Goethe's Faust he could not be more different from Don Juan.

The convivial 'southern' manager

For de Madariaga, Tirso de Molina's Don Juan encapsulates the ebullience of the south, the spontaneous wilfulness of a culture that is innately opposed to rules and regulations. The bonds that hold such a Latin society together, be it in Spain or Portugal, Italy or Ireland, are inherently communal rather than managerial or organizational. The convivial manager is full of the joys as well as the sadnesses, the loves as well as the hatreds of life. The humanistic philosophy that he or she espouses combines personal and social impulses to make 'people and love' as important as profit and loss, in the way, for example, that Anita Roddick has exhibited through her Body Shop.

The artistic form that most readily lends itself to such a communal culture is that of dance, with its pulsating rhythms, coupled—in the Italian case—with the drama of opera. The 'southern' economic structure builds upon the family network, Mafia-like at its worst and Benetton-like at its best. A so-called socio-economic network, most particularly in central Italy, has taken root as an upgraded and duly extended form of individual/organizational and product/market family. In that context, family structure and infrastructure merge synergistically together, albeit in a local setting. Such a feeling-centred community, moreover, lends itself to personnel management of the intrinsically social as opposed to an extrinsically institutional kind. Such is the fourth of the European characters, so often identified as hot 'southern' as opposed to cool 'northern', innately communal as opposed to overtly institutional.

All four characters, moreover—experiential, developmental, professional and convivial—change over time as well as across European space.

The European learning cycle

Faust passes from self-knowledge and damnation in Marlowe to self-giving love and salvation in Goethe; Don Juan passes from selfish sex and damnation in Tirso to self-giving love and salvation in Zorilla. Both the mind and the will of

Europe change their polarity between 1600 and 1900, from dare not and you shall be damned to dare and you will be saved—if your daring is pure.

(de Madariaga, 1968)

A HERITAGE OF IMBALANCE

Europe has not stood still. Over the course of the last century, together with the rest of the developed world, it has moved out of an industrial and into a post-industrial era. As such, it has entered the information age. Economic progress, however, has been uneven. The European south, in general terms, has lagged behind the north. That having been said, central Italy has experienced an economic growth rate in recent times that has surpassed that of all its European neighbours. Britain, seemingly, reached its zenith towards the middle of the nineteenth century and Germany has taken up the economic reins ever since. However, Eastern Europe has dragged its economic feet, while France, and more recently Spain, as well as the Benelux and Scandinavian countries have gained apace.

The problem is that, until now, business and economic performance in the different 'western' European countries have been mainly compared and contrasted quantitatively rather than qualitatively. Unlike in the arts and sciences, where European interchange has been prolific, in management theory and practice there has been amazingly little mutual exchange. While implicitly and practically each European nation has 'done its own thing', explicitly and conceptually the Anglo-Saxon mould has been universally cast. Ironically, and counter to de Madariaga's more broadly based proposition, genuine debate between the four European managerial and organizational characters has been minimal. This has served to stultify the European intellect as far as management is concerned, duly inhibiting European-wide learning. However, the times they are a-changing!

THE LEARNING CYCLE

Management as learning

In 1971 Reg Revans submitted a paper to the Polish Academy of Sciences. Entitled 'Management as Creativity and Learning', it set out to identify five orders of learning. The first four of these (Fig. 19.2) mirrored closely both Jung's pychological types and also our philosophical domains. Interestingly enough, we can trace a learning path from 'western' economic action/pragmatism/sensation; to 'northern' conceptualiza-tion/rationalism/thought; to 'eastern' reflection/wholism/intuition; to 'southern' concretization/human collaboration/feeling. If any part of the whole is missing, as we shall soon see, then learning is inhibited. In other words, if any one of our European quartet is missing then there will be managerial and organizational imbalance. For example, an overdose of

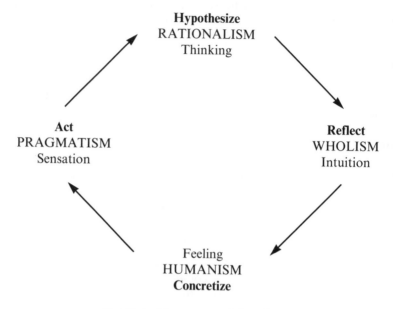

Fig. 19.2 Management as learning

'westernness' results in short-termism, an excess of 'northernness' creates alienation, an overdose of 'easternness' results in totalitarianism, and an excess of 'southernness' yields nepotism.

Interestingly enough, already in the early 1970s Revans was arguing that Europe as a whole had reached a fifth stage in its evolution:

> At Stage Five we enter the here and now of contemporary Europe. The intellectual insight into the world around us that we gain by scientific method must be assimilated to our personal convictions, necessarily at a level more profound than formal logic. The results of experiment are no longer to be regarded simply as some detached relationship for use at our convenience; they are for us to absorb and make part of ourselves.
>
> (Revans, 1984, page 503)

Revans goes on to liken the phases of the learning to the stages of life. Having developed from childhood through youth and young adulthood, full adulthood and mid-life, we fifthly and finally reach 'the mature man, not only rational but also humane, not only respectful of evidence, but also willing to assimilate into his own conduct and his personal values the lessons that hold for him' (Revans, 1984, page 505). Such an individual or society, moreover, only gains maturity once it has progressed through pragmatism and rationalism, wholism and humanism. The full set of

European characters have to be brought interactively into play before maturity can be reached. In other words, European business has to become a learning community (Lessem, 1993).

The dialectical learning process

In a seminal piece of writing, almost a decade ago, David Kolb, a Professor of Organizational Behaviour at Canada's Case Western University, advanced his case for managerial and organizational learning. Kolb maintained that learning is by its very nature a tension- and conflict-filled process, in that new knowledge, skills or attitudes are achieved through confrontation among four modes of learning:

> Learners, if they are to be effective, need four different kinds of abilities—concrete experience (CE) abilities, reflective observation (RO) abilities, abstract conceptualisation (AC) abilities, and active experimentation (AE) abilities. That is, they must be able to involve themselves fully, openly and without bias in new experiences (CE). They must be able to reflect on and observe their experiences from many perspectives (RO). They must be able to create concepts that integrate their observations into logically sound theories (AC), and they must be able to use these theories to make decisions and solve problems (AE).
>
> (Kolb, 1984, page 30)

Learning therefore requires abilities that are polar opposites, and the learner, as a result, must continually choose which set of learning abilities he or she will bring to bear in any specific learning situation. In addition, the way in which the conflicts among the dialectically opposed modes of adaptation are resolved determines the level of learning that results. If conflicts are resolved by the suppression of one mode and/or dominance of another, learning tends to be specialized around the dominant mode and limited in areas controlled by the dominated one. Active experimentation, for example, is most vigorously embodied in the entrepreneurially based free enterprise that emerges most naturally out of Europe's Western heritage. It has served to create an international stock exchange, a robust venture capital market and a nation of shopkeepers. However, if left purely to its own devices—thereby dominating the other three modes—it can degenerate into rampant acquisitiveness, financial engineering and social exploitation. Milliken in the United States and Robert Maxwell in Britain are recent examples of such unbalanced 'Western' self-centredness.

The learning modes

Kolb's four learning modes—active experimentation, abstract concept ualization, reflective observation, and concrete experience—in fact run closely parallel with our Europeannesses:

(1) *Westernness*: An orientation towards *active experimentation* focuses on actively influencing people and changing situations. It emphasizes practical applications as opposed to reflective understanding; a pragmatic concern with what works as opposed to what is absolute truth; an emphasis on doing as opposed to observing. Such people are willing to take risks in order to achieve their objectives.

(2) *Northernness*: An orientation towards *abstract conceptualization* focuses on using logic, ideas and concepts. It emphasizes thinking as opposed to feeling; a concern with building general theories as opposed to intuitively understanding unique, specific areas; a scientific as opposed to an artistic approach to problems. Such a person is good at systematic planning, manipulation of abstract symbols and quantitative analysis. People with this orientation value precision, the rigour and discipline of analysing ideas, and the aesthetic quality of a neat conceptual system.

(3) *Easternness*: An orientation towards *reflective observation* focuses on understanding the meaning of ideas and situations by carefully observing and impartially describing them. It emphasizes understanding as opposed to practical application; a concern with what is true or how things happen as opposed to what will work; an emphasis on reflection as opposed to action. People with a reflective orientation enjoy intuiting the meaning of situations and ideas and are good at seeing their implications.

(4) *Southernness*: An orientation towards *concrete experience* focuses on being involved in experiences and dealing with immediate human situations in a personal way. It emphasizes feeling as opposed to thinking; a concern with the uniqueness and complexity of present reality as opposed to theories and generalizations; an intuitive, 'artistic' approach as opposed to the systematic, scientific approach to problems. People with practical experience orientation enjoy and are good at relating to others. They are often good, intuitive decision makers and function well in unstructured situations.

These four learning modes were positioned by Kolb in dialectically opposed pairs of 'prehension' and 'transformation', that is, comprehension versus apprehension, on the one hand, and intention versus extension, on the other.

Prehension versus transformation
The structural bases of the learning process, for Kolb, lie in the transactions among these four adaptive modes and the way in which the adaptive dialectics get resolved. The abstract/concrete dialectic is one of *prehension*, representing two different and opposed processes of grasping and taking hold of experience in the world—either through reliance on

conceptual interpretation and symbolic representation, a process he calls *comprehension*; or through reliance on the tangible, felt qualities of immediate experience, which Kolb identifies as *apprehension*. In our own European terminology, rationalism comprehends and humanism apprehends reality.

The active/reflective dialectic, on the other hand, is one of *transformation*, representing two opposed ways of transforming our grasp of experience—either through internal reflection, a process Kolb calls *intention*, or through manipulation of the external world, called *extension*. Whereas, for us, wholism transforms experience through inner intention, pragmatism does so through outer extension (Fig. 19.3).

What you see, hear and feel around you are sensations, colours, textures and sounds that are so basic and reliable that we call them reality. They are simply there, grasped through a mode of knowing Kolb calls 'apprehension'. Through 'comprehension' we introduce order into what would otherwise be a seamless, unpredictable flow of apprehended sensations. Apprehension and comprehension as well as intention and extension are dialectically related to each other, so that, for Kolb, their syntheses produce higher levels of learning. Herein lies the power of the authentically European argument which, in business, is yet to be conducted.

Kolb drew heavily on his Swiss predecessor, Carl Jung. Jung saw a basic conflict between the specialized psychological orientations required for the development of society and the need for people to develop and express all the psychological functions for their own individual fulfilment. Hence a manager in France or Britain, Holland or Belgium—apart from the European whole—is inevitably underdeveloped. Jung's concept of individuation describes the process whereby people achieve personal integrity through the development of their non-expressed and non-dominant functions. These are then integrated with their dominant specialized orientation into a fluid, holistic adaptive process. As for the individual, so for the whole of business and society. In that context, all of Europe is still to become economically integrated, and the field for such integration is quite the opposite of what the Anglo-Saxons call a 'level playing field'. Rather, it is an inherently dialectical one.

Learning and development

THE LEARNING PROCESS

For Kolb, the way learning shapes the course of development can be described by the level of integrative complexity in the four learning modes. First, behavioural complexity in active experimentation, results in higher-order actions. Such behaviour is characteristically pragmatic.

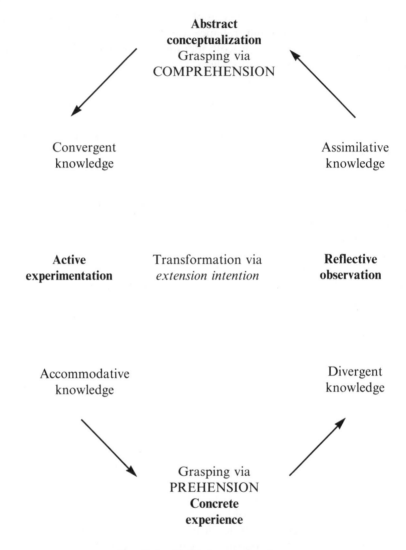

Fig. 19.3   Kolb's learning cycle

Second, symbolic complexity in abstract conceptualization, results in higher-order concepts. Such appreciation of complexity is typically rational. Third, perceptual complexity in reflective observation results in higher-order observations. Such reflective thought is associated with wholism. Finally, affective complexity in practical experience results in higher-order sentiments, characteristic of humanism.

According to Kolb, development on each dimension proceeds from a state of embeddedness to one of specialization, and ultimately integration. Such 'embeddedness', in our context, represents the current state of European management, where culturally laden attributes are largely undifferentiated except at a level of surface complication. Consequently, managers merely immerse themselves in the European world without being able to distinguish clearly one culture from another (Fig. 19.4).

What we have attempted in this book is to develop some basis for cultural specialization along the lines of our European quartet. Ultimately, though, a European manager must aim for integration, whereby he or she accommodates the dialectical nature of management but from his or her own acknowledged cultural vantage point.

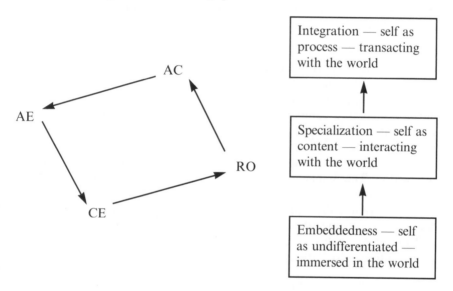

Fig. 19.4 Learning and development

This integrative process is marked by increasing complexity and relativism in dealing with the world and one's experiences, and by higher-level integration of the dialectical conflicts among the four primary 'nesses' or learning modes.

THE DEVELOPMENT PROCESS
In the early stages of development, progress along each of these four dimensions can occur with relative independence from the others. The child and young adult, by way of an analogy, can develop highly sophisticated symbolic proficiencies and remain naive emotionally. At the highest stages of development, however, commitment to learning and creativity produces a strong need for integration of the four adaptive modes. Development in one mode precipitates development in the

others. It is in this context that the European quartet came together, each with a view to playing an integral part in the compositional whole.

For Kolb, the human developmental process is divided into three maturational stages: embeddedness, specialization and integration. Development in the *embedded* phase is marked by the gradual emergence of internalized structures that allow the individual to gain a sense of self that is separate and distinct from the surrounding environment. So we declare ourselves to be Englishmen or Frenchwomen, based on such tangible *attributes* as place of birth, use of language and taste for food. Learning at the earliest developmental stages is primarily enactive, that is, knowledge is externalized in actions, leading in our case to 'managing across cultures'.

According to Kolb, increasing freedom from undifferentiated immersion in the world begins with basic discrimination between internal and external stimuli and ends with that delineation of the boundaries. Managers shaped by cultural, educational and organizational socialization develop increased competence in a specialized mode of adaptation. The managerial self in this stage is defined primarily in terms of content things that he or she can do, experiences each has had, goods and qualities he or she possesses. The primary mode of relating to the world, for Kolb, is interaction. The manager acts on the world and the world acts on him or her, but neither is fundamentally changed by the other. So the rationalist remains a rationalist and the pragmatist a pragmatist, pure and simple. The focus is on objectified data, such as comparative demographic trends, and on depersonalized frameworks, such as different training establishments or trade associations.

The specialized accomplishments of stage two bring security and achievement, often paid for by subjugation of the need for personal fulfilment. Therefore each European nation remains partially unfulfilled. The personal experience of the conflict between social demands and the need for personal fulfilment precipitates the transition into the *integrative* mode. This level contains ideas and images, such as the 'free' versus the 'social' markets; the 'island race' versus Germany or Japan Inc. The nature of this shift depends on the specifics of the manager's or organization's dominant and non-expressed, adaptive modes. For the reflective, developmental manager in Germany or Holland, the awakening of the active mode brings a new sense of risk to life. Rather than being influenced, he or she now sees opportunities to influence. For the British or American manager who has specialized in the active, experiential mode, the emergence of the reflective side broadens the range of choice and deepens the ability to sense the implications of actions. For the Italian or Spanish manager in the practical, humanistic mode, the abstract perspective gives new continuity and direction to experience. The abstract, French or Swiss rationalist manager with a new sense of immediate experience finds new life and meaning in abstract constructions of organizational reality.

The net effect of these shifts in perspective is an increasing experience of self or society, management or organization as process. A learning process that has previously been blocked by the repression of the non-specialized adaptive modes—for example, the pragmatist suppressing his or her humanism—is now experienced deeply to be the essence of a manager's European self.

Raising European consciousness

In Kolb's learning model there are three distinct levels of adaptation, representing successively higher-order forms of learning. These are governed, in turn, by qualitatively different forms of consciousness. Kolb refers to these successively higher-order forms of adaptation as performance, learning and development.

In the embedded phase adaptation takes the form of performance governed by a simple 'registrative' consciousness. Hence management is characterized in everyday terms as practical or impractical, approachable or remote. We 'perform' by taking due account of surface attributes, such as greeting rituals and body language, in managing across cultures. In the specialization phase adaptation occurs via a learning process governed by an 'interpretive' consciousness. Much of this book has been written in such a vein. We learn about more deeply ingrained cultural forms like *dirigisme* and *Mitbestimmung*, in the process of developing a cross-cultural appreciation of management and organization.

To that extent, we have deliberately overdone the specialization, thereby associating the British and the Germans, the French and the Italians with all-inclusive attributes and frameworks, ideas and images that are actually more widely spread. In effect, these are prevailing tendencies rather than absolute prerequisites.

Management, and indeed life, cannot be contained in such neat packages. One flows into the other, as westernness flows into northernness, and easternness into southernness. The northern Italians, for example, are both Latin and Germanic; the southern French are Latin and Gallic. However, there is a need to differentiate before we integrate so as to extricate ourselves from an ill-defined European morass that has hitherto been swamped by the more clearly distinguishable Americans and Japanese.

Having differentiated between pragmatic, rational, wholistic and humanistic approaches, we then need, as managers and as firms, to integrate. Such integration, as we have seen, represents, on the one hand, a process of managerial and corporate individuation, and, on the other, one of individual and organizational learning. In effect, as Peter Senge at MIT has pointed out in his book, *The Fifth Discipline* (published in 1992 by Century Business), such organizational learning is a composite of experientially oriented 'personal mastery', professionally based 'mental modelling', developmentally oriented 'systems thinking', and convivially based 'team learning', all of which together contribute towards a shared business vision.

An authentically European approach to managerial learning would, however, need to be simultaneously individual (Anglo-Saxon), organizational (Gallic), industrial (Germanic) and communal (Latin) in orientation. In fact, conventionally based management education is hugely biased towards the individual, thus precluding the parallel and integrated development of the organization, industry and community. Organization development, therefore, has remained pitifully underdeveloped, as well as the facilitation of learning among whole industrial complexes. Finally, from a societal perspective, in *Making Democracy Work* (published in 1993 by Princeton University Press) Robert Putnam at Harvard has recently pointed out that the rapid economic development of whole communities within modern Italy is the result of their particular civic traditions. Such 'civic virtues', he argues, lie within a communal orientation (reflected both economically and politically) that provides the 'social capital' underpinning successful enterprise in north-central Italy. Management development of the convivial variety therefore involves nothing less than the development of cooperation, solidarity and public-spiritedness—that is social capital—within a whole community.

Within our emerging European Community the development of such a consciousness is becoming ever more of a business/economic as well as a socio/political imperative. The longstanding economic depression in the UK has now been overtaken by ever increasing unemployment in France, a sudden reversal in the economic fortunes of the newly united Germany, and a combined political and economic malaise in Italy. From the perspective adopted in this book each of these four European domains is suffering from its undue isolation, excessive differentiation or, to put it nicely, its 'overdone strength'. While the pragmatic British suffer from their rampant short-termism, and the rational French from their excessive bureaucracy, the wholistic Germans are inclined to 'over-engineer' their products, and the humanistic Italians are prone towards nepotism. Each needs the other to 'individuate' culturally and economically, and such smaller countries as the Benelux and the Scandinavian nations have a vital role to play in fostering such integration. Whereas for the Dutchman Alfons Trompenaars and his Anglo-Saxon colleague Charles Hampden Turner, the cast of characters represented across the newly global stage are *The Seven Cultures of Capitalism* (published in 1993 by Doubleday); for ourselves, within Europe, four management systems represent the diversity out of which needs to be forged our European, if not global, unity.

Bibliography

Years in square brackets [ ] are years of first publication.

Adair, J. (1964) *Action Centred Leadership*, Aldershot: Gower.
Albert M. (1991) *Capitalisme contre capitalisme*, Paris: Editions du Seuil.
Assagioli, R. (1974) *The Act of Will*, Aldershot: Wildwood House.
Backhaus, J. (1987) 'The emergence of worker participation', *Journal of Economic Issues*, **21**, No. 2, June.
Bacon, Francis (1961) *The Advancement of Learning*, London: Dent [1605].
Barsoux, J. and P. Lawrence (1991) 'The making of a French manager', *Harvard Business Review*, July/August, 67.
Barzini, L. (1974) *The Impossible Europeans*, London: Weidenfeld & Nicolson.
Bergin, T. and M. Fisch, (1968) *The New Science of Giambattista Vico*, Cornell University Press.
Bleicher, K. (1989) *Chancen für Europas Zukunft*, Frankfurt: Frankfurte Allgemeine.
Cassirer, E. (1963) *Rousseau, Kant and Goethe*, New York: Harper.
Chandler, A. (1990) *Scale and Scope*, New York: Bellknapp.
Coates, W. *et al.* (1965) *The Emergence of Liberal Humanism*, New York: McGraw-Hill.
Croce, B. (1965) *Guide to Aesthetics*, New York: Bobbs-Merrill.
Crozier, M. (1964) *The Bureaucratic Phenomenon*, London: Tavistock.
Danco, L. (1980) *Inside the Family Business*, Ohio: Center for Family Business.
De Madariaga, S. (1992) *Englishman, Frenchman, Spaniard*, Oxford: Oxford University Press.
De Madariaga, S. (1968) *Portrait of Europe*, London: Hollis and Carter.
Derossi, P. (1984) *The Italian phenomenon*, Amsterdam: Elsevier.
De Santis, O. (1980) *La Struttura dell'Impresa Cooperativa in Emilia-Romagna*, Bologna: Franco Angeli.
D'Iribarne, P. (1990) *La logique d'honneur*, Paris: Editions du Seuil.
Durant, W. (1962) *Outlines of Philosophy*, London: Benn.
Eckerman, J. (1930) *Conversations with Goethe*, London: Everyman.
Eisler, L. (1962) *Francis Bacon and the Modern Dilemma*, Nebraska University Press.
Farrington, B. (1973) *Francis Bacon*, London: Macmillan.
Faulkner Jones, R. (1932) The English Spirit, London: Steiner Press.
Fayol, H. (1949) *Industrial and General Administration*, London: Pitman [1916].

Fisch, M. and T. Bergin (1944) *The Autobiography of Giambattista Vico*, Cornell University Press [1818].

Fisher, A. (1992) 'Grass at home for German industry', *Financial Times*, 20 March.

Gardner, H. (1974) *Quest for Mind*, New York: Wiley.

Garelli, S. (1992) *The World Competitiveness Report, Edition 12*, Lausanne: World Economic Forum.

Gelfand, M. (1979) *African Crucible*, Harare, Zimbabwe: Mambo Press.

Glasser, R. (1977) *The Net and the Quest*, London: Temple Smith.

Glouchevitch, P. (1992) *Juggernaut*, New York: Simon & Schuster.

Graham, R. (1992) 'A godfather retires', *Financial Times*, 19 October.

Grochla, E. (1978) *Einführung in die Organisationtheorie*, Frankfurt: Poeschel.

Hallenstein, D. (1991) *Doing Business in Italy*, London: BBC Publications.

Hampden Turner, C. (1970) *Radical Man—Towards a Theory of Psycho-Social Development*, Schenkman.

Hampden Turner, C. (1991) *Charting the Corporate Mind*, Oxford: Blackwell.

Hampden Turner, C. and F. Trompenaars (1993) *The Seven Cultures of Capitalism*, New York: Doubleday.

Handy, C. (1980) *The Gods of Management*, London: Pan.

Handy, C. (1990) *The Age of Unreason*, London: Hutchinson.

Harvey-Jones, J. (1990) *Making it Happen*, London: Collins.

Havel, V. (1988) *Living in Truth*, London: Faber.

Hofstede, G. (1991) *Cultures and Organizations*, Maidenhead: McGraw-Hill.

Holmstrom, M. (1989) *Industrial Democracy in Italy*, Aldershot: Avebury.

Illich, I. (1972) *Convivial Technology*, London: Marion Boyars.

Inzerelli, G. (1990) 'The Italian alternative: flexible organization and social management', *International Studies of Management and Organization*, **20**, No. 4.

Jacobi, Y. (1962) *Modern Man in Search of a Soul*, London: Faber.

Jantsch, E. (1974) *Design for Evolution*, New York: Brazillier.

Jaques, E. (1976) *A General Theory of Bureaucracy*, London: Heinemann.

Jaques, E. (1989) *Requisite Organization*, London: Cassell.

Jaques, E. (1991) *Executive Leadership*, Oxford: Blackwell.

Kirsch, W. (1984) *Das Management Strategischer*, Munich: Kirsch.

Kolakowski, L. (1972) *Positivist Philosophy*, Harmondsworth: Penguin Books.

Kolb, D. (1974) *Organizational Psychology*, Englewood Cliffs, NJ: Prentice-Hall.

Kolb, D. (1984) *Experiential Psychology*, Englewood Cliffs, NJ: Prentice-Hall.

Kroeger, O. and J. Thuesen (1988) *Type Talk*, New York: Delta.

Lamb, D. (1980) *Hegel—from Foundation to System*, Leiden: Martinus Nijhoff.

Lamont, C. (1965) *The Philosophy of Humanism*, New York: Barrie and Rockliff.

Lawrence, P. (1980) *Managers and Management in West Germany*, London: Croom Helm.

Lawrence, P. and J. Barsoux (1990) *Management in France*, London: Cassell.

Lawrence, P. and J. Lorsche (1968) *Organization and Environment*, Cambridge, MA: Harvard Business School.

Lazonof, W. (1991) *The Myth of the Market Economy*, New York: Cambridge University Press.
Lehmann, H. (Ed.) (1974) *Systemtheorie und Betrieb*, Hanover: Opladen.
Lessem, R. (1987) *Intrapreneurship*, London: Wildwood House.
Lessem, R. (1989) *Global Management Principles*, Englewood Cliffs, NJ: Prentice-Hall.
Lessem, R. (1990) *Developmental Management*, Oxford: Blackwell.
Lessem, R. (1991) *Total Quality Learning*, Oxford: Blackwell.
Lessem, R. (1993) *Business as a Learning Community*, Maidenhead: McGraw-Hill.
Lievegoed, B. (1990) *Managing the Developing Organization*, Oxford: Blackwell.
Lorenz, C. (1992) 'High time to turn around R&D', *Financial Times*, 9 October.
Lowith, K. (1965) *From Hegel to Nietzsche*, London: Constable.
Marx, K., F. Engels and V. I. Lenin (1977) *On Dialectical Materialism*, Moscow: Progress Publishers.
Maslow, A. (1964) *Motivation and Personality*, New York: Harper & Row.
Mito, S. (1991) *The Honda Book of Management*, London: Kogan Page.
Mole, J. (1991) *Mind Your Manners*, London: Industrial Society.
Myers Briggs, I. (1962) *The Myers Briggs Type Indicator*, New York: Educational Testing Service.
Myers Briggs, I. (1980) *Differing Gifts*, New York: Consulting Psychgologists Press.
Oakshott, R. (1978) *The Case for Workers' Cooperatives*, London: Routledge and Kegan Paul.
Pascale, R. and A. Athos (1982) *The Art of Japanese Management*, Harmondsworth: Penguin Books.
Peters, T. and R. Waterman (1982) *In Search of Excellence*, New York: Harper and Row.
Pinchot, G. (1985) *Intrapreneuring*, New York: Harper and Row.
Piore, M. and T. Sabel (1984) *The Second Industrial Divide*, New York: Basic Books.
Porter, M. (1990) *The Competitive Advantage of Nations*, New York, Macmillan.
Pugh, D. *et al.* (1971) *Writers on Organizations*, Harmondsworth: Penguin Books.
Reich, R. (1991) *The Work of Nations*, New York: Simon & Schuster.
Reill, P. (1975) *The German Enlightenment and the Rise of Historicism*, University of California Press.
Revans, R. (1965) *Science and the Manager*, London, MacDonald.
Revans, R. (1967) *Big Firms: the Managerial Gap*, New York: New Society.
Revans, R. (1980) *Action Learning*, London, Blond and Briggs.
Revans, R. (1984) *Management as Learning and Creativity*, London: Chartwell Brett.
Roll, E. (1953) *A History of Economic Thought*, London, Faber.
Röpke, W. (1960) *A Human Economy*, Oxford: Oswald Wolff.
Schwartz, P. (1979) *Morphologie von Kooperation*, Mohr
Shonfield, A. (1965) *Modern Capitalism*, Oxford: Oxford University Press.
Smiles, S. (1986) *Self-Help*, Harmondsworth: Penguin Books [1859].
Smith, A. (1975) *The Wealth of Nations*, London: Everyman [1776].
Smyser, W. (1992) *The Economy of United Germany*, London: Hurst.

Spiegel, H. (1971) *The Growth of Economic Thought*, Duke University Press.

Steiner, R. (1947) *Social Renewal*, London: Anthroposophical Press.

Steiner, R. (1972) *World Economy*, London: Steiner Press.

Stevens, A. (1980) *On Jung*, Harmondsworth: Penguin Books.

Stoner, J. A. F. (1982) *Management*, 2nd edn., Hemel Hempstead: Prentice-Hall.

Thurow, L. (1992) *Head to Head*, New York: Morrow.

Toynbee, A. (1968) *A Study of History*, London: Thames & Hudson.

Ulrich, H. (1978) *Unternehmungspolitik*, Munich: Haupt.

Van der Post, L. (1978) *Jung and the Story of Our Time*, Harmondsworth: Penguin Books.

Wachter, H. (1992) 'Human resource management in Germany', *Employee Relations*, 14 April.

Wever, K. and C. Allen (1992) 'Is Germany a model for managers?' *Harvard Business Review*, September/October, 36.

Womack, J., D. Jones and T. Roos (1990) *The Machine that Changed the World*, New York: Macmillan.

Wrong, D. (Ed.) (1970) *Max Weber*, Englewood Cliffs, NJ: Prentice-Hall.

Zuboff, S. (1988) *In the Age of the Smart Machine*, London Heinemann.

Index